# ABO

# A WEE BOY'S PROGRESS

## Allan Neil

# DEDICATION

This book is dedicated to all those wonderful men and women who served with me through all the times; good, exciting, boring, dangerous, happy, laughing, sad and downright tragic that made up the life of a working copper in the second half of the twentieth century in our small country.

I especially dedicate it to Toby Pratt and John Rist who, shamefully, never received proper recognition for their deeds just before and after 03.00 hours on 12th October 1984.

I recognize the value of the family support I received throughout my time in the Police Forces in which I served and another dedication is to my parents who brought me up with certain values that I have always tried to adhere to and to my late daughter Jo who got the roughest possible deal of cards just when her life should have been opening up before her.

========================================

# Acknowledgements

Photographs:

Harper's Brae – my distant cousin Jim Neil

Grand Hotel aftermath – with kind permission of The Editor, Brighton Evening Argus

Police Helicopter, Jason Willcox and Chief Constable Whitehouse – with kind permission of the Chief Constable, Sussex Police.

Assistance with formatting for printing – Fred McAllen

Cover design – Fred McAllen

*Also by Allan Neil*

*A Lost Connection (a novel)*

*A Week in the Life of Chairdog Bongo (Fiction for children and dog lovers)*

*Via Baltica (a travelogue)*

ABO 4

# Contents

**Where it all began**

# CHAPTER 1

## In the Beginning: A Wartime Boyhood

It all has to start somewhere. In my case, it was on December 28, 1938, though some might say it actually began some forty weeks earlier; the moment of my conception; the coming together in ecstasy (I like to think) of my mother, Janet Mitchell Allan (known as Jessie), and my father, William (Wullie) Neil. That would have been around the twenty-first of March, my father's thirty-second birthday. Two days prior to that, Scotland had beaten England at Twickenham to gain rugby's Grand Slam. My father would have been in a euphoric mood as he would equally have been had we beaten the English at a doughnut-eating competition or shove-halfpenny.

The town of my birth was Penicuik, then a small burgh with a population of around two thousand. It lay ten miles to the south of Edinburgh, almost surrounded by countryside; the Pentland Hills to the west, the Moorfoots to the east, and Auchencorth Moss, which formed, with Harlaw Muir, a wild moorland to the south. To the north were well-maintained mixed farmland and coal mines between the northern boundary of the burgh and the southern suburbs of the capital city.

The two main industries of the area at the time, apart from farming, were coal mining and the manufacture of paper.

I first drew breath in a wee flat over Peggy Dodds's sweetshop, Angle Park, John Street, Penicuik at 3:00 a.m. on a crisp, cold Wednesday morning. I was bright yellow from jaundice, so my mother had to take a lot of ribbing about where on earth she had found a Chinaman in Penicuik! I was given the name William James Allan Neil, immediately shortened to 'Billy.

Life had not been too good for either of my parents. Both their fathers had been miners. Both were long dead.

My maternal grandfather, Angus Allan, was a miner in the Lanarkshire coalfield.

Granny Greegor and flock.  Children left to right – Agnes, Jessie, Kate, Willie

He died in late 1913 of an indeterminate lung condition when my mother was less than one year old and her sister Kate was already in utero. With her four children, William, Agnes, Jessie, and Kate, my grandmother moved to a cottage in the back of beyond, some four miles from Lanark, where she commenced to bring them up on practically nothing.

William became an apprentice cobbler—the trade of his grandfather. He had a very unhappy marriage in Lanarkshire and moved south to Buckinghamshire, where he remarried and did very well for himself and his new family.

Agnes married John (Black Jock) Bryson, a miner and a widower with two children of his own, when she herself, at just sixteen years of age, was no more than a child. She bore him ten more children—John, Angus, Donald, George, Margaret, Nancy, Isobel, Catherine, Jean, and Danny. Agnes lived her life on a knife-edge of poverty and schooled her offspring so that only one got in any trouble with the law. Of the one that did, more later in this narrative.

My mother's sister, Kate, was a vivacious, outgoing girl and woman right to the end of her life. She married Hector Kyle, a soldier, just before the war and bore him three children, Hector Junior, Angus, and Jim. Hector Senior was a very adventurous man in the field of business. Soon after the war, he had a fish vending round with a small van in South Lanarkshire, before taking over a lorry company called Dalziel Haulage (Dalziel pronounced Dee-ell, so the company logo was DL Haulage.) He sold that off in the early 1960s and moved the family to Canada, where the sons all did very well for themselves. Hector Senior died prematurely, as did his son Angus, and Kate never did recover from those deaths.

In the abjectness of their youthful poverty, my grandmother taught her daughters that nothing should be discarded until it was absolutely of no further use. Other people's thrown-away woollen garments were painstakingly unravelled, the wool washed and stretched, and then knitted into new clothing or crocheted into bedcovers. Cotton and linen rags were either cut into geometric shapes, to be fashioned into patchwork articles, or painstakingly cut into strips. Old hessian sacks would be washed and dried and the rag strips woven through them to make carpets and mats. Articles made from those recycled materials that were not needed by the family were sold for a few pennies or exchanged with local farmers for food and milk.

Larger pieces of material could be shaped into smaller garments after the holed or worn patches were cut away. My mother never lost these skills, and many were the jumpers, cardigans, and socks, knitted in unusual colours that I wore totally unselfconsciously as a boy. Mum's sister Kate developed into a seamstress of some note, actually teaching at evening classes after the family's arrival in Canada, helping to make ends meet while husband Hector got himself on his feet.

My mother was ever a girl and lady of duty. Staying at home in her early teens and earning nothing was always going to be a burden on her mother.

Lanark was then an important market town, leaning towards the agricultural. From the age of twelve, my mother would walk into the town on market day trying to find a local farmer or businessman who would engage her as a cleaner or a nanny. This way she was able to bring valuable money into the family home.

One day in 1926, when she was thirteen years of age, my mother was, as usual, touting herself for business around Lanark Market when she met Robert Craik, a farmer from Milton Bridge, near Penicuik. Robert (Bob) had just become the father to his second child, a girl, Dorothy, and was looking for help around the home for his wife. He hired my mother on the spot. I guess Bob must have run her home before taking her to Milton Bridge, and this would have been the first my grandmother knew that her daughter was leaving home.

Sometime around 1930, my grandmother moved to the town of Carluke in Lanarkshire, where she took in a lodger called Mr. McGregor, of whom I have no more details. Mr. McGregor looked after my grandmother who, around this time, gave birth to my Uncle Jimmy. Did they marry? I do not know.

Shortly afterwards, or maybe just before Jimmy's birth, Mr. McGregor left the scene and, sadly, I heard no more of him. His legacy did not die, though. From the start of my memories, my mother's mother was always known as "Granny Greegor." My second-born son is called Gregor in remembrance of a lovely old lady.

As a small boy, I often stayed at Granny Greegor's, frequently travelling alone on school holidays. Nowadays, going from Penicuik to Carluke takes a matter of forty-five minutes. Then I travelled by bus from Penicuik to Lanark—about an hour and three quarters, followed by a walk across the bus station at Lanark and boarding a central number 240 bus for the half-hour leg to Carluke. Actually, I was not quite alone, as the Edinburgh-Penicuik-Lanark bus had a regular driver and a conductor who had worked with my father at the SMT factory in Edinburgh during the war. When we got to Lanark, Jimmy the conductor made sure I was on the 240 bus before going for his tea break.

At Carluke my Auntie Kate shared the Milton Crescent Council House accommodation with her mother along with her sons Hector and Angus, while her husband went about his army duties. Not far from the house the main Glasgow to London railway line ran. I have vivid memories of walking down to where the track crossed over a bridge on a farm road and lying at the side of the railway while huge locomotives hauling twelve carriages thundered through at God knows what speed. Health and Safety? Phooey!

Another potent memory is of climbing into Granny Greegor's high bed, at the age of around four years, and burying myself in its warm, musky sheets, being sound asleep long before she joined me.

Granny Greegor's son Jimmy became a hardworking man in the steel mills of Motherwell, marrying Rose Cliens and fathering one son, James, who became a respected haematologist in the NHS at nearby Law Hospital. Sadly, both Jimmy and Rose died prematurely. By marrying Rose, Jimmy had created some family ripples. Rose and her family were Roman Catholics, while my mother's family was Protestant. Jessie had, in fact, been a Baptist and could not have cared less about anyone else's religion.

My mother worked devotedly for the Craik family. It is a sure sign that she was appreciated that the Craiks, then Dorothy, kept in touch even when she had married my father, and Jessie's own children had grown up and become grandparents. In 2002, Dorothy, at seventy-six years of age, turned up at my mother's funeral and wept real tears of sorrow.

I am not sure exactly when my mother met my father. What I am sure of is that they never had any quarrels or disagreements that I knew of. Of course they must have had some fallouts, but these were always conducted out of the sight and hearing of their children.

I do know that my mother was never short of admirers. I met several elderly men in Penicuik who only had praise for her and who said that my father, Wullie, had been a very lucky man.

My father's background was not dissimilar to my mother's. His father, James Neil, was a shale miner in the West Calder area of Midlothian—my father was born in the mining village of Bellsquarry. My great-grandfather, also James, was killed in a 1906 cave-in at Whitehill Colliery, near the village of Roslin, a few miles north of Penicuik a month before the birth of my father.

This event prompted my grandfather to give up mining and get a safer job—in the Roslin Gunpowder factory, even though his cousin Samuel Neil and five of his workmates had died in an explosion there on January 22, 1890! My grandparents and their first three sons, Jimmy, Sandy, and my newly born father, moved to the mainly mining enclave of Shottstown in Penicuik, where the two younger sons, Andrew and Peter, were born.

Shottstown had been built by the Shotts Iron Company to house their workers. The company operated a dual-purpose mine on the edge of Penicuik. Coal and iron stone were taken from the ground there. The pit was called Mauricewood, and on September 5, 1889 it was the scene of a disastrous underground fire in the coal mining part, in which sixty-three of the seventy men working underground were killed—two catastrophes that happened within five months in such a small area. Local legend used to have it that the fire still burned 960 feet—282.5 metres—below the surface. Whatever the truth of it, the legend did not deter the building of a new housing estate on the site in the 1960s. At the location of the original pithead, there is a monument to the miners killed that day.

In my boyhood, Shottstown was a closely knit slum mining community of the type detested by Tories. It was torn down in the early 1950s to be replaced by shiny new council accommodation.

My grandfather died in 1927 of liver carcinoma. His five sons had been forbidden from going down the mine and, when reaching working age, had found work in the Valleyfield paper mill in Penicuik. However, in 1928, possibly feeling released from the moratorium, my father got work four miles away underground at the Moat Pit, located on the edge of the village of Roslin, at the age of 22. My father's mining career came to an abrupt end after a few years when he contracted meningitis. He lost his right eye and the hearing in his right ear, and he also lost his employment in the pit. Had his disability resulted from a mining accident, the union would have made sure he had continued employment on the surface. Because it was the result of a medical condition, there was no such fallback, and he found himself out on the streets, happily with a good strong mother behind him.

Eventually he got a job in another paper mill—James Brown and Co., Eskmills, Penicuik—a long-established company that had been founded in its current form in 1847, although it had been in the Browns' hands for thirty years before that. Because of his condition, he was taken on as a disabled worker at a lower rate of pay than the able-bodied. It was obvious to me, when I worked in the same mill, that there was no difference in what he was doing as opposed to the so-called fully fit. Typically, he never once complained.

He was a very religious man with strong beliefs centred around the Scottish Presbyterian Church—sadly, a source of regular irritation between us. He was an elder of the South Kirk in Penicuik and never missed a service. Fortunately or otherwise, I went to a school that encouraged freedom of thought, and I found the creed of the Kirk negative and restrictive. I tried very hard to honour my father's beliefs, but it was very difficult and only my love of the man (it was impossible not to love him) prevented serious alienation between us.

My father never missed a day's work that he would have been fit to undertake and also went to work on many days when, frankly, he was not fit.

James Brown and Co. folded around 1966, when my father was sixty years old. He could quite easily have gone on benefits for five years before drawing his state pension. Not Wullie! Jobs for the able-bodied were very hard to find with so many miners and mill-men out of work at that time, but he took a job as a street sweeper for Penicuik Town Council. Many lesser men would have felt humiliated and downtrodden doing such a menial job in the public gaze, but not my father. His cheerfulness and his ability to talk with any person he might meet made him a highly popular character around the town, and I, for one, never felt demeaned by his doing such a job.

My parents were alike in that both had many friends and not a single enemy. During the war, my dad went to work for SMT—Scottish Motor Traction—in Edinburgh. In peacetime they were a company that built and maintained buses, but during the war their factory was given over to the production of Spitfire fighter aircraft components. He worked on nightshift there and also joined the local detachment of the Home Guard. It did not occur to me at the time, but much later, when I was in the Royal Navy learning how to kill people, I wondered how he could sight his rifle, being short of a right eye!

Through all this, we lived in a flat over a shop. The flat had two rooms, one being a combined sitting room and kitchen; the other was a bedroom. There was no hot water other than what could be heated in the coal-fired range in the sitting room. At the top of the stairs behind the shop was a cold-water sink for washing up, and in the backyard was a solid-fuel wash boiler and an outside lavatory. The range was the only cooking facility in the place.

My father's mother, Granny Neil, lived just round the corner in council accommodation, with her second—unmarried—son, Sandy. These houses had been built just before the war, so were modern and had hot and cold running water and, best of all, a bathroom! We used all to go round one evening a week, going in as Wullie Neil and his scruffy lot and coming out as Wullie Neil and his brand new pins!

I still have a scar from those days when I was careless getting out of the bath and cracked my forehead! I got a cut that needed stitching, and as, in those days, you could call the GP out in the evening, or go to the surgery outside hours, it was dealt with without the need to go to Accident and Emergency.

My mother was fully engaged in bringing up not only me, but also my sister, Catherine, who arrived in April 1942. On top of that, she took in soldiers from the nearby infantry barracks who were billeted on us prior to D-Day.

I remember only three of the soldiers. One, called Norman Wright, was a ruddy-cheeked, cheerful barge builder from St. Osyth in Essex. Another was a taciturn Yorkshireman from Leeds—Vince Kelleher by name. I think I have spelled it correctly. The most memorable by far to a little boy's mind was Titus. He was a colossal African from Nigeria. My friends and I used to gather round just to gaze at him as none of us had ever seen a black man. The poor guy must have been sorely embarrassed, but I always recall him having a huge, beaming smile on his face. The soldiers got the use of the bedroom, and the three of us had the sitting room—Catherine in her cot, Mum and I in a bed-settee. Dad, on night shift, slept during the day.

When I look back at Penicuik in the 1940s, it is black and white, monochrome as in the old newsreels.

Bridge Street Penicuik, in the 1940's

Maybe that has a lot to do with the coldness and austerity of wartime and immediate post-war years. As a family, we must have been sorely stretched to make ends meet. I recall being sent more than once by my mother to buy "a fourpit o' tatties" and half a neep from Old Mrs. Sneddon's corner store across the road from our flat. A fourpit was a quarter of a stone—three and a half pounds, or 1.6 kilos of potatoes. Half a neep was a swede sliced in two through the middle, top to bottom. This would be combined with a half-pound of the cheapest minced beef to make a meal for three adults and two children.

Of course, having soldiers billeted on us had the occasional bonus when our guests would bring home prizes smuggled from the barracks—roast meat, vegetables, or fruit unavailable to the civilian population.

When I go back to Penicuik now, I see the main street—John Street—with cars parked along its length, and a modern, pedestrian shopping centre at its heart. My mind goes back to the same road and centre, available to, but totally free of cars, with the odd speciality shop like Tom Fell the Baker, Pepper Lamb the Butcher, and the Co-operative Store (simply known as "the Store.") Incidentally, the Midlothian pronunciation of "Co-operative" is "koh-per-<u>ai</u>-tiv."

None of my friends' parents had cars. In fact the only person I knew in John Street to own one was Jack Welsh, who had a tobacconist and ice cream shop opposite and had a Morris 8. I did not ride in a motor vehicle other than a bus (or a police van—see ahead) until I was about nine years of age, when I went out with my Uncle Hector, husband of my mother's sister Kate, in his van on his fish round.

In the days of the war, of course, rationing precluded children like myself from enjoying what children of later days took for granted; sweets, for example. Heaven knows how bad my teeth would have been with access to Mars Bars and Dairy Milk chocolate! Oral hygiene was difficult enough given the soft water on tap in the town, devoid of calcium and, of course, fluoride-free. My mouth bears witness to that, even today! Rationing also controlled what even the most doting of mothers could dress their offspring in.

One of the most shameful incidents of my young life lies stark in my memory even today, some almost seventy years later. My mother must have made a huge sacrifice to dress me in a white sailor suit to go to the Kirk one Sunday. She used also to curl my long, platinum blonde hair into ringlets and I must have been crimped and polished into an object of real maternal pride.

I don't remember how I came to be so incensed. Perhaps some well-meaning old lady had patted my head, saying "Whit a bonny wee lassie."

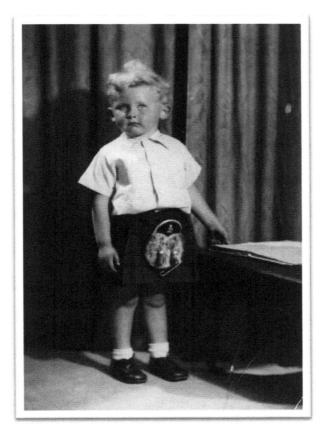

The Author aged 3 in 1942

That happened more than once, but on the way home from the Kirk I found a pile of soot and stood kicking it for several minutes until my dad dragged me away and chastised me as severely as he was ever able to do.

Another memorable incident happened in early 1943, when I was four years old. My parents and Granny Neil had clubbed together to buy me a tricycle as a combined birthday and Christmas present. It must have been secondhand, but I was extremely proud of it. One day an older boy—a Glaswegian evacuee, I learned much later—took my tricycle from outside Dodds's shop. I shouted for him to stop, but he kept riding down John Street, then Edinburgh Road, with me in pursuit. I chased him all the way into Fairmilehead, on the southern fringe of Edinburgh, a total of six miles, before he and I were collared by a patrolling policeman and taken to the local police station. My parents, who had been frantic with worry, were contacted and a Black Maria conveyed the boy, the trike, and me back to Penicuik.

That summer, before I was due to start school, I contracted scarlet fever, of which there was something of an epidemic at the time. This meant a spell in Loanhead Isolation Hospital, some five miles away. I do not remember too much about it except that I was not allowed any visitors. My parents were allowed only to look at me through a window into the ward whenever they visited. The only lasting effect I have of this disease is, apparently, the ability to make my eyeballs shiver in different directions!

There was a strong belief at the time that when a child recovered from scarlet fever, he inevitably contracted diphtheria. Happily that did not happen to me, possibly because I was immunised against it. I did, however, suffer the usual catalogue of the time of childhood ailments—measles, chickenpox, and whooping cough (pertussis), managing to avoid only the mumps.

My first day at school was in August 1943. The school was Penicuik Infants, which formed part of an imposing 1930s building overlooking the Public Park in Carlops Road. The primary shared the building with the junior secondary—the then Scottish equivalent of the old English secondary modern. The edifice still stands and is now called Penicuik High School.

My first teacher was called Mrs. Murdoch, whom I remember as mumsy and kind. My other memories of the school are dim, apart from the fact that I got involved in a fight with a boy whose reputation as a tough meant that not only did I get a bloody nose but also I achieved a measure of respect from other pupils.

In July 1946, my younger sister, Janette, arrived, and our already overcrowded little flat began to resemble the Black Hole of Calcutta.

Before she was a year old, Janette contracted polio, then known as infantile paralysis. My Uncle Peter's daughter Agnes also fell victim to the disease. Janette was whisked away to an isolation ward, and the flat had to be fumigated. Janette did not suffer a serious handicap but for years walked with a limp. Many children, Agnes included, had to have metal calipers fitted to support their seriously weakened legs.

Our last winter in the flat was the most severe that the country had suffered in many years. Penicuik took more than four feet of snow with much drifting up to ten feet or more. We were trapped in the flat because the outdoor staircase to it had been enclosed with a door at the stair foot, which opened outwards, except when it had that depth of snow deposited against it. My parents had to call for help from the windows until a neighbour was able to fight his way to the door and shovel enough snow to allow us to open it. We then took over and cleared the path to the pavement, then cleared that across the front of the shop.

To me, as an eight-year-old, this was paradise. Snowmen, igloos, tunnels through the drifts, and snowball fights—wonderful.

The time had come, however, to move out of our cramped accommodation, and this was precipitated when the Dodds family sold the shop and the buyers, the Bairds, required the over-the-shop accommodation.

There was no Rent Act protection in those days, so it was a big rush for my parents to find somewhere for us all to live.

Happily, the Craiks' respect for my mum paid off. We were given the farm cottage at New Milton in return for my mum carrying out some domestic duties for the farmer and his family.

Political correctness? Penicuik South Kirk Junior Choir 'minstrels.'
Author is back row far left, aged 10 in 1949.

# CHAPTER 2

## Life on the Farm, School, and Work: A Move to the Country, a Good Schooling, and Starting Work

How well I remember the leaving of Angle Park.

After my parents had moved into the flat in 1938, the open staircase at the back had been enclosed. This had added to the comfort of the dwelling by reducing the effect of the prevailing wind, but when it came to moving the family's bulky 1920s and 1930s furniture out, the improvement meant the wardrobes and other cumbersome items could not be taken out by way of the stairs.

My dad had arranged someone with a lorry to move us, and we ended up having it parked on the pavement outside the shop. Some brave soul then climbed a ladder to one of the sash windows and removed the two halves so that everything could be lowered out of the gap and then manhandled down the ladder and onto the back of the truck.

The farm cottage was well built and comfortable; the only amenities it did not possess were an interior toilet and an electric immersion heater for hot water. I say "only," but the improvement in lifestyle must have been quite dramatic! The absence of a "range" meant less work for Mum, but we then had to rely on an open coal fire, on which meals were cooked, which kind of balanced that for her. There was no bathroom, and baths were taken in the kitchen sink.

Of course, I soon began to explore around the farm. To me it was straight out of wonderland, giving me the chance to climb over lots of farm machinery. The health and safety Gestapo would have been horrified.

The farm was a mixed dairy/arable affair. Bob Craik used to follow the three-year cycle whereby each field would have a root crop, e.g., potatoes in year one. Year two would be cereals, usually oats or barley. In year three, the field would be grassed and the cattle left to graze it and fertilise it again for year one after a cut or two of hay had been taken.

I could give a hand on the farm by "singling" swedes (thinning them to a hoe-width when they were young) or howking tatties—following the digging machine around when potatoes were harvested and bagging those missed by the machine.

There were two shire horses on the farm, used for ploughing or for hauling the reaper/binder round at grain harvest and any other locomotion that was required. Their minder, the ploughman, Bob White, used to let me ride on their backs while they worked (more horror from the H & S KGB). They were so broad that I had to sit cross-legged on their backs. I was allowed to tie their nosebags full of oats on at the end of the day or to give them the odd carrot. I just loved these old cuddies, as we called them. Gentle giants, they are long gone now, victims of the cult of mechanisation.

I started at Glencorse Primary School, a small rural establishment with just four or five teachers. The headmaster, Mr. William Lawrie, took the top class of boys and girls who would be twelve or so years of age at the end of the school year. His deputy, Miss Annie Allan, took the previous year, and it was into that class that I was decanted after taking some kind of examination. This was a full year higher than I had been at Penicuik so that, at nine years of age, I was in a class of ten-year-olds. It also meant that when I progressed to senior school my contemporaries from Penicuik would be one year behind me.

The school was situated right alongside Glencorse Barracks, the headquarters of the First Battalion, The Royal Scots. One or two children in my class were the offspring of soldiers who lived in the married quarters of the barracks, and I found it especially easy to make friends with these boys and girls. I was fascinated by the fact that most of them had lived abroad at some time in their young lives. This probably fuelled my lifelong interest in foreign travel.

My first Glencorse teacher, Annie Allan, was an inspiration. She paid me special attention because a year difference in age at nine is quite large.

I moved into Mr. Lawrie's class in 1949 when aged ten. In that particular year, there was no qualifying exam to go to senior secondary (grammar) school. As a Scottish Office experiment, pupils were judged on their work throughout their final year.

At the end of the school year, my parents told me I had come top of the class and would be going to Lasswade Senior Secondary. Annie Allan took me to one side and told me she was very proud of me because I would be going into the top "stream" at Lasswade. From that day, until her death, Annie asked after me every time she met my parents.

I will never be able to thank you enough, Annie. Together with another lady teacher called Katie Williamson, you shaped my character much more than you ever knew. It would be another eight years before I encountered anyone equally influential.

At Glencorse I struck up a friendship with a boy who lived in an old cottage in a pre-Victorian row called Milton Cottages, just down a track from the farm. His name was Archie Affleck, and his father, Archie Senior, was a woodsman employed by the Forestry Commission. By a huge coincidence, my great-grandmother, Agnes Waugh, who married James Neil, killed in Whitehill Colliery, had been born on May 5, 1855 and brought up in that very house. Agnes was the sixth child of Peter and Janet Waugh. She was one of only two who survived beyond young childhood.

Archie and I used to wander the woods daily looking at nature's wonders. We fished for minnows in a burn that ran through Milton Bridge, identified birds and other wildlife in the woods and for hours played a game we claimed to have invented—football tennis, which involved kicking or heading a ball over a rope between two clothes-drying posts.

We also trawled the local golf course searching for lost balls to sell back to the club for a penny each. The golf course was, and still is, also called Glencorse and had the distinction of having a burn cross the fairway an incredible number of times. A sharp-eyed boy could spot lost balls in the burn with amazing regularity. The burn also had some high clay banks into which a ball could become plugged. We learned how to tell the difference between martins' and dippers' nesting tunnels and holes caused by wayward golf balls.

The other distinction the course had was that the professional was the father of a boy in my class at Glencorse School. That boy was called

Ronnie Shade—R. D. B. M. Shade—the initials widely believed to be an acronym for "Right Down the Bloody Middle." Ronnie went on to become the British amateur golf champion, followed by a career as a professional.

Ronnie arranged for one or two of us to have a lesson from his father. I took the offer up, but on taking hold of the club it appeared that the club head was the wrong way round. This was, of course, because when I hold an implement that requires two hands I am left-handed. Mr. Shade insisted that if I wanted to play the game I would have to change to being right-handed.

Unfortunately, playing kack-handed, as I saw it, I could not get the club head to connect with the ball and very quickly lost interest in playing the game of golf, soon picking up cricket, where left-handedness not only was accepted, but also could be used to your team's advantage.

One snowy winter's day, Archie and I took our little sledges over to the vacant golf course to ride down a steep track from the eighteenth tee down towards the main road. Near the bottom of this track lay the ubiquitous burn, over which was a narrow footbridge some twelve inches wider than the space between the runners on my sledge.

I was wearing an imitation leather jerkin, which had been a Christmas present a week or so earlier. It zipped up the front and had a tight waistband at the bottom.

I hurtled down the track at a dizzy speed and, of course, misjudged the footbridge. I was decanted off the bridge and into the stream through half an inch of ice. The burn is only a few inches deep so there was no danger of drowning, but my jerkin filled up with icy water.

I remember racing back home and arriving blue with cold. My mother had a few choice words for me, but typically could not be stern for long, and pretty soon we were rolling around with laughter!

In August 1950, at the age of eleven years, I started at Lasswade, some seven miles northeast of Penicuik. I went by school bus, which picked me up with a couple of others at Milton Cottages, where Archie lived. He had another year to do at Glencorse. The others lived in the village of Auchendinny, about three quarters of a mile away off the main road.

The school, the teachers, and the other members of my class overawed me. It was Class 1A1, as Annie Allan had said, the elite. I could not believe I was in such distinguished company.

I thoroughly enjoyed the challenge, spending as much as four hours in an evening completing homework that was really, in theory, beyond my capabilities.

Many of the teachers at Lasswade were memorable. It was, like all state schools in Scotland, a mixed-sex school, with male and female teachers and pupils.

Miss Cameron taught French; she was known to all the pupils as Wiggy, as it was apparent that her orange hair was not her own. To this day, I remember the first bit of French I had to memorise: "La Jeune Fille a la Grande Bouche," "The Young Girl with the Big Mouth," taken from a textbook. This was to get us used to pronunciation before we got enmeshed in declension and all that rote stuff.

The geography teacher was Miss Lind, known of course as Jenny, after the famous opera singer—the Swedish Nightingale. She was disabled and taught from a wheelchair. She had, however, an unerring eye for any miscreant in her class and possessed a laser-accurate aim with piece of chalk or duster! I have to say I enjoyed her teaching, and my skills in geography have served me well on many occasions in pub quizzes. Just ask me—what is the capital of American Samoa?

The art teacher was Mr. Russell, known as Tubby. He was also the school's rugby coach. Rugby was the only winter sport for boys at Lasswade. I enjoyed it and threw myself into it but, sadly, was not good enough to make any of the school XVs. "You're far too wee to be a forward, and what's more you cannae pass for toffee!" was Tubby's verdict. "Also," he said, "your tackling is just fine, but the fella ye hit's got to be carrying the ball!"

Football became my game, played with Penicuik friends and, later, clubs, but I never lost my love for the game of rugby and came back to it later in my life, playing at a very modest level before graduating to refereeing and then referee coaching and advising.

Mrs. Winnie Laird taught Latin. I was reasonably good at the subject but had to work hard to sustain interest. Latin contributed hugely to my homework load, owing to the time it took me to complete it. Mrs. Laird was miffed when I decided to drop the subject at the end of the third year.

Mrs. Dolly Wood was the maths teacher. She had a big job on her hands with me. Have a look at my final report from Lasswade and you will understand. Not until some forty-five years later, when I got computerised, did mathematical logic have any part in my thinking.

Scientific subjects were a mixed blessing. Physics had rather too much mathematical content for me to be comfortable with it. Chemistry, however, was exciting. This played a big part in consoling me when I had to leave school for employment in a paper mill laboratory.

To me the most memorable of all the teachers was Miss Williamson—Katie—who taught English. Somehow there was a spark between this skinny, gauche eleven-year-old boy and a tall, cultured grey-haired spinster in her fifties. I used to hang onto her every word, and it felt as though I was receiving the same sort of personal attention as I had had from Annie Allan at Glencorse.

I loved everything in the English curriculum with one notable exception. I could not abide Shakespeare! I used to make such a hash of reading it and of writing about it that one day Miss Williamson took me aside and asked why I was so bad at the Bard when everything else seemed to come easy to me. I stuttered and stammered, but she smiled and told me not to worry because everyone has a blind spot and Shakespeare was mine. Now in my maturity, I still cannot relate to Shakespeare and would not cross the street to get a free seat to any performance.

Although I was now living at New Milton Farm, Penicuik was less than three miles to the south and it took ten minutes on the bus, of which there were five an hour. Apart from woodcraft and playing on the farm, there was little of social interest at Milton Bridge, and for these pursuits I inevitably ended up back in Penicuik. In that way, I maintained contact with all my boyhood pals.

When Bob Craik's lease on New Milton Farm was up, he decided not to renew it, so the Neil family had to move again. The farm reverted to being the active property of the Bush Estate, which, many years later as part of Edinburgh University Research Facility, found fame or notoriety as the creators of the first "cloned" mammal—Dolly the sheep.

This time we ended up in a flat in a large house, previously the grand home of the Jardine family of Esk Mills—of whom we will learn more later—but now subdivided into small dwellings and already condemned by the council as not fit for human habitation.

It was named Southbank and was at the top of a steep hill called Harper's Brae on the very northeastern edge of Penicuik. The town centre was a mile and a half away, reached only on foot or by bike, but it became again the hub of my social life. Daily I walked or jogged the mile and a half to catch the school bus to Lasswade.

Harper's Brae (Hill), Penicuik, early 20th century. It still looked exactly the same when I lived there in the 1950s.

Our flat at Southbank was fairly spacious, but there was no private toilet and we had to share one with the other tenants. There was no electricity either, and lighting and cooking were by gas. There wasn't a bathroom, but behind the house at the top of the precipitous south bank of the River Esk there was a brick outhouse, in which were two large concrete bowls in brick bases over coal fires. The bowls were filled with buckets of cold water from an outside tap and the fire lit. When the water was hot enough, we took it in turn to have our baths. By now everyone in Health and Safety will be apoplectic. (Don't fall asleep in the bath, Billy!)

Behind the tubs was a sluice, through which the bath or laundry water was released to run freely down the steep bank and into the river, some twenty-five metres below. Do I hear the word "pollution"? Yes, but the bath waste was as nothing compared to the unspeakable horrors that three paper mills were dumping into the river, and in addition there was a very primitive sewage settling pond upstream from which raw liquid sewage from Penicuik went into the river too. There were even more paper mills between Penicuik and the sea, each contributing its own nasties to the flow.

The river was dead. How different now that the paper mills are long gone and the sewage works have been brought into the twenty-first century. The river has been regenerated, and it is now alive with fish, flora, and fauna. The riverside walk along the track bed of the also defunct railway that used to serve Penicuik and its mills provides one of the most intense pleasures of any visit to Penicuik.

After less than two years in Southbank, we got a council house—in Eskvale Crescent, in the Kirkhill area of Penicuik. This was a new development much closer to the centre of town with half the distance to walk to the school bus stop and of course to meet up with my pals.

What else in Penicuik registers as memorable? Well, my friends, of course, all unforgettable in their own ways. Drew Craven, my best pal; my cousin Drew Neil; another cousin, Ian Neil; Alec Peden, Harry Wright, and Tommy Easton. Now, like me, old geezers in their early seventies, with the exception of poor Tommy, who died in his late teens.

What did we do with our young lives? Mostly we kicked a ball around, either in the public park or in the yard behind a tenement block in John Street called Pryde's Place, opposite my birthplace of Angle Park. Pryde's Place is long gone and has been replaced by comfortable modern dwellings. Most of my friends lived in Pryde's Place; the rest lived in the local council estate.

How about girls, then? Well, it did not take long for me to realise that they had no interest in me, and, as I had (and still have) a horror of rejection, I soon stopped trying to make them get one.

Then there were the lads I played football with in the Penicuik Boys' Club side—Martin Stark, Duncan Livie, Charlie Gordon, and Charlie Brown (Chic Broon). In the same team was Brian Paterson, whose elder brother Jock was a star centre half in the championship-winning Hibernian side of the time and who would have won many "caps" today. In those days, Jock could not play for Scotland as he had been born in England—at Colchester—where his father had been in the army.

There was Peter Borrowman, Jim Main, Tommy Banner, and a couple of others whose names escape me. Jim Main was an occasional player for us, preferring rugby, and in fact he went on to become a highly respected rugby coach in the border town of Galashiels, where he was an equally highly regarded maths teacher. Tommy Banner was a talented musician, classically trained, who became a professional entertainer and, subsequently, a member of the Somerset fun group, The Wurzels, who had a number of hit records in the 1970s. As I write, the Wurzels are still going strong, though Tommy has had his health problems, like the rest of us.

Penicuik used to have two slum communities, Shottstown and Fieldsend. Most commonly the inhabitants of these two enclaves were miners, although mill workers were also to be found among the inhabitants. In the rush of modernisation of the 1950s, they were demolished and replaced by modern, comfortable, and soulless terraces of identical council houses. I don't expect the erstwhile inhabitants of Shottstown or Fieldsend had any derogatory comment to make about them, however, finding themselves with access to running hot water, not to mention non-communal, flushing inside loos and bathrooms.

In July 1953, my school report showed me in the top five in the top class of the third year at Lasswade. I was asked by the school which subjects I wanted to drop and chose Latin and woodwork. Why woodwork when I was seriously attracted to joinery? Well, in three years of it, all we did was cut bits of wood and learn how to use a mallet and chisel enough to drive a groove across the grain of a bit of timber. It was all far too slow for me. I did not have the option of dropping any of the mathematical subjects and, in fact, had a mysterious discipline called trigonometry added to them for the following term. In the first term of the fourth year, I had to struggle with that on top of the other math's disciplines.

I was really flying in English, French, geography and history. The sciences, art, and sports I could get stuck into, but it all came to nothing when my parents notified the school that I was to be withdrawn at the end of that term and that my father had found a job for me. I was summoned to the office of Mr. William Binnie, the headmaster, and asked if I really wanted to leave. I told him that I did. Well, my parents had spoken and, as the Bible says, "Honour thy father and thy mother."

Miss Williamson took me aside and asked me the same. I gave her the same answer, although I recall with shame that I was examining the floor as I did. Her reply was, "Don't stop educating yourself, Billy. There is so much to learn. You'll never know it all, but it can be so rewarding trying." She knew how I really felt. I wish she could read this humble offering.

Try to understand how it was in a small place like Penicuik in those days. The divide between the learned or lucky and the great unwashed "oiks" was vast. My parents and I were from the latter category. University was "not for the likes of us." When you were old enough to work and fit to work, you worked. You brought a wage in, however small. My father had not missed a day's work in his life except when he was seriously ill. My mother had gone out to clean for the more privileged when she had three children to support on my father's meagre income.

Now that the family had a male of earning age and capability, it was expected that he pull his weight. Also, to be fair, the job my father had found for me was as good as anyone could have expected me to get, given my total lack of qualifications. He had tried and failed to get me an apprenticeship as a joiner. You had to be "family" in those days to get one.

## SCHOOL LEAVING RECORD

Name of pupil  William Neil                                     Date of birth  26.12.38

| Secondary schools attended | Dates of attendance | Course(s) followed | Number of years spent in course | Year of course reached |
|---|---|---|---|---|
| Lasswade Secondary | 26.8.50 to 22.12.53 | 2 Language | Three Years One Term | IV |

Proficiency in the subjects studied is shown by the placing of the cross entered under each.  Years in which a subject was studied only as a subsidiary are shown by the numbers denoting those years being ringed.

My final school report.  No Einstein, you'll agree.

I was to be an assistant in the laboratory of James Brown and Company, Paper Manufacturers, Esk Mills, Penicuik, my father's employers. I was to start work there on December 28, 1953—my fifteenth birthday.

The school's Christmas Carol service in Lasswade Kirk that year was poignant to me. Life was going to change beyond recognition. I was never going to see many of my school friends again. Some, like me, were also leaving the school. David Learmonth and Willie Watson were going to Rhodesia to be cadets in the British South Africa Police. Harry Golding was off to the Merchant Navy College to train as a ship's officer. Most of the others in my class were staying with it and going on to university and the like, or at least going to tackle their Lowers and Highers—the Scottish equivalent in those days of the "O" and "A" levels of English education.

My last day at Lasswade was forever marred by an unfortunate incident on the way home on the school bus. I was sitting in the front seat by the door and when it stopped at Milton Cottages, and as my friend Archie Affleck was getting off, I thumped him heartily between the shoulder blades and said, "Good luck, Archie. I won't be back in the New Year."

A couple of days later, Archie Senior turned up on our doorstep and informed my father that I had pushed his son off the school bus. Many times since I have wished that my last memory of school had been other than that misunderstanding.

James Brown and Company was a long-established firm in Penicuik. The mill dated back to 1775, when it was founded to produce cotton and paper. As it was on the banks of the River Esk, power was derived from a huge water wheel. During the Napoleonic Wars, the buildings had been used as a prisoner of war camp for captive Frenchmen. After the Battle of Waterloo in 1815, Mr. James Brown bought the mill. He ran it successfully, and he and his successors always made sure the mill was in the forefront of industrial progress. In 1847 the mill dropped its cotton production and began to concentrate solely on papermaking.

In 1852 a Mr. Thomas McDougal, Brown's son-in-law inherited the business. In 1898 it became a public limited liability company. The McDougal female side married into the Jardine family, and when I started in the last few days of 1953, the general manager was Mr. John Jardine, the managing director was Mr. Edward McDougal Jardine, and my boss, the chief chemist, was Mr. Andrew Jardine. As befitted its stature in the community, the mill's telephone number was Penicuik 1.

John Jardine and his family lived in a rather grand dwelling called Eskmills House, the garden of which backed on to Eskvale Crescent, and our council house was number 6 in that street. The family was absolutely without "side," and I became friendly with their sons, Ewan, Douglas, and James, all pupils at the well-known private (in England, public) school, Edinburgh Academy.

My job in the laboratory was less than arduous. It involved going round the mill and collecting samples from every part of the papermaking process, which I shall now try to summarise.

Paper can be made from a number of fibrous raw materials, from straw at the cheap end to linen at the top. James Brown and Co. was a middle-of-the road outfit. Their products included decent quality writing paper such as "Basildon Bond." They made huge quantities of duplicator paper, mainly for Her Majesty's Stationery Office, who would distribute in turn to government and military recipients. They turned out good quality "art" paper, used for glossy productions, such as the photograph pages in books, and they also made printing paper for the rest of the books.

The main ingredients for the paper made at Eskmills were esparto grass, imported from North Africa, and wood pulp, usually from Finland or Sweden, but sometimes from Poland. The mill also bought in good quality waste paper. "Broke"—substandard or torn paper from the mill itself also went into the mix. There are two kinds of wood pulp, known as mechanical and chemical. The mechanical stuff is basically just softwood ground to a pulp with all its impurities and was used mainly in the manufacture of newsprint—the paper made into newspapers and cheap magazines. That process was alien to Eskmills.

Chemical wood pulp was "digested" on site in the country of its origin, so that impurities were removed, and the resulting pulp, which arrived in the form of thick boards, consisted almost entirely of cellulose fibres.

Esparto grass is a tough, wiry desert plant, which has high cellulose content. In North Africa it is often made into baskets and similarly woven products.

The grass was imported in bales, which were broken up in the "cooking house" and passed through a dusting machine before being dropped into huge pressure cookers along with measured quantities of sodium hydroxide, also known as caustic soda, or, especially in the mill, as lye, pronounced "lee." Nobody who has ever lived downwind of an old-fashioned paper mill can ever forget the smell of esparto grass being cooked in lye and of used or "spent" lye being burned off to rid it of its waxy esparto solids to reclaim it and use it again. Eskvale Crescent was downwind of the mill for at least three hundred days in every year!

Given the grass's geographic origin, it was not unusual to find various specimens of desert fauna in the bales. Mostly these were dead, but there was the occasional alarm when a live spider, locust, or scorpion was discovered. If they escaped the boots of the workers, these creatures were usually donated to Edinburgh Zoo.

All the ingredients met up in great circular vats known as "beaters," where they went round and round, being ground under a huge bladed wheel for a given amount of time, depending on the qualities required of the finished paper. The esparto pulp was piped here and measured amounts of wood pulp, waste paper, and "broke" added. Measured in just after this stage would be bleach, which would be washed out before other substances such as size and china clay were added, along with dyes if coloured paper was required.

At various intervals, I would take samples of any coal deliveries (the steam required to drive the machinery was produced by solid fuel boilers). The coal was tested for calorific value, a measure of the heat produced, and any poor result led to bargaining between the company and the Coal Board.

In the event of agreement not being reached, the public analyst would be called in to arbitrate. He—Mr. Thin by name—was a frequent visitor to the mill, as similar disputes could arise with the suppliers of wood pulp (too much moisture). The junior (that was I) would take wood pulp samples from each delivery. These would be weighed, dried, and weighed again and the resulting equation expressed as "air dry" and "bone dry." I also gathered samples of prepared lye and of paper at each stage of its manufacture. These would be analysed by the more senior members of the staff—Mr. Andrew Jardine or my immediate senior, Archie Dempster.

Soon I was allowed to run the simplest of tests, to determine the clay content of the paper. China clay, brought in by rail from Cornwall, was an essential component of most papers, adding body and opacity to it.

Put too much china clay in the pot, though, and customers would have a similar plea to Mr. Thin that they were buying clay and not paper. The process involved weighing a square of paper to be tested, rolling it up, and pushing it into a Pyrex glass tube that had an electrical filament bound around it. After setting fire to the paper, it would be allowed to smoulder until the only residue left would be white china clay. After cooling the ash, it would be weighed and the result expressed as percentage clay.

As junior, it was part of my job to take all the day's results in to Mr. Edward Jardine, who was as deaf as any post. I had to read the results out before leaving them with him, and if I were to recite one with which he did not approve, he would make no attempt to hide the fact that he was switching his hearing aid off!

In September 1954, I started evening classes in paper technology at Heriot Watt College (Now University) in Edinburgh. My tutor was one Dr. Kenneth MacBean. He was the head research chemist at James Brown's great rival mill, Valleyfield, in Penicuik.

As my knowledge and experience progressed, I was allowed to do more serious testing, including assessing whether a paper was composed of the correct percentage of wood and esparto fibres, distinguished under a microscope, as each has a distinctive shape. A piece of paper would be pulped and then spread on a microscope slide with a dye that coloured each component fibre differently, and the numbers of each fibre would be counted.

Around the beginning of 1955, the company introduced a new range of "art" papers, those shiny pages that would bear the photographic content of books. It was called "Supawhite," because it was so brilliantly white it stood out from any other.

This astonishing whiteness was achieved by the use of a substance called "Tinopal"—a fluorescent whitening agent. These agents transform ultraviolet light into visible light, tinged with an unmistakable blueness, which appears as a dazzling white. When it first came out, Tinopal was apparently so expensive that the operatives in the "coating," or "enamelling" house where the "art" paper was produced could not be trusted to use it economically.

It fell, therefore, upon the laboratory, and me in particular, to measure it out in exactly the right quantities, using laboratory scales. In the "enamelling house," the Tinopal would be added to the coating material, which also included china clay, titanium dioxide, casein (a by-product of milk), and a mysterious substance called "blanc-fixe." The subsequent gloop was coated onto the base paper using sophisticated machinery, dried, polished, rolled, cut into manageable lengths (my father's job) on yet another machine, and then guillotined to the exact size ordered.

The problem with Tinopal in those days was that it was a fine, powdery yellow substance that became airborne at the slightest rash movement. The job was carried out in a little locked room close to the coating house. After I arrived back at the lab with bright yellow lips and face a couple of times, Mr. Andrew obtained a gauze mask at huge expense to the company.

The substance is still around. I don't know if it is still used in the manufacture of paper, but it is found in the kind of detergents that "add white-white-whiteness."

One definitely non-PC activity at the mill was when new female workers started. Paper mills use huge quantities of felt during the final machining of the pulp into paper, and there was one particularly surly gentleman employed in the washing and refurbishment of used felts. On their first days, these naïve youngsters would be despatched to the felt house to tell the man that the foreman had "sent them to get felt." They usually ended up being chased back to their foreman!

My starting pay in the mill was £2 10s a week net—£2.50 in today's money. I gave Mum the two quid and kept the ten shillings, which was usually enough for me to haunt Tony Valerio's coffee bar at weekends and get the bus to Hearts "away" football matches when my dad put a coach on, plus get me in the grounds. I was playing football in the winter by now, but our fixtures tended to be on Saturday mornings.

I'd been in the mill about two years when Archie Dempster vanished for his national service in the Royal Scots and his place was taken by his older brother Drew, newly demobbed from the RAF. Drew got me back to playing rugby, but, although I turned out a few times for Penicuik Second Fifteen and enjoyed the games, I was still better at football and therefore more in demand.

Drew was a big lad—he played in the second row—but had not an ounce of aggression in him. He had a lovely sense of humour and liked to sing. He knew all fourteen verses of "Abdul Abulbul Amir," and, do you know, I can still remember the tune and some of the verses.

You don't know it? Try Google!

# CHAPTER 3

## The Navy: National Service

Archie Dempster's going off reminded me that, at eighteen—in less than a year's time—I'd be liable for my national service. It was around then that I lost a friend, Peter Ketchen, to a piece of EOKA terrorism in Cyprus while he was serving with the Royal Scots, and when Archie came to the lab on a visit and told me about infantry training, I was less than keen on it.

Thanks to Mr. Andrew, I was now playing cricket in summer for one of the lesser Penicuik sides. One of the other youngsters in the team worked at Penicuik House for Sir John Clerk (Baronet) of Penicuik, the local laird and a descendant of the celebrated seventeenth/eighteenth-century lawyer, judge, and composer of the same name.

The lad, Hugh, told me that he had joined the RNVR—Royal Naval Volunteer Reserve, of which his employer was a commodore, and, as a result, it was guaranteed that he'd get in the Royal Navy for his service.

I told him I was interested in doing the same, and he promised to ask Sir John about it. I gave him my details.

A week later, he told me to go to the RNVR Forth Division HQ, HMS Claverhouse in Granton Square on the north side of Edinburgh, on the banks of the Forth. He gave me a date and time about two weeks ahead and told me that it was a recruiting day and I was expected. A day or so later, I received an official letter confirming this.

I did not see Hugh again before the appointed time, as the following week's cricket match was rained off, but I arrived on time.

I was given a medical, which did not bother me, and then was put before an officer of lieutenant-commander rank. All I remember of the interview was one question: "Why do you want to join the Reserve?"—to which I replied, as prompted by Hugh, "I want to finish my evening classes and qualify in my trade, but I also want to see what the Navy is like with a view to joining up."

I was in and given three choices of branch. I could be a visual signalman, a radio operator, or an EM—engineering mechanic, i.e., stoker. I chose the first, as it seemed to deal with communications in the open air and I might not be below decks if we copped a torpedo! My Uncle Andrew's accounts of the wartime Arctic convoys had a part in that decision, no doubt. Hugh was also a signalman, "bunting tosser," or "bunts" in naval parlance, the term coming from one of the signalman's duties as semaphore sender, naval flags being bunting.

With three other guys, two some way older with actual naval experience, I was taken to another room, where we took an oath before being led to the stores. For the first time, I caught a whiff of that uniquely seafaring smell of tarry rope. Wherever I am in the world, if I catch that odour, I am immediately back in the stores of HMS Claverhouse.

I was measured up and kitted out, and then given a brief tutorial on how to dress and how to press the uniform (seven horizontal creases in each leg, four inches apart, alternately convex and concave, and two verticals, both concave down the sides of the trouser legs.)

Back to the office, then, and I was handed my paybook, details of forthcoming nights, known as "drills," and copies of recent "routine orders" and the "Naval Ratings Handbook." The last contained everything a matelot—British sailor—needs to know, including naval discipline regulations. I still have my copy.

To avoid being kicked out, it was necessary to attend one drill a month. As they took place every Tuesday and Thursday, it was not going to be difficult, as my Tuesdays were blank in the diary at that time.

They were actually fun, consisting of learning Morse code and semaphore, naval custom and lore, and listening to old salts' wartime stories. It was still only 1956; guys had served in the navy through the war who were still in their thirties and early forties. Several of these men were now ratings at HMS Claverhouse, including George Gagan, a leading signalman with a great fund of stories about his service in the war, most suspiciously apocryphal.

After drills, if Hugh turned up, we got into the habit of going to the "All-in Wrestling," which used to be held each Tuesday at 7:30 p.m. at the El Dorado in Leith. The actual hall is long forgotten, but Hugh and I used to arrive around 9:15 p.m., in uniform of course, and get in free with time enough to see the last three bouts.

I can't remember any of the wrestlers except a giant called Pye, who was particularly hated by the crowd and who, naturally, played up to them. I remember one venerable old grandmama standing by the ropes, foaming at the mouth and screaming, "Bite his balls off, Charlie!" This may have been "Dirty Jack" Pye, known as "The Doncaster Panther," who was still wrestling in his fifties and had never been knocked out!

Going home meant getting the bus from St. Andrew Square, and one night we cut it too fine and missed ours. We had a twenty-minute wait at that time, and Hugh propelled me into a pub where, in naval uniform, I had my first strong drink—a rum and peppermint.

I got my initial taste of life at sea in the division's coastal minesweeper, HMS Killiecrankie, sailing from Granton Harbour to Portland, taking part in a minesweeping exercise, and then steaming back to Granton—a week's trip in all.

I had my first, and thankfully my last, experience of seasickness on that trip, spending the whole southward leg being wretched and wishing for death. It must have sorted me, though, because despite being in some horrific weather at sea since, I have not felt the slightest hint of "mal de mer."

Hugh's family—miners—moved to Bathgate in West Lothian, and our wrestling nights came to an end. He still came to the RNVR, though, until he was called up about six months before I was.

These were also the days of my musical ambitions. Lonnie Donegan had just got half the youth of the country hooked on "skiffle" music. Skiffle groups were springing up everywhere, and Penicuik was no exception. I had got hold of a guitar from somewhere and taught myself to play about twelve chords.

I teamed up with three other boys, Alex Hutchinson, Tommy Easton, and Ron Wilson, to form a group, which consisted of Alex and me on guitars, Tommy Easton initially on washboard before he got some drums, and Ron on an improvised double bass. It consisted of a plywood "Tinopal" drum, begged from the mill, a broom handle, and a length of bass piano wire. The notes were fairly approximate, but the beat was great.

We kitted ourselves out with identical shirts, bootlace ties, and blue jeans and called ourselves, rather unimaginatively, "The Blue Jeans."

We practised in each other's houses, driving our parents up the wall, but eventually went out and played in public. We were very well received in the Penicuik area, playing at various functions and, a couple of times, in the interval of the Saturday night hops in the Cowan Institute, now Penicuik Town Hall.

Ron Wilson's father was a foreman in the coating house of Eskmills, and Ron had to pull out when his family moved away. Another local lad, Bill Young, took Ron's place but we only had a few gigs together when I went on my way to the Navy.

I had actually just completed my City and Guilds Paper Technology exam when I received my call-up papers in April 1958. I was nineteen by then and beginning to hope that they had forgotten me.

On the afternoon of May 6, I got on a train at Princes Street Station, Edinburgh, and made my slow way, changing twice, to Plymouth, where, at about 8:00 a.m. I reported as instructed, at the main railway station, to a naval patrol unit.

With a couple of other lads, I was put into the back of a van and whisked, via the Torpoint Ferry, to HMS Raleigh, on the Cornish side of the River Tamar.

It is the custom of the RN to give all its establishments, floating or ashore, the title of Her Majesty's Ship. HMS Raleigh was the sixth establishment of that name, its predecessors all being real ships of the line.

On May 8, 1958, I ceased to be William James Allan Neil and became Ordinary Signalman P/J979999 Neil, WJA.

Joining was a blur. Each arrival was given a card marked "Joining Routine" and had to visit each of the departments listed, do whatever had to be done there, collect a stamp on the card, and move on. Included were medical and dental examinations, weighing, photograph, uniform issue, and so on.

In my case, on arriving at the uniform issue, I placed my kitbag on the counter and took out all my RNVR kit.

The rating muttered something like, "Effinnell! Another effing amateur effing sailor!" before consigning my beautifully pressed and cared-for kit to a heap at the back of the room and handing me a distinctly worn-looking set of clothing—unpressed—plus the badges for me to sew on.

My wonderfully "bulled" boots met the same fate in the footwear store, and I was handed a pair that looked as though they'd been rubbed in particularly matt soot and treated with rough sandpaper.

The first meal was dinner (they don't have "lunch" in the navy, except in the wardroom where the officers hang out).

Now I have always contended that my mother, for all her admirable qualities, would have picked up Olympic Gold had there been an event for cooking catastrophes. I had been eighteen years of age, on an RNVR trip, before I found that cabbage was not actually the same colour and consistency as porridge! It seemed the problem was that my father did not like onions—they disagreed with him—so Mum wouldn't have an onion in the house.

Wartime restrictions probably had a bearing on things, but so did my dad's poor wages, and it was always the cheapest meat that found its way into the Neil kitchen.

Mum would buy mince that was probably 30 percent fat and 30 percent gristle, the remainder being cut from some unspeakable part of a cow. She put it in a saucepan with some water and boiled it for an hour, and then let it cool before taking the solid fat off the top. That fat would find its way into the frying pan; the mince would be boiled up again, thickened with "Bisto," and served with liquid mashed potato and something grey and mushy.

Stew was done the same way. Bless Mum. In the latter years of her life, I had her eating food with garlic in it, not to mention mild curries!

Dinner at HMS Raleigh that first day was carrot soup followed by Irish stew. Many in that intake were from a refined and educated background, their call-up having been deferred until they finished university, and noses were wrinkled all round with cries of "Ugh, what on earth is this?"

I thought, "What are they going on about? This is the best food I ever tasted!"

My stay at HMS Raleigh consisted of six weeks of basic "square-bashing." The communications ratings were separated from the other incomers, so that there were not too many of the confrontations that took place between the slightly sophisticated former and the bog-standard latter.

One of the signalmen in my group, a certain Steve Berrisford, with whom I became very friendly, was splashed in the shower with cold water. The villain was one of the seamen intakes, a Glaswegian.

Steve said something to the effect of "Would you mind not doing that?" delivered from an erect six foot six to the little Glasgow tough, who reached up, grabbed Steve by the throat and muttered, "Any mair o' yer high horse an' I'll cut ye tae ribbons."

With his normal insouciance, Steve replied, "Well, we'd better make sure it doesn't happen again."

Baffled, the aggressor returned to his own friends.

Later, Steve confided, "What was he going to cut me with? He was as naked as I was!"

Raleigh was also where I ceased to be "Billy," which I had always hated, and became Allan to all but my immediate family and Penicuik friends. Unbelievably, the short Glaswegian who had threatened Steve was also called William Neil. On the drill square soon after arrival, the GI (gunnery instructor—they always took drill) pointed this fact out. The nametag on his shirt said "W. NEIL," while that on mine announced "WJA NEIL."

The GI enquired what the J and A stood for, and I told him. "Okay," he said. "He will be Neil W and you will be "NEIL J" or "NEIL A." "Can you make it A, sir?" I asked. That was how it happened.

There was no "shore leave" until three weeks were completed, when all those who wanted to "go ashore" had to board a "liberty boat" and be marched through the gate. Steve and I wandered down to a little place called St. John's, entered a cider bar, and indulged for the first time in a couple of pints of scrumpy. It did for me. Walking out of the pub into the fresh air, the ground came up to meet me, and I woke up in my bunk in Raleigh in the morning.

After the Raleigh experience, the communications trainees were sent off to HMS Drake—the signals school part at St. Budeaux, just across the Tamar in Devonport.

There the radio operators and visual signalmen were separated, and I found myself in a class of eight. They were Ray Johnson from York, John McKellar from Kilmarnock, Mike Boden from Liverpool, Steve

Berrisford from Barnes, London SW13, Peter Lillington from Reading, Peter Dimbleby from Uxbridge, Harry Hart from somewhere in London, and me.

Royal Naval Signals School, St Budeaux 1958. Author middle row far right, Steve Berrisford centre back row.

Training went on apace. Learning Morse and semaphore was done on the parade ground in the form of what were known as "biffers." The students paired off (always Steve and me, the crafty bugger). Someone sent a semaphore message, and one of the pair read it while the other wrote it down; then we changed over, so that the original "reader" was now writing. That was followed by one of the pair reading a Morse message in the same way, then again changing over.

The difference was, as Steve had realised, that eighteenth months' experience in the RNVR meant my semaphore and Morse were near perfect, so at the change-over, instead of a 180-degree turn, we did a 360-degree one, so Steve and I always came top of the class. On the final test, Steve came top because I made a small error on my "read"!

The subterfuge was not discovered until Steve had to take a genuine Morse message on HMS Adamant, months later. Other skills learned were how to use voice radio, how to encode messages, and, most valuable, because I still use it—touch-typing. I am using that skill right now!

On my first leave from St. Budeaux, it was obviously a little far to go to Penicuik for a long weekend, and Steve kindly invited me to spend it with his family at their splendid house on the edge of Barnes Common.

This was an atmosphere as alien to me as if I had been landed among kindly Venusians of an intelligence I could only dream of. Steve's father, A. G. Berrisford, was an academic of some renown in educational circles and had written and published plays. His mother had been a teacher and was efficiency with two capital Es.

The food at table was ethereal, the conversation breathtaking. I felt they must think I was some kind of primeval creature dragged from the bog by the arcane workings of the Royal Navy, some tongue-tied little Scottish idiot from a council estate. If they did, they never once showed it.

Steve had a car! The only person I had known to have a car had been Jack Welsh, the owner of a sweetshop opposite the Dodds' in Penicuik. Jack was ancient, and Steve was only nineteen, yet here he was driving me round the capital of the United Kingdom at two in the morning in his Riley 1.5, which backfired every time he took his foot off the throttle.

We drove around Buckingham Palace three times, and each time we passed the sentry he made the Riley backfire. Today we'd have been shot as terrorists!

After leaving St. Budeaux, Steve and I, plus Mike Boden, found ourselves posted to the submarine depot ship HMS Adamant, almost permanently stationed in the Gareloch, near Helensburgh, Dunbartonshire.

I learned to sleep in a hammock. There were nearly forty ratings in the communications messdeck (living quarters), while there were only six bunks. People crashed out on and under tables, and the rest found somewhere to sling a hammock, either in the messdeck or in a corridor somewhere. I got quite attached to the hammock life, and when given the opportunity to upgrade to a table I declined it.

Life was simple. I'd spend the day taking messages off the teleprinter, typing them up and duplicating them, before forwarding them to whomsoever they were of interest.

Mealtimes were great—something different every day, and the soup getting better daily as the leftovers were consigned to the cauldron. And the bread! It was freshly baked and I've never tasted better. Evenings were spent aboard playing card games, except on pay day, when we would foray into Helensburgh to sample the beer and, for others more fortunate, the girls.

One weekend in three I spent back home in Penicuik. I took Steve the first time and my family loved him. They'd never met anyone like him and had only seen his educated kind with the laconic turn of phrase in the Playhouse cinema on a Saturday night. My twelve-year-old sister Janette told Steve that she would marry him one day! Whenever our leaves coincided, I took him home with me.

Adamant had a trip to Belfast in early 1959, which I missed out on, being taken to Cowglen Military Hospital in Glasgow to have my inflamed appendix removed. As I lay on my bed, the grizzled old surgeon who was to do the job came to see me and prodded my stomach. I could not miss the unmistakable whiff of whisky on his breath or the fact that his hands were shaking as he prodded. I was too far gone to worry. I just wanted the pain to go away.

Appendectomy scars nowadays are two inches long, maximum. Mine is nine inches, as if that surgeon had needed a bigger hole to peer into.

I was back on board in time to go on a NATO exercise with Adamant that took the ship to Gibraltar and the Atlantic off the North African coast, with a visit to Casablanca.

Gibraltar was an eye-opener. There must have been twenty sizeable ships, British, Canadian, French, and US in the harbour. The little town of Gibraltar was bursting at the seams, and getting to any bar was nearly impossible in the crush. Enough matelots made it, though, judging by the drunken bodies littering the road back to the harbour and the constant to-ing and fro-ing of naval patrolmen siphoning them into paddy wagons.

Offenders' Parade was the naval term for when defaulters (offenders) were hauled up before the "skipper" (captain) or "jimmy" (first lieutenant). These must have been major events aboard many vessels the following morning.

At that time, the Royal Navy had a long tradition of distributing rum just before dinner at midday. Ratings were divided into three categories for the purpose of the grog ration. "G" meant you took your grog. "T" meant "temperate"—in other words, you did not want a rum issue—and "UA" meant you were underage. Woe unto any rating who elected to be "T." If you did not want your rum ration, it was expected that you would still register as "G" and your grog would be distributed among others in the messdeck.

Up to and including leading hands got their grog as one part rum and two parts water. As the rum was around 100 proof, that meant you got over a third of a pint of booze at around 33 proof. Nothing could be saved; it all had to go down the hatch immediately.

Chiefs and petty officers were able to take it neat.

The main effect of this was that if a ship were to be called into action at around 2:00 p.m., not only would the junior ratings be drunk, but also their NCOs would be paralytic! God help Great Britain if WWIII had broken out on any afternoon in 1959!

Each chief or petty officers' mess had an elected "bubbly bosun," the man who arranged to collect and distribute the rum ration. On Adamant there was one particular yeoman of signals—a petty officer signalman—who had the job. Notoriously he used to manage to retain a double issue for himself and then spent the afternoon sound asleep beneath a gun sponson—a circular mounting on which smaller defensive weapons such as the Bofors anti-aircraft guns would be fastened to give them the facility of swivelling.

En route from Gibraltar to the NATO exercise, the captain of HMS Adamant elected to have a full-scale anti-aircraft gun drill.

Around 3:00 p.m., all the Oerlikons and Bofors guns on Adamant fired off, with a certain yeoman of signals fast asleep under one sponson, emerging thirty seconds later, staggering around, chalk-white and with his eardrums shot away!

Adamant was at Casablanca for two nights, and half the crew got ashore on the first day, the remainder the next. Steve and I got ashore on day two. Apart from the crush of Gibraltar, which was really much like Plymouth, only warmer, this was my first time on foreign soil, and the sights and sounds entranced me.

Like most British matelots, however, Steve and I succumbed to the lure of hard drink. Morocco was a French colony in those days, so booze was readily available.

We got hold of some cherry brandy dirt-cheap and got totally blinded, and after miraculously getting aboard past the naval patrolmen at the top of the gangway, I was promptly sick over the seaward side of the ship. Adamant went back to sea with a bright pink stain down her starboard side! Boozing and being sick were a large part of my life in those days.

With Adamant back in the Gareloch, the powers that be in The Admiralty decided that they wanted nothing more to do with national servicemen on board live ships, and in August 1959 Steve and I found ourselves posted to HMS Mercury—the other RN signals school.

Mercury was situated in the picturesque Meon Valley near Petersfield in Hampshire. Steve and I had elected to be "Pompey" ratings on passing out from Budeaux, which meant that all our records would be held at HMS Nelson—Portsmouth Barracks. Mercury was under Pompey's wing. Mike Boden, on the other hand, was a "Guz" rating—a Plymouth man, so he went off back to St. Budeaux.

The rest of my service was spent swanning around Mercury. I did a course to qualify as a leading signalman and passed with no problem, meaning an immediate promotion to TO1, just below leading rate.

I was a chief's messman at the base, a post that meant skivvying for the chief yeomen and other chief petty officers—no big deal, as it just meant laying tables and clearing them and shoving the dishes through the washer. Defaulters took care of the heavily soiled cooking pans and trays as part of their punishment.

Every other weekend was taken off. On many of these, I went back to Barnes with Steve and was admitted into his eclectic circle of friends, got drunk, got sick, and got to know and love jazz music. The Bull at Barnes and Humphrey Lyttelton's Jazz Club at 100 Oxford Street, W1 were two favourite experiences.

Release from the navy came four months earlier than expected, as someone realised they were paying us money for nothing. Steve and I saw our time out navigating brooms around the naval barracks at Portsmouth, and I was home in time for Christmas 1959.

The navy did put a tempting offer in front of me. I had qualified in August as a leading rate—the equivalent of a corporal in the army or Royal Air Force—and the discharging officer told me that if I were to sign up as a regular for nine years, I'd be promoted straightaway with back pay as a regular leading hand to the date of passing the exam. Before that my pay would be adjusted up to the regulars' rate—all backdated to the date of my joining. In those days, it was a healthy sum of money.

I did consider it, to be sure, but I thought I had a good and secure job to go home to; plus at twenty-one years of age, nine years is one hell of a chunk of one's life! Also, in October I'd met a girl, the first ever to show any interest in me, and I was smitten. I'm not going to mention the poor kid by her real name. I was wrong for her, and she was wrong for me, and it all ended in tears and a hurt that affected me for years to come. I guess it did for her too.

Let's call her Jean.

# CHAPTER 4

## Hard Times: A Move to London and a First Love That Didn't Work Out

The first two momentous events of my regained civilian life both came as complete shocks.

Firstly I introduced Jean to my family and found that she was disapproved of in no uncertain manner. My father, as usual, tried not to show it. My mother's opinion was plain, even if she said nothing. My sister Catherine left me in no doubt about where she and my parents stood. My girl was not welcome. It did not take a lot for a girl to acquire "a bad reputation" in Penicuik, and it seemed that local opinion was that whatever it was, Jean had done it. Whatever "it" was had happened before my time, so I considered it irrelevant tittle-tattle that people referred to "it" without actually telling me what "it" was.

I'd never had a girlfriend before, and I saw no prospects of ever getting another, and, anyway, I was hooked on her and believed she was on me.

The second shock came when I presented myself back at the paper mill. There was no job for me. On finishing his army service, Archie had been despatched to work at the London office, and of course there was my successor as junior—Edmond Pendrich. There would be no national service for Edmond, so he would be going nowhere. Ergo, all jobs filled.

I, too, was offered a job in the London office; otherwise, I was out of work. My parents were of the opinion that I should take the London offer. Jean was unhappy but said she would let me get settled and then follow me down when I had found a place to live.

In 1960, that an unmarried couple should live together was unthinkable, especially in a Church of Scotland environment, my father being an Elder of the Kirk, too.

New Year's was spent in a dreadful atmosphere, tears being shed all round. There was a confrontation between my parents and me, when I declared that I was twenty-one years old, a child no longer. I was going to London, and Jean was going to follow soon after.

I went to Steve's first, of course, while I searched for a place to live. I could not have afforded to stay in SW13 as accommodation was well out of my price range. The cost of commuting on the train to the City of London, where James Brown & Co.'s office was, would have meant I could not afford to eat given what my pay was to be—all of twenty-one pounds, ten shillings and six pence a month! There was a promise of a "substantial rise" once I had settled in—in six months!

I found a bedsit near Swiss Cottage tube in Hampstead and paid a month in advance from cash given by the company to cushion the blow. Before the month was up, I realised I couldn't afford to stay there. The landlady, a rather straitlaced and severe Mrs. Hodson, was happy to let me go, fortunately without further charge.

I'd started to look within walking distance of the office and had found a filthy basement just off Commercial Road, Whitechapel, right in Jack the Ripper territory. It consisted of a bedsit with a dirt-encrusted, one-ring electric stove for cooking, a blackened sink, and a toilet with a cracked bowl. Water would have to be heated on the stove, and there was no bathroom, not even a communal one. The wallpaper and paint were both in horrible condition, and the carpet was manky. The place stank of neglect and abuse.

The only three things the slum had going for it was that it was within easy walking distance of the office, it had a half-decent lock, and the rent was only £8 7s 6d a month. That's just under £8.40 in today's money, half the rent of the place at Swiss Cottage. Interestingly, if you compare that to today's value, using average earnings in your calculations, the rent would have been £332.77. My wage of the time, £21 10s 6d a month, computes as £855.26 today. Work it out for yourself!

The landlord was a little East End weasel, some five feet three inches tall, who owned the rest of that terraced slum and several other properties in the area. He told me I could do the place up at my own expense, and I paid him a month up front.

I borrowed a wheelbarrow and spent the weekend searching demolition sites, of which there were several in that area, and I managed to acquire a replacement toilet bowl and a slightly less battered and greasy electric cooker. Miraculously, I managed to change the toilet without a plumbing disaster, and I used the wheelbarrow to take the old one away, plus the hotplate and the rancid carpet. These were dumped on various demolition sites. I found a reasonable bit of carpet indoors on another site.

I bought some cheap lining paper and paste, some sandpaper, and Woolworth's paint and got to work over the next two weeks whenever I got the chance.

Jean was writing to me at the office, as there was no telephone available to her. I kept her informed and received a letter stating that she was coming down in the bus on a date three weeks ahead.

At the end of the month, a Friday evening, the landlord called for his rent. I had it ready for him. Proudly I showed him my handiwork.

His response was to shake the money in my face. "That's only half the rent. This place is worth twice that now."

I protested that we had agreed a rent and also that I could do the place up. His response was, "Oh, yeah. Where's the rent book?"

He had been due to give me that document that day, but it was still in his pocket. I told him as much and that I could not get any more money until Monday. My dwindling money was actually in the post office, but to gain time I told him it was in the bank.

He informed me he'd collect Monday evening and when I tried to protest he called to someone waiting outside. An enormous thug with no neck and shoulders like a gorilla came in. The landlord said to him, "Tell the boy here what happens on Monday if he doesn't have the rent money."

"I get to rip your fucking head off."

The landlord honoured me with a greasy smirk and told me that either I handed over another £8 7s 6d on Monday evening or, if I were still here, he'd turn me over to his friend. If I didn't want to pay him, I was free to sling my hook over the weekend.

When he'd gone I sat and pondered. The money given me by James Brown & Co. for the move and settling in was getting frighteningly low. I dashed a letter off to Jean asking her to put the move off, telling her why. I was boiling with rage and shame, knowing I'd have no chance against King Kong. I decided to sleep on it, and then rang Steve, asking if I could stay a couple of days. It was no problem.

I got up early on the Saturday and systematically undid all my handiwork, tearing the wallpaper off the walls and hitting the toilet seat with a brick until it broke. I carried the cooker to a site and dumped it and threw the carpet into the back yard in the rain.

I packed my bag and set off to Barnes, and left my bag there before going out to an area just north of the city to look for another place.

Steve knew somebody who suggested an agency near Arsenal Football Ground in Highbury, and on the Tuesday or Wednesday I actually found a tiny attic room, which masqueraded as a double as there was a foot of space all the way round the bed! At £3 a week I could just about afford it and agreed to move in the following Monday evening.

I reckoned I could easily walk to and from work from there. It was in a back street called Framfield Road, close to Drayton Park Station on the Moorgate Underground line, which I could use if the weather was really bad.

Steve and his parents were great, and I could have stayed there had I been on my own.

I duly moved in on the Monday. On Tuesday afternoon, there was a phone call at the office from Jean. I called her back at a phone box in Penicuik. She wanted to know what was happening, and when I told her I'd found another place, she told me she'd be down as planned, by train to King's Cross.

The landlord at Drayton Park, an African gentleman called Mr. Phillips from Sierra Leone, lived on the ground floor. I told him my wife was coming down from Scotland, still sure I would be bound for Hell for living in sin.

I had everything sorted out when she arrived a week or so later, and I met her at King's Cross. That night I told her about wrestling with my conscience about how we were going to live, and she suggested we fix a register office wedding.

A friend of her father, "Dasher" Logie (I never did find out his Christian name), had a job fixed up for Jean in a little factory near Essex Road tube station, just two stops from Drayton Park.

"Dasher" and Dennis—a young foreman from the factory—were the witnesses when Jean and I married at Islington Register Office on Wednesday, May 18, 1960.

The "reception" took place at Dennis's tidy little terraced house not far from the factory and was supposed to finish around 7:00 p.m. However, Dennis realised that the European Cup Final was on TV, dived out to get some drinks, and returned with enough beer to float a battleship.

The wedding party continued with Real Madrid beating Eintracht Frankfurt 7-3 while everyone got plastered and Dennis's wife (I can't recall her name for the life of me) provided food and persuaded Jean and me to stay the night. Jean was not expected at the factory for the remainder of the week. In the morning, I phoned in sick to the office. With my prize headache, I hardly had to pretend! I had told nobody about the wedding, either at the office or at home in Penicuik.

Even with both of us working, we found it was impossible to save more than a few shillings a week. It was out of the question that we could raise a deposit to buy any kind of house or flat in the London area, and local authority or trust housing was not an option.

The crunch came when the factory laid workers off, and Jean, being the last in, was one of those that had to go. The only work available to her that she could find and fancy doing was right at the bottom end of the menial scale.

"Dasher" had disappeared. I had met a couple of his friends and was not at all keen to associate with them, so I had not seen him for some weeks.

Jean had a bit of a disagreement with Mr. Phillips, our landlord. It got nasty, and she decided to take herself off back to Penicuik, with or without me. With her went the last of the money, to pay the train fare. I'd bought some basic stuff for the bedsit on credit and had to work it off before I could go back north, as had become my intention.

Quite apart from anything else, there was no prospect of decent pay for at least a couple of years. My promised "substantial raise" turned out to be of a very small percentage. The company was "experiencing difficulties" according to the London manager, Mr. George Dever. In fact it went to the wall within two years. My duties themselves were less than challenging—a bit of simple ledger work and acting as a message boy on foot within the city, taking urgent correspondence and samples to and from various paper merchants' offices.

Archie was firmly ensconced in the office, and no promotion above junior was anywhere in sight.

I was living on a 2/6d luncheon voucher i.e., just 12.5p each day from Monday to Friday. In a city café, it bought two sausages that tasted like and probably were composed of sawdust and some chips, and that was my diet during the week. At weekends I was living on meat-free stovies—a Scottish dish made from potatoes, dripping, salt and water. It should have had bits of mutton or corned beef added, but I could not afford that, pay off my debt, and save up the fare home.

In a desperate attempt to get some money together, I went to an agency that found jobs for casual bar staff and got a job Friday evenings and all day Saturday at a pub called the Rose and Crown in East India Dock Road, about four miles' walk from Highbury. The pub actually closed between 2:30 and 6:00 p.m. on my Saturday. After I'd had a bite to eat and a half hour nap on a chair, the landlord had me tugging and heaving crates and barrels around in the cellar and cleaning the bar out ready for the evening's trade.

Dockland, in those days, was nothing like the "yuppie" haunt and banking centre that it has become. In 1960 East India Dock was still a bustling top-end port, handling shipping from around the globe. The pub was a dive, full of visiting sailors, prostitutes, and Limehouse duckers and divers. Fighting was a regular pastime among the punters, and the landlord kept a shillelagh behind the bar to repel anyone trying to dive for the till during a fracas.

One of the working girls, a bottle blonde called Donna, used to talk to me in quiet periods, and I got an insight into the mind of a prostitute that was a valuable resource in a later life.

The bar job was hard work, especially the cellar stint, but sometimes the tips were good, and I began to put away a few shillings a week towards going home to Penicuik after paying off my loans. Besides, as I was working all day on Saturday, I copped for pie, mash, and beans, courtesy of Mrs. Hoolihan, the landlord's wife, who thought I was "Far too t'in!"

The walk home at midnight was a worry, though, as the route took me too close for comfort to the eastern end of Commercial Road, and I had a weather eye open for my erstwhile landlord and his pet Tyrannosaurus Rex.

I was getting the odd phone call at work from Jean, and she sounded happy in October when I told her I'd put in my notice both at work and to Mr. Phillips, the landlord.

I had seen Dennis a couple of times during this period and called to tell him I was off back to Scotland. We went for a drink, which turned into a drunken, maudlin evening, during which Dennis confided that on my wedding evening, while I was slumped in a drunken stupor in front of the television, Dasher had persuaded an equally drunk Jean to accompany him to the bedroom. Even in my inebriated state, I told Dennis I didn't believe him, and it would have come to fisticuffs if either of us had been able to stay vertical long enough to throw a punch.

In the first week of November 1960, I lugged my bags to Arsenal tube station, caught a train to Victoria Coach Station, and said a not-too-fond farewell to London. I'd written a few days earlier and was expected at Jean's parents' house in Penicuik, catching an early morning bus and walking the last four hundred yards.

I did not go round to see my parents. My fear of rejection was as binding as ever, even more so as I loved them dearly.

Life with Jean's parents was one long round of violent arguments between her mother and father. In the meantime, I was job hunting in Edinburgh, walking the ten miles each way to save money and getting nowhere until Jean's Uncle Harry turned up on a visit to his sister one day.

Harry was a clerk on the railway at Waverley Station in Edinburgh, and when he found that I could touch-type and also read and send Morse, he promised to put a word in for me.

How did we exist in those days without a telephone? The arrangement was that I call Uncle Harry at his work at the Waverley from a kiosk a few days later. The news was good. I had to go into the office for an interview and a test.

Was the road to take an upward turn?

# CHAPTER 5

## Dr. Beeching and Joining the Police: Working on the Railways, Getting Wed, and Becoming a Policeman

I got the job, which was as a telegraph clerk, bottom of the heap, at the Waverley. My knowledge of Morse code did it for me, plus my ability to touch-type, as the job involved the sending of railway telegram messages by Morse and the operation of the teleprinter.

After a brief period of training, I was let loose as a clerk, Grade 4. There was no Grade 5.

Meanwhile, things at Penicuik had gone beyond remedy. Jean and I were now subject to daily abuse, mainly from her mother, who, when in full flight, would have scared the living daylights out of the previously mentioned wrestler, Dirty Jack Pye.

Jean knew a guy with a two-bedroom flat in West Maitland Street, in the Haymarket area of Edinburgh. He was a bachelor in his mid-thirties, a lecturer at the Royal Dick Veterinary College, where she had worked as an animal handler for a while on leaving school. Jean told me she had bumped into him in Edinburgh, and he had offered us temporary accommodation in his spare room. We moved in. Let's call him George.

The flat was of a classic Edinburgh design, spacious, with high ceilings and bay windows with a view over busy West Maitland Street. It was beautifully furnished, and the walls were hung with prints of the works of the Impressionist painters. I couldn't thank our benefactor enough and told him I would be looking for permanent accommodation straightaway.

The job at the Waverley involved shift work—early mornings, days, late evenings, and the occasional night shifts. The railway ran round the clock, so this was necessary, as it needed a reliable flow of up-to-date information to function efficiently. In those days, the telegraph and teleprinter were the main means of distributing information quickly and accurately.

Messages were ranked in order of importance, MTs—Moving Train Messages—being top of the list, relaying information as to punctuality or problems down the line ahead of moving trains. Other messages included details of vulnerable goods consignments like whisky, train compositions, sleeper bookings, and seat reservations. Nowadays, of course, a computer does all that in a hundredth of the time, using a tenth of the labour.

George, our temporary landlord, appeared to be in no hurry for me to find permanent accommodation, and I'd been working at the Waverley for about three weeks when I did my first week of night shift. About the fourth night, I must have eaten something disagreeable as I got pretty sick, and the shift supervisor packed me off home. I walked to West Maitland Street, a distance of about two miles at around 2:00 in the morning. Feeling wretched, I let myself into the flat very quietly and on going to our bedroom I found it was empty. The rest is obvious.

When the dust had settled, Jean told me she had been in love with George since first meeting him three years previously, and she should never have left him. She was not going to leave him again, and I could do whatever I wanted to do without her. No wonder George was not in any hurry for the two of us to find our own accommodation!

I packed my things and was on the first bus to Penicuik, where I threw myself at the mercy of my parents, spending the next two days locked in my old bedroom. There was no fatted calf, but my mum and dad otherwise followed the narrative of the prodigal son pretty closely.

I was at rock bottom. Since then I have realised what it is that can make otherwise sensible people obliterate reality by use of drugs. I didn't have that option then, thank heavens.

Salvation came from an unlikely source. Steve Berrisford turned up on the doorstep to visit my parents, having no idea that I was back in Penicuik. He was working for the company that made Aspro painkillers and other para-pharmaceutical stuff and had just been appointed as their sales representative for the east of Scotland.

Pleading continued stomach problems, I stayed off work for around four days before going back. Steve stayed with my parents for two weeks until he found a flat in Fettes Row in Edinburgh New Town, and the two of us moved into it.

I was working shifts, of course, and Steve travelled around a lot, but we found time to hit the town whenever possible.

We found a couple of girls—Steve doing the spadework, of course. My girl was about five years older than I was and one hell of a lot more mature. We got on extremely well, and my parents liked her a lot. She might read this, so I'll call her Judy. She was very good for me and, together with Steve, got me back on track. Unfortunately she had a young son with whom I simply could not relate and after a year or so we split. I heard a few years later that she was happily married, and I felt pleased and not a little relieved.

On July 14, 1962, Sheila came into my life. It's her real name, and there is no point in pretending otherwise.

I remember the date because it was my younger sister Janette's sixteenth birthday; our parents were away, and I organised a party for her. Steve had just gone back south on promotion from his company.

Working in the office in the Waverley Station was a girl called Norma. I invited her and a couple of others, and she asked if she could bring her sister. I said she could.

On the evening of the party, Norma turned up with her sister, just about the most beautiful girl I'd seen in my life. I didn't dare even to speak to her, but into the party Norma got much the worse for drink and was violently sick. Being the party organiser, I felt responsible and was trying to take care of her when I was aware of Sheila helping me.

We got Norma cleaned up and into my bed, and I found myself alone with Sheila. I could not believe it, but she had taken an interest in me. The upshot was that we started going out, and Jean began rapidly to recede into the past.

One day in December that year, we were alone in the house at Eskvale Crescent and things took their natural course.

When Sheila announced that she was pregnant, there was only one course of action in the Penicuik of the day, and we were married in February 1963. On everyone's advice, I had divorced Jean as soon as possible after the Haymarket business.

Apart from her sister, Norma, Sheila had three brothers, John, Lawrence, and Colin. Her mother was an absolutely lovely and sweet lady called Edith, and her father was Willie.

Willie was a dyed-in-the-wool socialist and, as I had (and still have) definite left-wing leanings, we got on famously. He liked my own description of my political stance. In an election, given a straight fight between a Tory and a member of the Flat Earth Society, I would vote for the latter every time.

I had picked up a bit of a promotion in my railway job, which involved transferring to Buchanan Street Station in Glasgow. I had reached the dizzy heights of Railway Clerk Grade 3! Instead of moving in with either set of parents—the norm at the time—I took my new bride to lodge with my uncle and aunt, my mother's half-brother Jimmy and his wife, Rose, in Wishaw, in Lanarkshire, before moving into furnished rooms in the Burnside area of Glasgow.

With our child's birth becoming more imminent, we were anxiously trying to find better rented accommodation, but all we would be able to afford were in very downbeat areas of Glasgow. After the Whitechapel experience, I had no wish to deal with slum landlords.

Bless my dad. He stepped in to offer the loan of a deposit on buying a flat. We had to move out of Glasgow to afford it, but we found a place—a first-floor flat up a back stair—137 Bellshill Road, Motherwell.

Nominally it had two bedrooms, but in fact the second bedroom was a box less than two metres square. Never mind—it was ours, and on August 23, when Sheila went into labour, we got her to Bellshill Maternity Hospital, five miles up the road, and my boy Stephen came into the world.

The flat was beside the railway line on the opposite side to the huge Ravenscraig steelworks, noisy and grimy, but it was home, and the big advantage was that it was just five minutes' walk from Motherwell Station, with trains every twenty minutes into Glasgow Central. From there it was a ten-minute uphill walk to Buchanan Street.

Being a railway employee, of course, my season ticket cost a fraction of full price. The first ten miles were free anyway, with the remainder at around 30 percent of the normal.

I was working hard, maybe too hard, taking any overtime that was offered. One morning, coming off a double night shift (4:00 p.m. to 7:00 a.m.), I got on the usual train for a 7:00 a.m. finish—the 7:30 from Glasgow Central to London Euston, promptly fell asleep and woke up as the train was leaving Carlisle, next stop Preston!

We were not on the telephone, and mobile phones were pure science fiction in those days. When I got home, Sheila had been frantic but was now furious. As a result of this, I got the phone number of the little convenience store across the road, in case of future emergencies.

Sheila was pregnant again when the first shock of the Beeching era hit the railway. Dr. Richard Beeching had been appointed by the minister of transport as chairman of the British Railways Board in June 1961. His report "The Reshaping of British Railways" was published in 1963 and stated that only half the routes covered the cost of operating them, and that half the stations produced about 95 percent of all the revenue. His answer was a totally ruthless wielding of a big axe. Whole lines were closed down, their stations demolished or boarded up and their staff chucked on the scrap heap. Of the five lines from Scotland across the border, only two—the East and West Coast main lines—survived.      One      village—Riccarton—on      the

Edinburgh/Galashiels/Carlisle line had no road access. All households in the village had at least one member employed by British Rail. They found themselves not only out of work, but also cut off except for a rough forest track that was laid hurriedly in 1963. Riccarton residents were only little people, so their fate was unimportant.

Glasgow's Buchanan Street station was in the first wave of the chop. I was made redundant, with the offer of a similar job at Queen Street Station, which I accepted. It was a shorter walk from Central Station than Buchanan Street!

Meanwhile our second son—Gregor—was born on St. Patrick's Day, 1966, and life went on. A couple of weeks later, the word came that the Queen Street operation would also be closed down under Beeching. Again I was made redundant, this time with no option, my own personalised axe being timed to hit my neck in July.

I applied for several vacancies within the British Rail family, with totally negative results. Thousands of railwaymen were hunting a handful of jobs.

One day in early May, on my way in for a 4:00 p.m. start at Queen Street, I bought a copy of the *Glasgow Evening Times*. I turned to the Sits Vac pages and was astonished to see advertisements from around thirty police forces and constabularies in England and Wales, who had, it seemed, just been given Home Office authority to swell their ranks. Most of the ads had cut-out forms attached, where you could fill in your name, address, age, date of birth, and telephone number. I think I completed twenty-three such forms, posting them at Central Station on my way home to Motherwell. The day after the next, when I came in to work at 4:00 p.m., there was a message to ring an Inspector Osborne on a Lewis (sic) number. I was puzzled. "Inspector" suggested police, but I couldn't recall applying to the police on the Outer Hebrides. All was clarified when I asked the operator for the number. Lewes, with two "Es," is in East Sussex and in those days contained the headquarters of the East Sussex Police. Inspector Osborne was the force recruiting officer.

I confirmed my interest in joining, and it was obviously a very competitive market, as the inspector asked me for the identity of my local police station. I told him it was Motherwell, and he asked me if I would be prepared to go in there in two days' time to take a written exam.

I replied that it was no problem. He asked me to send him a photograph of myself, and I agreed to post one off first thing in the morning.

The next day I was on duty at 2:00 p.m., and the inspector rang again soon afterwards to confirm that I was expected at Motherwell Police Station at 10:00 a.m. the next day. The exam paper had been sent by telex and an acknowledgement duly received.

I hadn't told Sheila up to that point, not wishing to get her hopes up, and she was intrigued and not a little worried when I told her where I was off to at 9:30 the next morning. Why, she asked, did I not apply for a Scottish force? There were two reasons. Firstly at five feet ten inches, only one force in Scotland would take me—Glasgow. Secondly, the only force in Scotland recruiting was, yes, Glasgow. Having worked there round the clock and having seen some of the gratuitous violence meted out after pub closing hour, I had no wish to be a policeman in that city.

The exam was fearsomely difficult; at least it would have been to the average five-year-old. It took me about ten minutes of the sixty allocated, and that was after double-checking everything! I also had to fill in a form stating my job history.

The results must have been sent to Lewes by telex too. The next day was Friday, and I was working 10:00 a.m. to 6:00 p.m. to be followed by a long weekend off. Mr. Osborne was in touch before lunch. The exam result was satisfactory. When could I come to Lewes?

I told him I could be there by overnight train on Monday morning. That was excellent, he replied, as there were others to be seen that morning. As a redundant employee of British Rail, I was entitled to a free return ticket, which I arranged quickly, and the inspector sounded pleased that I would not be making an expenses claim.

Rien n'a changé!

Sheila said she had doubts about moving so far away, until I told her that East Sussex was a favourite holiday destination. If I got in, which I still doubted, I could end up working at a nice rural or seaside town far removed from the grot and grime of Glasgow and Motherwell. That cheered her up.

I got the night sleeper from Motherwell on Sunday evening, promising to ring the shop opposite with any news.

I'd worked out how to get to Lewes and, as instructed by the inspector, I rang him on arrival. Ten minutes later, a police car collected three other men and me and conveyed us to Malling House, the police headquarters.

The ensuing medical was as derisory as the exam had been, and I was soon ushered into the austere presence of the deputy chief constable, Mr. Pat Ross, and Inspector Osborne. The latter complimented me on my choice of wife (the photo I'd sent was of the two of us on our wedding day!). Much was made of the fact that I had experienced naval discipline, with Mr. Ross bemoaning the fact that it was difficult to recruit young ex-servicemen these post–national service days.

I was accepted and given a starting date of June 6, 1966, my own personal D-Day! Being redundant, I had no need to work any notice; I just wanted some time to sell the flat. I phoned the shop in Motherwell with the news.

I was told at the interview that I would be posted to Hove, abutting Brighton to its west and nowadays part of the City of Brighton and Hove. As I had a young family, I was going to need some assistance with accommodation, as I knew housing was going to be much more expensive down there.

Inspector Osborne told me to get a train to Hove and gave me a number to ring on arrival, when I would be collected and shown a police house, which I would be invited to accept.

I was met at Hove Station by Sergeant Bill Crawford. He was personnel sergeant and a phlegmatic fellow Scot. He drove me to Chalky Road in Portslade, where a block of four new houses, numbers 2–8, were in the final stages of completion. Number 2 was to be mine, end-of-terrace and three-bedroomed. This was heaven. I couldn't sign the agreement quickly enough.

I was instructed to present myself with my family and furniture on Friday afternoon, June 3, and to ring Sgt. Crawford, who would come out straightaway with the keys.

I got a shock on my arrival home. It had been announced in the local papers on that very day that all the dwellings on our side of Bellshill Road were due for demolition under a grandiose plan for the "regeneration" of the town. In the event I got exactly what I'd paid for the flat, less legal fees and the cost of removal, I would not have enough money left repay my father at that point and was going to arrive in East Sussex stony broke.

Steve and I had kept in touch, and he had visited me at Motherwell with his wife and baby. I arranged for us to stay over with them in Barnes on the night of June 2, giving the removers time to get to Chalky Road. I worked a bit of a flanker with British Rail by giving notice to expire June 6. This enabled me to get free tickets for the family and me from Edinburgh to Portslade.

On May 28, our pitifully small collection of furniture and effects was taken away by removers. As a part-load, it would take some time to get to Portslade and the company was happy to deliver on June 3. We stayed in the Blacks' very crowded flat in the centre of Edinburgh until it was time to go.

Of course, we visited Penicuik, and I broke the news to my father that I would not be able to repay his loan for some time.

He replied, "It's okay, son. I'm very proud of you for joining the police. I don't expect to see it back."

My life direction was changing again, and this time it looked very bright for the future.

Come in Police Constable 420 Neil of the East Sussex Police.

# CHAPTER 6

## Police Training School: How a Policeman Was Trained in 1966

On June 3, we all arrived at Portslade Station in the late morning. I rang Bill Crawford from there, and we took a taxi to Chalky Road. We didn't have to wait long. He arrived within fifteen minutes with the keys, just as a Croydon-based removal van stopped outside. It did not take long to unload, and I gave the guys ten shillings from my shrinking purse.

Bill instructed me to present myself to the duty inspector at Hove at 8:00 a.m. on the sixth, and we busied ourselves sorting out the furniture. We hadn't brought carpets, but the house was floor-tiled throughout the ground floor and had splinter-free flooring in the bedrooms.

One of our new neighbours came to introduce himself and his wife. His name was Jo Pannett, and, by a quirk of fortune, he has been working with me at Sussex County Cricket Club as a steward for the last two years! I met the others very shortly afterwards—Dave Fickweiler and Belle, and John Atkins and his wife. Dave became a very skilled fraud investigator and went on to leave the police to work in the City of London a few years later. Poor John died as a serving detective sergeant at Newhaven, just along the coast.

After sorting everything out on the Saturday, the family got on a bus and familiarised itself with Brighton, to all of us a very exciting town in those days.

I duly presented myself at Holland Road, Hove Police station, at 8:00 a.m. on June 6. Two other newcomers arrived that day, Roger Brace and Alan Gully. We were shown around the station and introduced to Chief Superintendent Lou Weeding. About noon we were piled into a van and taken to Lewes Magistrates' Court, where, along with other young men and one woman from various East Sussex stations, we were sworn in as constables.

From there it was HQ, where I was first introduced to the charms of Sergeant Myatt, the clothing officer—surely the inspiration for the film *Grumpy Old Men*. I arrived back home in the van with a huge bag of uniform, all provided except boots, for which an allowance was then paid. I still had my boots from my navy days, which had lain undisturbed in my parents' hall cupboard and which, apart from a good layer of dust, were still in pristine "bulled" condition, i.e., with toecaps so shiny you could almost shave using them. I had actually remembered to bring them south with me.

The afternoon was spent pressing trousers and tunics and brushing helmet and cap. When it came to the shirts, I had a moment of panic. They were the old-fashioned kind with separate collars, which had to be attached using two studs, a short one at the back and a longer one in front. I had no studs. None of the shops in the area supplied them, and I ended up getting a bus into Hove and buying two pairs from a bespoke tailor's shop just as the proprietor was closing shop for the day.

The next two days were spent at Hove, firstly getting the correct wearing of uniform sorted out. In those days, PCs were supplied with not only a fairly heavy raincoat, but also with a cape, made of thick navy blue serge. It came in one piece, a lot like a poncho with a hole to put one's head through and a chain and two hooks to close it around the neck. It was the ideal garment for walking around on dark, cold winter nights. There was no way for anybody to tell if you had your hands in your pockets, or if you were carrying a bag of chips!

For practical policing purposes, it was also the ideal garment for prowling around in the dark, as the chain and hooks were coated in matt black paint and there was nothing to reflect light. It also concealed your shape. The best coppers watched without being seen, unlike today's high-visibility presence. The PC himself decided when he ought to be visible, to deter or reassure.

On Tuesday afternoon and Wednesday, we read the report of Hove's biggest incident in years—an infamous fire that had destroyed the Old Town Hall and Magistrates' Courts in the early hours of January 9, some six months earlier.

I don't recall much of the ensuing ten or so days, except that there was a three-day induction course at HQ to give us an idea of the basics of police work, without going into all the theory stuff that was to be our fate soon afterwards.

On Thursday afternoon, June 16, Bill Crawford gave the three of us rail vouchers to Folkestone Central, where we would be met and taken to the Police District Training Centre at nearby Sandgate. We had to report there on Sunday the twentieth between 1:00 and 5:00 p.m. We were then sent home to have Friday and Saturday with our families.

Trains to Folkestone from London were half-hourly, and a car, which ran recruits to the Centre, met each arrival. Two others arrived on the same train as I did. Roger got there a little later, and Alan made his own way there in his Ford Consul, despite having been told there was no parking for students! The course was fifteen weeks long with two weekends off to return home. Students were allowed out of the grounds only on Saturdays, so Alan had to fret for a week about his pride and joy being parked out on the streets of Sandgate.

My course was number 220 and my class was A2. There were twenty recruits in the class, forty on the course. The other nineteen in my class were, from East Sussex, Roger Brace, Allan Gully, Barry Jackson, Don Jeffery, and Marvin Tribbeck; Brighton Borough supplied Peter Dacey, Jim Dawes, and Graham Hill; from Hampshire and Isle of Wight came Brian Buffin, Ray Croucher, Roger Smith, and Ray Whitear; Chris Cook, Roger Davis, John Lawrence, Tony Leach, David Sleath, and Dave Weston were all Southampton City men. The final member of the class was Mike Walker, all the way from Jersey in the Channel Isles.

The class instructor was Sgt. Ernie Quant of Southampton City; the course instructor was Inspector Dick Clay from Brighton Borough. Mr. Clay impressed us straightaway when we saw a BEM medal ribbon heading the military stuff on his tunic. The Brighton guys told us it was for an act of heroism as a PC at Brighton.

As John Lawrence had been a sergeant in the army, he became drill leader. The drill instructor was the famous (among Sandgate alumni) Sgt. Will Squires. He was a Kent officer and was always hardest on Kent recruits, of which there were several in Class A1, the other half of the course.

Mention Will Squires to anyone who went through Sandgate and the words "Will's Hill" always come up. Will's way of punishing slackers was to make them double up the steep drive from the main gate with arms in "traffic signals 1 & 2" position—in other words, right arm aloft and left hand out at right angles to the body.

Physical training was the domain of Sgt. Ray Wallace, also of Kent. Not many people actually knew his Christian name, as he was universally known as "Punchy," having been a bit of a boxer in his time.

For some reason, "Punchy" kept picking on John Lawrence. Now John was the biggest man in the class, and, had he wanted to end his career, he could easily have flattened Punchy. John had been a heavyweight champion boxer in the army! Punchy was the least popular of all the instructors, and I achieved fleeting fame when he insisted on taking part in a football match on the right wing. I was in the opposing side at left back, and when Punchy came floating like a fairy down the touchline, he showed me a bit too much of the ball. I put him and ball into touch with a fair tackle that the notorious Norman "Bites yer legs" Hunter of Leeds United would have been proud of. Punchy went sick for a week, and John Lawrence took over the PT sessions.

The first weekend off came after five weeks. No assistance was given with the cost of getting home and back, so it was fortunate that Alan Gully had his car handy. We did not get away until after breakfast on Saturday and had to be back by 10:30 p.m. on Sunday. Going home by train, apart from the expense, meant I would not have got back to Chalky Road until the afternoon and would have had to leave again before teatime on Sunday.

Not surprisingly, those recruits who had transport brought their cars back that Sunday. In those days, parking was free and unrestricted in the majority of streets in Sandgate. I don't know what they'd do now, as the town today is the usual tangle of double yellow lines and time-limited pay-and-display parking bays!

No motorway route existed in 1966, so it was a lengthy cross-country journey back home inland after Rye via Udimore, Battle, and Lewes, avoiding the "trundlers" of Hastings and Eastbourne.

Sheila was unhappy, not surprisingly, having been left for five weeks with two small children and not much money. My first four weeks' wages had gone in the bank three weeks previously, all £60 of it, and already it was nearly all gone. There was not much I could do, though. I could hardly chuck the job in and make us all not only broke, but homeless to boot. At least, being stuck at Sandgate, I was not spending money, except on rolling tobacco, on which I'd cut right down, and a contribution to Alan Gully's petrol costs at 6 shillings or 30 pence a gallon!

Being confined to the training centre had that bonus, but the course itself was very intensive. Just before going off on the weekend, we had done the first exam, split into three parts—crime, traffic matters, and general police duties, the last covering everything from betting, gaming, and lotteries, through diseases of animals to the Vagrancy Act. There were over one hundred "definitions" to be learned verbatim, e.g., "Betting is the staking of money or other valuable thing on an event of a doubtful issue."

Lesson matters had also to be learned word-perfect from the unwavering authority of "Moriarty's Police Law," a copy of which was issued free to East Sussex recruits, but which had to be purchased by recruits from some other forces. I think it cost £1 at the time. Everything that a probationary constable had to know was contained between its austere, dark blue hard covers.

Back from our "weekend," we learned the results of the exam, and we had all done fairly well, although there were some who were going to have to work harder to get to the pass mark of 80 percent in each part of the final exam.

It went on as before, with another Saturday to Sunday break after ten weeks, following a second exam. Again I travelled with Alan Gully.

Five weeks were left on the course, four of these leading up to the final exam, which took place on the last Monday of the course. Everyone passed, and I was pleased with my average of 90 percent. The star performer, though, was Graham Hill, who got 100, 100, and 99 in the three tests. Sgt. Ernie Quant confided that there was no way he was going to be permitted to get 100 x 3! Years later Graham played a significant part during a tough time in my life.

The remainder of the course was spent on "practical exercises" and practice report writing before the passing-out parade on the final morning, September 17, taken by the chief constable of Kent with addresses from him and from the training centre commandant, Chief Superintendent Parkin. We learned from the latter that we had been the first intake ever in Sandgate's history to complete its initial course without losing a single one of our forty members along the way. The following course, 221, had already lost some of its number by its halfway mark!

A lot of proud parents attended along with the odd spouse. It was out of the question for Sheila to get there with the two children and no means of transport.

Back to Hove then, and police work for real.

# CHAPTER 7

## Hove First Time Around: First Posting and Learning the Practical Ropes

As well as a relieved wife and two happy boys, an envelope awaited me on my arrival back home.

Compliments of Sgt. Crawford, I would be working on C-section, commencing at 1400 hours on Monday. Briefing was at 1345 hours. After briefing I was to see him in his office.

Sheila was peeved. She had thought I would have a few days off before going in to work. She could not understand why I had not refused to go in. I think in retrospect that was when she started to become disenchanted with being a policeman's wife and when things began slowly to unravel between us. The fact that we were permanently broke did not help matters.

I duly reported on time and met my section. My inspector was to be Lawrie Finlay, and my sergeants were Jack Kitchen, Pat Regan, and Alec Hunt. I was introduced to the PC who was to be my "tutor" for the duration of a cycle of shifts. His name was Barry Godden, and he'd only been back from training himself for six months.

After briefing I was taken by Bill Crawford to see Superintendent Frank Cutting, the 2ic at Hove. My report from Sandgate was in front of him, so it must have been sent off before the end of the course, but after the final exam results.

Mr. Cutting complimented me but was at pains to point out that I could forget most of what I'd learned at the Centre because now the real learning was about to start. I reckon I heard the same statement from four other officers that day, including Barry as we walked out onto the streets.

Before going out, though, I had to make my "points card." These were the days before personal radios, and the only way information could be relayed to officers on the beat was to phone them at fixed locations at set times. Each beat had "points," where you had to arrive five minutes before a given time and wait until five minutes afterwards.

'Points' card, Hove Police 1966

Most of the "points" were police telephone boxes, and the officer would ring in from there. Others were just ordinary telephone kiosks where you waited to see if anyone contacted you. A few "points" were just locations where your sergeant would meet up with you. If the station wanted to contact you more urgently, the operator would call the police phone box where you were next due and an amber light would flash on it.

Woe betide the constable who missed a point without good reason. It was the only way the station could check on your safety, and a missed point would get people out looking for you. I still have my points card. It is divided into four sections, "A" to "D," and at briefing the sergeant would announce which points were in force that day. You noted that in your pocket book straightaway.

On the first day, Barry and I were on 4 beat. There were three points on it, Sackville Road South End, The Drive, and Woolworth's. Sackville Road was a normal telephone kiosk; the other two were police phones.

If we had been on "A" points that day, the point would have been made at twenty minutes past each hour. As we were on the 1400–2200 shift, the first would have been 1420 at Sackville Road South, then 1520 at The Drive, and 1620 at Woolworth's. On occasion the timing made it physically impossible to make the first point—for instance, on 11 beat on "B" points, the first point would have been 1405 hours, almost a mile from base. You just had to make sure the lady on the switchboard knew you were going to miss it before you went out.

Every copper will tell you that when you first walk out of the police station, you imagine every eye in town is on you. It's true!

That first afternoon we made our way slowly on to 4 beat. It was long past the times for the first two points and the next, Woolworth's police box, was the closest. Barry instructed me on the first duties of the beat officer. These were "Don't get wet," and make sure you get your tea stops sorted out.

The first of these was in the underground toilet for men right opposite Woolworth's, where the attendant's room was spotless, like the toilets in his charge, and was equipped with kettle, teapot, and "the makings."

This might sound like an easy life, but the whole idea of tea stops was not just to skive off, but also to maintain a network of information. You would not believe what two petty crooks talk about when standing at adjacent urinals, forgetting that on the other side of a thin door was a pair of receptive ears. By way of fair-trading, any problems at a tea spot received swift attention.

Barry was a good tutor. A no-nonsense South Londoner, he had a good way of putting information over. We started with the basic diet of probationary constables—things like two boys on a bike, bikes with no brakes, untaxed cars, and parked cars with bald tyres. Barry would demonstrate on the first of each category and show me how to speak to the public, firmly and fairly. He normally got the right reaction.

I learned that it was not a matter of totting up offences in the book, but of dealing with every incident on its merits. Unless the offence was serious or the offender was of the serial type, Barry told me, it was far better to let the offender correct matters himself.

One motorist on a subsequent day on 6 beat whose car had a bald tyre and a spare that was worse was booked up. Barry told him that if he showed up at our "point" at Montefiore Road in an hour and a half with a new tyre and a receipt for it, the offence report would be torn up in his presence. He did, it was, and isn't that a much better way of dealing with offenders than the grim-faced "only-doing-my-job" attitude shown by the current crop of "parking wardens," whose discretion in such matters is nonexistent?

Of course, that worked two ways also. If that driver had snarled the old question, "Haven't you got anything better to do?" I dare say the outcome would have been different, and no doubt Barry would have explained why!

The next week was nights, and a totally different way of policing.

The crux of the job, as previously explained, was that you were seen only when you wanted to be. You lived in the shadows, watching. People out walking late at night expected to be checked and frequently were. Unless they were drunk, they were almost always co-operative. Anyone thought to be acting suspiciously would be kept under observation from cover before being checked over.

People submitted to searches without demur. There was no obligation to have or give a reason for the stop, and the only record would be a pocket book entry of name, address, and date of birth. They usually ended up with a "Good night, sir, thanks for your cooperation," and "That's okay, mate, have a good night yourself."

Nowadays you must have a valid reason for the stop, one that you can back up at any inquest—such as a complaint of harassment—and a complicated form has to be filled in. While you're doing that, half a dozen better "stop" candidates might walk past unmolested.

Another essential duty on nights was "shaking hands with doors." Each shop door on your beat had to be checked, as had any opening windows, front and rear, if accessible. Any insecurity was reported on the next point after you'd kept an eye on it for as long as possible. If you missed one, you had some explaining to do.

Tea stops on nights were scarce, unless you were fortunate enough to have a hospital, railway station, or signal box on your beat.

One pub landlord, however, at the long-gone Clarence in North Street, Portslade always left a pint of beer and a pie, sausage roll, or sandwich out the back for the night bobby. The pub was slightly rough, being close to the harbour, and a night PC had once helped the licensee out of a sticky spot. He also liked a visit around 11:30 p.m. to dislodge those punters with no beds to go to so he could go to his.

A dentist in Western Road, Hove was equally kind with a thermos of coffee left outside his basement for the night PC on 6 beat. The other side of Western Road was on 1 beat, but the PC on that beat dared not cross for a coffee in case he was spotted "off his beat" by the sergeant!

Later in my probation, I was on 13 beat—South Portslade—waiting at a "point" outside the Kayser Bondor factory on the main coast road, twenty-five yards or so from the county boundary with West Sussex.

It was about 1:00 a.m., and as I waited there was a loud crash on the West Sussex side of the boundary. A car had been driven into a lamppost some fifty yards from where I stood. I ran to it to check if anyone had been hurt. The driver was okay—he told me he had nodded off at the wheel. I had been there a few minutes when I saw my sergeant's white A30 van pull up at my "point," and I ran to it, as he had a radio to contact West Sussex—in those days every road accident was recorded.

Sgt. Hunt's first words to me were, "What are you doing off your beat? For God's sake, man you're not only off your beat. You're off your Force area!" Even after I had explained, and he'd radioed a message to be relayed to Shoreham, he still grumped for a good five minutes till the West Sussex patrol car arrived.

I soon found out that early turn, 0600—1400, was going to be my least favourite shift. Having to be at briefing at 0545 meant I had to get the first bus from Chalky Road into Hove at 0515 hours, meaning getting up at 0445. Turning up at briefing unshaven was courting serious disapprobation from Jack Kitchen, a stickler for appearance.

In 1966 briefings were called "parades" and were held in the "parade room." Constables lined up at attention holding their "accoutrements" for examination—pocket book, whistle, and truncheon. I got into serious strife with Sergeant Kitchen one morning on early shift, when my front collar stud disintegrated and I improvised with a paper clip on arriving at The Nick. I was a whisker away from being "stuck on" for improper dress!

After the set of three shifts, I was on my own. On almost my first day on 1400–2200, I got my first "collar." I was on 1 beat, the smallest beat in Hove, but the busiest, right alongside the Brighton Borough boundary. I had my final "point" of the shift at ten past nine at the police phone box at Brunswick Place.

I was slightly early, so I had faded into the doorway of a nearby bank when I saw the figure of a man in a raincoat dodge into a similar aperture of a shop on the other side of the street. It aroused my suspicion, especially when I saw a girl in a miniskirt walking towards the shop from the opposite direction. As she reached the shop doorway, the man moved out and threw his raincoat open. The girl squealed, and I realised the man had his goods on display.

I ran across the road and grabbed him. The girl was laughing hysterically. I asked her if she knew where Hove Police Station was and she said she did. I asked her to go there and dragged "matey" across to the phone box. Within two minutes of calling in, a car arrived and we made our way back to The Nick. There was no sign of the girl on the way, and in fact she just vanished into the night. Fortunately (for me) the flasher, whose name I have long forgotten, "put his hands up," was charged, and kept in for court in the morning. Because I was the only witness, I also had to turn up in court, which pleased the family not at all!

Our flasher pleaded guilty to indecent exposure and was weighed off with a fine and given time to pay. He lived in Worthing, and on leaving court he got on a bus and promptly groped the conductress, who felled him with her ticket machine. Next day he was dragged back to court and remanded in custody.

After court I was told to stay on until 5:30, walk the "main roads," and then go home. I was picked up by a sergeant in Church Road and conveyed to the junction of Western Road and Holland Road, where the traffic lights were out of order. The sergeant instructed me to do a traffic point at this busy junction until the engineers sorted the problem out.

It was raining steadily, and I could think of a few dozen other jobs I'd rather be doing. At one point, when I was facing into the rain, a large bead of water gathered on the front of my helmet, just where it came down between my eyebrows. I had my right hand up stopping the traffic in front of me and my left hand out to the left holding those vehicles behind me. I became almost mesmerised by this growing drop of water, which seemed reluctant to drop off.

Unthinkingly I nodded my head to dislodge it, and the driver in front of me took it as a nod for him to come through. There was a wet skidding of tyres as a car coming from my left only just managed to stop right in front of me, avoiding both the oncoming vehicle and me by a whisker!

My next "body" came on nights when I was given 6 beat, which included a park known as St. Anne's Wells Gardens. In the middle of this park was a public toilet. About 1:00 a.m., I was walking past the toilet when I heard noises from within. I went to investigate, and in a whirl of movement a male person raced past me. I shouted for him to stop and was ignored so I gave chase. I was reasonably quick, but I was matched by the fugitive, whom I pursued south in Holland Road past the front door of The Nick. As I said, we had no radios. I pulled my whistle out and blew loud blasts as I ran past the police station.

Nobody came out!

I continued to chase my target south in Holland Road until we reached the Esplanade. He ran straight across it, jumped down onto the pebble beach, carried on, and threw himself into the sea, swimming away from land.

Well, enough was enough. I ran to the police phone at the southern end of Holland Road and rang in breathlessly. Sergeant Regan arrived within minutes, and we stood on the Esplanade and watched in the moonlight as our friend decided that it was a bit cold in there in November and swam back.

He had a number of old pennies in his pocket, and a search of the park revealed more near the toilet and the fact that the coin mechanism had been forced off the doors in the Gents. My "collar," a fellow-Scot named McNish, was charged. He had a long record of extremely petty crime and "went down" for three months.

A few months later, about midnight, I disturbed someone coming out of the back door of a social club. I gave chase as he tossed coins out of his pocket before tripping over some shuttering containing a recently laid concrete base for a garage. The builder had only finished it a few hours earlier, so it had not properly set. My quarry flew full-length into the softish concrete, gouging out a ragged gash. As I "felt his collar," I realised he was my old friend McNish, fresh out of

Lewes Jail, obviously having gone upmarket from his penny days, as the swag this time had been sixpenny pieces (2.5p in today's money!)

In the winter of 1966–1967, Brighton and Hove buses withdrew the early service from Chalky Road. I had to find another means of transport to get in for early turn, and I bought an old Ariel Leader 250-cc motorbike. Although I'd ridden bikes in my teens up in Penicuik, I hadn't bothered with a test, so I had to ride this one on "L" plates. The purchase of it seriously damaged my already weak finances but, as the other three (car-owning) Chalky Road residents were all on different shifts, I had to find a way to get in at that time of the morning.

The bike ran very well, and in the summer of 1967 I used it to go back to Sandgate for my "continuation course," this time held at Shorncliffe Barracks on the hill above the town. The students were accommodated in army huts, twenty to each.

It is only memorable for one incident, when a very patrician hyphenated Surrey officer began to get up everyone else's noses, and when he went out one evening everybody in the hut collaborated in moving his bed and locker out. The other beds and lockers were then closed up so that when he arrived back, with everyone else in bed, he had nowhere to go.

In the summer of 1967, East Sussex Police decided to go with the "unit beat policing" system that had been tried out in a northern force. It involved beats being given one officer who would not be moved off it and who would vary his shifts to cover it the best he could.

Panda cars—Morris Minor saloons liveried in distinctive sky blue and white—would liaise between these beat officers, one Panda to two beats, conveying paperwork and doing enquiries on the beats.

Hove had fourteen beats, three being light motorcycle patrols, which remained outside the Panda system, meaning we had five Panda cars. Only those beat officers whose areas were in close proximity to The Nick ever went in there; the remainder booked on and off and did their paperwork at police boxes.

This was also the starting point for the regular issue of two-way radios, facilitating instant communication between the various units in the system.

People point to this change as being the beginning of the deterioration of relations between the police and their public. I think there is more than a grain of truth in this, as the beat man on foot could be around for only 42 hours out of the 168 in a week, less the time spent on paperwork, court appearances, rest days, and annual leave. In addition, those constables with beats fairly close to The Nick were prone to being called in to do temporary jailer or prisoner escorts. The public had been used to having one around for most of the 168 hours. Officers driving around in cars, they said, and still do say, are not in real contact with the public.

Prior to the introduction of the unit beat system, it was not unusual for all fourteen beats in Hove to be covered on nights, with other foot constables patrolling the seafront and main roads. When I returned to Hove nineteen years later, there were no foot patrols at all on nights, and precious few on days.

Beat officers from the two Portslade beats (including the motorbike beat) worked from the former Portslade police station in St. Andrew's Road, as did four PCs from beats in West Hove. The West Hove foot beats shared a common corner at the old cinema, by then a bingo hall, in Portland Road. The nice thing about the bingo hall was that beneath it there was a boiler room, accessed from the rear of the building. This would still be very warm during the night and a good refuge from winter weather at 3:00 in the morning, after shaking hands with all the doorknobs on one's beat. If the weather was particularly foul, you could find the officers from 9, 10, 11, and 12 beats warming their hands in there!

On the domestic scene, we'd made friends with the Blundell family, not police, who lived in Hillbank Close, backing onto Chalky Road. They were Charlie, a mechanical genius, his wife, Marion, their two daughters, sixteen-year-old Sandra and Corinne, aged fourteen, and adopted eight-year-old son, Clive. Charlie had got hold of an ancient Mini in totally unroadworthy condition, which he put in my garage and worked on. He got it going and legal and proceeded to give me driving lessons in it.

Hove was crying out for qualified officers to drive the Pandas, and I put myself forward, without confidence, for a driving test, to be taken by the traffic superintendent, a man given governmental authority to conduct such tests. I carried it out in a large Commer van with all the gears the wrong way round and by some miracle I got through.

Returning to the police station, the superintendent pointed to my bike and said, "That's a nice Leader." I told him it was mine. He said, "Why has it got "L" plates on it?" He found out I'd been riding bikes off and on since I was sixteen and told me he'd borrow some riding gear from the traffic office and test me on the bike while he was there.

Unbelievably I passed that too. I don't know of anyone else who has passed his car and motorcycle tests within an hour and a half. Not only that, but also I was authorised to drive and ride some less demanding police vehicles, two or four wheeled. I have always harboured the suspicion that the police were more desperate for drivers and riders than even they cared to admit!

In the meantime, I'd been nominated as relief "collator." The position was an important one under the unit beat system. For the first time, each beat officer and those in Panda cars were encouraged to submit even the tiniest bit of intelligence about anything on the ground. The collator sorted it out into a card system, issuing a bulletin every week, which included details of all crime and incidents in and around Hove and drawing attention to active criminals and their vehicles.

The first tangible result of passing the bike test was that I was given the North Portslade and Mile Oak beat, which included my house, on a Velocette motorbike. The bike was supposed to be kept overnight behind the former Portslade police station in St. Andrew's Road, by then used as a police box only. I soon discovered that I could, with everyone's blessing, keep it overnight locked in the garage of 2 Chalky Road.

This meant that I could book on by radio from home the minute I was dressed, saving myself a good forty-five minutes on my earliest starts, and the same at the end of a shift. This was the amount of time it would have taken to go down to St. Andrew's Road and back up to my beat, and if something had needed attending to when I called in I would be there in a few minutes. I could also have my meal breaks at home. Both the job and I benefitted as did, I like to think, the residents of North Portslade and Mile Oak. When necessary I rode into Hove to fill up with fuel.

As the beat was large and spread out, the idea was that you rode to, and parked the bike at, any one of the four shopping parades and the two industrial areas, and walked those areas for as long as it needed on the day. As on the foot beats, a lot of time was taken up in completing enquiries for other parts of Sussex, and for other forces.

I enjoyed that part of the job, although I did have one seriously embarrassing moment. I was riding past a bus stop on a bend one very cold morning. Some girls were waiting for a bus. I raised my right hand to wave, the throttle shut off, the bike wobbled, and I was on icy water on top of spilt diesel. Off I came. I was at walking pace, so there was no damage or injury, just a very red face under my helmet and a bunch of tittering teenage girls.

Meanwhile, things were not going well on the domestic front. Sheila was bored with life. She got a job as a nursing auxiliary at a nearby hospital and worked when I could babysit. At other times, the aforementioned Corinne, now sixteen years old, helped out with those duties.

A friend at her work told Sheila that with her looks she should enter a beauty contest. I encouraged her in this, believing it would get her some purpose. She heard of one in Portsmouth, and I took her down there in the Mini. I'd sold the bike by then and taxed and insured the car. She won the contest and was hooked.

This had a big effect on her morale, and I took every opportunity to take her to more, Corinne sitting in as necessary.

In May 1968, I completed my training by doing the second continuation course, this time at Nutfield Training Centre, near Redhill in Surrey. It must have been pretty uneventful because I can't remember anything about it, except that a number of men who had been on initial training with me had fallen by the wayside for one reason or another!

On return to Hove, no longer a probationer, I applied for and got a spell as aide to CID, the first step in becoming a detective constable. It was a three-month attachment and not the happiest time of my life. I couldn't hit it off with the sergeant in charge of me and was given jobs to deal with that were real no-hopers, where all I could do were door-to-door enquiries and fill in forms. I was close to the end of the three months, and actually looking forward to it, when Sheila entered, and won, the Brighton Carnival Queen contest, the first stage of the Miss World thing, as with the title went another—Miss Brighton.

My standing increased in the CID office with all the young bucks wanting to meet Sheila! My younger sister Janette came down from Penicuik with her fiancé, Brian. We took them to the Police Social Club at Hove, where the young guys all swarmed over Sheila—and Brian won the jackpot on the fruit machine!

Just before the end of my three-month CID Aide, I was given the crime of the theft of a ladder off a building site on 6 beat—the usual no-hoper. There was nothing else on, so I spent the day walking around 1 and 6 beats on Hove plus the adjacent beats on Brighton, looking for an extending ladder with "J. Watts" burned into the side.

About 6:00 p.m., I found it at the back of a jobber's site, the "J. Watts" filled and overpainted but obvious when viewed from an acute angle. I got back to the station and reported to my DS, offering to come in at 8:00 the next day instead of the scheduled 2:00 p.m. The DS told me there was no hurry. I could still cop the thief at 2:00 p.m.

I came in at 2:00 p.m. and told the DS I was going out to collar the ladder thief, but he told me not to bother, he had already nicked the guy.

I was livid and very unwisely gave the DS my honest opinion, so that was the end of my hope of getting on CID.

In 1968 the five separate police forces in Sussex merged into the Sussex Police. They were East and West Sussex Counties and Brighton, Eastbourne, and Hastings Boroughs. On the ground, nothing much changed. The East Sussex style of uniform was adopted by the whole force, and Brighton Borough lost its proud tradition of wearing white helmets in summer, something the surviving Brighton pensioners still grumble about.

I became Police Constable AN042 of the Sussex Police. Sussex had adopted a novel way of numbering its officers. The "A" meant I was a male officer, the "N" was the initial of my surname, and the "042" was the rough position that "Neil" took in an alphabetical list of surnames beginning with "N" between 001 and 999!

Soon afterwards things came to a head at home, and we split. I'd just dealt with a road accident involving a young boy being hit by a car on the Kingsway in Hove. He was not badly hurt, and I had taken him home. His mother had told me she had a spare room and would like to take in a single police officer as a lodger.

I walked out on Sheila at 3:00 in the morning on early shift after an ongoing row. I packed a bag and just walked around until it was time to book on. I was no longer on the motorbike beat, as I had been doing my CID Aide, and I was allocated to 12 beat, covering the Hove end of Shoreham Harbour, where Penny, the lady looking for a lodger, lived. I dumped my bag at the rear of her house about 4:00 a.m., wandered the seafront, booked on, and was knocking on her door around 7:30. I hadn't even begun to work out the finances, but she was happy to give me her spare room.

The money was a nightmare. Thanks to Charlie Blundell, I got a part-time job working for his company in Saltdean, making roller-towel cabinets. This was strictly illegal under the police discipline regulations, which rated it as an unlawful financial interest. As a serving policeman, you were not allowed any "moonlighting."

I also did a bit of "bouncer" work inside Brighton nightclubs, even more fraught because if there had ever been an incident requiring me to give evidence in court . . .

I moved from Penny's, as her estranged husband decided to come back and she thought that might be awkward. I found a bedsit in the middle of Brighton at a rent I could afford—just, allowing for Charlie's work and the bouncing.

I met Sandra Coleman at this time. She has stuck with me for more than forty years at time of writing—a girl with stamina. Obviously she did not have expensive tastes, going out with a guy living hand-to-mouth for the second time in his life. Soon she took me to meet her family.

Her mother, Eva, was a canny lass from County Durham, and she was appalled at how thin I was. She used to send Sandra round to my bedsit with hot meals, coinciding with my arriving home from the factory. Sandra was a "Hello Girl" working in the main telephone exchange in Brighton, only a short walk from my bedsit.

Thanks to her mother feeding me up and making at least some money on the side, I was just about making it through.

It did not matter in the end. Somebody grassed me up to "the job." I suspect it was someone who tried it on with Sheila and failed. I have a prime suspect but will leave that particular worm under its stone.

I was called in to see Chief Inspector Osborne—the same Osborne who as inspector had given me the job and was now 2IC at Hove, one rung further up his personal ladder.

There are two things I remember about the interview. One was Mr. Osborne telling me I should go home and make another baby! The second was when I laughed aloud at his solution, he read chapter and verse from police regulations, and I had no choice but to resign.

Suddenly, when I could have done it legally, I was no longer required as a bouncer. Another worker at Charlie's factory was a bit of a jobbing builder on the side, so I started to work on little jobs with him, outside factory hours. Work improved so much that we left the factory and concentrated on the building work.

It was not to be my time, though, because, taking his car to collect some materials, I got seriously hurt in a road crash in Peacehaven. I spent six weeks in hospital, in intensive care and later in a ward, coming out with no job, no money, and a big blank future.

Sandra visited me regularly in hospital, and when I came out the supply of hot meals was undiminished, thankfully, because I had no money coming in other than the promise of sickness benefit, which was, frankly, well below the breadline. After a week and against all medical advice, I went back to work for Charlie Blundell's employer full-time.

That was when Dave came into it.

Dave's parents had a fish and chip shop on my last beat at the foot of Boundary Road in Hove. It had been a regular tea stop and, latterly in my abject poverty, a place where I could get the odd bag of past-sell-by chips, having sorted out a problem for them.

I was in the area one evening and, flush with half a crown (12.5 pence) of spare cash, I decided to treat myself to a jumbo sausage and chips.

Dave was there, and when he found out my position he revealed that he had joined the British Airports Authority Constabulary and that they were desperate for men with regular police experience. The pay was the same as in the county forces, but a big plus was that they paid all overtime at enhanced rates. Overtime pay was an unknown phenomenon in Sussex.

He gave me a phone number to contact. I rang it, and a few days later the post contained an application form. I filled it in and returned it the same day. About a week later, I received a letter asking me to appear at Force HQ at Heathrow Airport.

Because, I suppose, of my recent road crash, the medical examination was much more thorough than when I had joined East Sussex, but after an interview with Chief Constable William Carson I was offered a job. I accepted, of course, and became Police Constable 320 Neil of the British Airports Authority Constabulary.

There followed a brief session with the personnel sergeant. I was to work at Heathrow and was informed that on top of my wages I would receive an "airport allowance" equivalent to the Metropolitan police rent allowance. At each airport covered by the BAAC, this airport allowance coincided with the rent allowance for the force in whose area it was located, as did the basic pay of the officers. Although police pay is negotiated nationally, the pay of the Metropolitan and City of London forces was set higher, because of the additional living costs involved.

The sergeant asked if I had arranged a place to stay, and when he found I hadn't he told me that there was a kind of "clearing house," where new PCs could stay till they found somewhere permanent. This was number 1 Sipson Road, directly opposite the main entrance to the airport.

I was given a starting day a week away, when I would be kitted out with uniform. At the end of the interview, I went to 1 Sipson Road, where I spoke to PC Peter Bryant, one of the only two permanent residents, in whose name the lease was held. I arranged to move in the day before my start across the road. PC Bryant was known as "Pete the Feet," and in that crowded house I soon found out why.

Things were most definitely beginning to look up again.

# CHAPTER 8

## The British Airports Authority Constabulary: A New Kind of Policing

I started at Heathrow in March 1970, moving into 1 Sipson Road the day before. This was a three-bedroom, two-reception semi, and there were eight of us staying there! We slept two to a bedroom in single beds and two in what was originally the dining room on camp beds. As the new boy, I was, of course, allocated one of the camp beds.

Two other PCs started the same day—Trevor Turley, a broad, powerful man of around thirty years who had just left the navy, and Gary Smith, a slim, young Scot from Perth, straight off Civvy Street. We were introduced to the set of discipline regulations that applied to the BAAC.

They differed in many ways from the ones that applied in Sussex, in that there was no control exercised over where an officer could reside, because of course nobody resided in the police area. If you got to work on time and were sober and suitably turned out, that was all that mattered.

Nor was there any control on additional earnings away from the job, provided these did not derive from the airport itself or clash with one's duties. I had no need to worry about this as, I was told, overtime was practically unlimited and paid at a third of an hour extra on a normal working day, half an hour extra if you worked a "rest day," and double rate for working bank holidays! Until I married Sandra, I was on my own away from home, and I opted for overtime every day except occasional rest days, when I travelled back to stay with the Colemans.

We were also given a broad briefing on the actions to be taken in the event of an aircraft emergency. These mostly applied to car crews and involved liaison with Met Police and London Emergency Services at designated "rendezvous points," although everyone with a radio made himself available for immediate pick-up and transportation.

Before working at the airport, I was required to take a two-week refresher course at Nutfield, where I had previously attended with Sussex. Other recruits were despatched to District Police Training School at Bruche in Cheshire for the full recruits' course.

Nutfield was pretty much a doddle for me, and the most enduring memory I have of the course is a confrontation with the commandant, Superintendent Cummings of Sussex, who could have made a better living by playing the "dour Scotsman" in the movies, by just being himself.

The airport police were the first in the country to introduce the clip-on tie—a very sensible move, taking one potential weapon away from anyone wishing to attack you. On the first day of the course, we were lined up on parade. Supt. Cummings stopped in front of me, peered at my tie, and enquired, "What kind of a knot do you call that? I call it a 'teddy boy' knot!"

I unclipped the tie and held it out. "I'm afraid I have no choice in the matter, sir."

Mr. Cummings went purple in the face and took a step back. "How dare you wear such an abomination with the Queen's uniform!"

It took several minutes for the parade sergeant and me to convince the superintendent that the tie was, indeed, uniform issue for the BAAC. While the rest of the parade was silently doubled up, he stomped off, muttering that he would take the matter up with the chief constable of this "cowboy outfit." Of course, nowadays every force in the country issues clip-on ties.

Back at Heathrow, I was given a lengthy tour of the airport, and shown the difference between "airside" and "landside," "airside" being everywhere beyond customs barriers in the airport.

I learned that policing on an airport, particularly one the size of Heathrow, was far from straightforward. At the end of the day, I was instructed to report the next morning for the early shift. That was when I received another pleasant surprise—early turns started at 7:00 a.m., and as I was going to be residing less than a minute's walk from the police station, the shift was going to be a lot more popular with me here than it had been at Hove.

In those days, there were three terminals at Heathrow. Terminal 1 was for domestic flights and those to and from the Irish Republic, Terminal 2 was European and Middle Eastern services, and Terminal 3, or "Oceanic," was for long-haul flights. Each terminal had foot patrols inside on landside; there were more men on foot airside, and at the front of each terminal PCs kept an eye on people arriving in cars and taxis and coming out of the arrivals side.

They had particularly to watch the taxi drivers. Rewards for some taxi trips were high, especially into Central London and beyond, and that fact led inevitably to some cabbies trying to circumvent the system. Briefly, taxis and their drivers had to wait in the taxi holding park near the police station until called forward to one of the terminals, where they joined the end of the queue waiting for custom.

Unless passengers had a prior taxi booked, the rule was that the first taxi in the rank took them. If the trip was a short one to, say, Twickenham, the first driver in the rank would consider himself unfortunate and might try to pass the fare to the rogue touts. They would have their minicabs waiting in the car park and would charge way over the odds, their vehicles not being metered like the black cabs.

Another trick was for a cabby to drop his fare off at the terminal and then try to attach himself to the end of the rank. Such a move was, naturally, not popular with drivers arriving from the taxi park, and it was not unusual for threats and sometimes a bit of pushing and shoving to occur.

On the whole, black-cab drivers were an honest bunch, although they had a well-deserved reputation for "pulling a fast one" and getting round the system. They had to work very hard for a year to obtain their badges, which gave them a good, if hardworking livelihood. The very worst thing that could happen to a cabby was to have his hackney licence withdrawn.

The real pains in the posterior were the touts who infested all the terminals, but mainly 2 and 3. Quite apart from the odd cabby that might, as mentioned, slip a short fare their way, the touts had a wealth of tricks to con unsuspecting travellers into using them. One was to stand at the arrival ropes holding a sign bearing a common Indian or Pakistani name, e.g., "Mr. and Mrs. Patel" or "Mr. and Mrs. Ahmed." Underneath, in pencil so that it could be changed easily, would be written the latest flight arrival, e.g., BA114, Karachi, taken from the flight arrival board.

Bearing in mind the number of travellers coming in from the Indian subcontinent bearing names like these, frequently to visit friends or family, this little trap used to work quite a lot. The travellers, often not fluent in English, might get in the "cab," thinking family had sent and paid for it, only to find out, on arrival at their destination, which might be as far away as Luton or Bradford, their driver demanding £100 to £300 for the trip.

Not surprisingly Heathrow police put officers on anti-tout patrol at the two main terminals concerned.

Most of the offences committed at Heathrow were governed by the airport bylaws, which among other powers included the ability of police to order offenders to leave the airport forthwith. Powers of arrest were attached to many of the bylaws (including "Failure to leave the airport having been required to do so by an authorised person"). Offenders were dealt with by being taken to West Drayton Metropolitan Police Station, where they could be detained overnight and put up before local magistrates.

Offenders against the Theft Act were dealt with by the airport's own CID, thence through West Drayton and, initially, the same local magistrates.

A major problem at Heathrow was theft of and from baggage in transit. Passengers could check their luggage in at the desks and never see it again until they reached their destinations, which might be over twenty-four hours' time in the case of a trip to New Zealand. Bags would go down to bays airside, where they would be placed on trucks or trolleys by handlers, taken to the waiting aircraft, and then stowed in the baggage hold.

Opportunities to rifle through bags were many, in the terminal, on the trucks, and, especially, in the baggage holds of aircraft. Getting evidence was a total nightmare as the loading bays and aircraft holds were perfectly situated against surveillance, and, as each shift of loaders was self-contained, all were involved, actively or passively, and witnesses were rarely found.

The thefts would not be discovered until the passengers arrived at the destination airport or in many cases at the end of an ongoing journey or even arrival at their hotels.

It was strongly believed, during my short stay at Heathrow, that handlers had access to many common suitcase keys, so some victims would not know their baggage had been searched right up to the very end. The thieves were clever enough never to have the keys in their physical possession anytime there was a danger of being turned over by police and therefore in peril of a charge of "going equipped to steal."

There were, however, other ways of opening apparently locked suitcases of a certain type without recourse to keys. I believe that such tricks have been exposed on YouTube, so there is no need for me to publicise them here.

Offences discovered at destination were normally reported to the airline or operator concerned, who in most cases filled out a "world tracer" form, good enough for an insurance claim, but the crime would never be reported to police either end of the journey. Unlike police, operators, and airlines' insurance companies are not required to produce statistics relating to theft claims. In my time at LHR, as Heathrow is known, it was the considered opinion of CID that the offences reported to them were less than 10 percent of those committed. A popular name for the airport was "Thiefrow."

It was not until the late 1990s that Detective Chief Superintendent Stevens, later Metropolitan Police Commissioner Sir John Stevens, activated a full-scale operation using covert microfibre-optic cameras that the problem was finally taken a grip of. With the full co-operation of British Airways and the loaders' Trade Union, a major successful operation was carried out against this form of crime, and a huge group of British Airways' crooked loaders was taken out of circulation.

This appeared to have just a braking effect on offenders, and the thefts continue, albeit on a much smaller scale. Between late 2006 and mid-2007, twenty-two baggage loaders at Stansted Airport were arrested. Most were cautioned, but one, said to be the ringleader, copped eight months' imprisonment. For sneak thieving like this, which at the very least ruined many holidays, those sanctions might seem pretty light.

Meanwhile, shortly after starting at Heathrow, my divorce from Sheila came through. It was uncontested, but I may have caused some concern when I turned up at Brighton Domestic Proceedings Court, just to keep an eye on things. Just as well, because I was thus prepared for the shock when the legal bill arrived, as the man Sheila's advisors had hired was not only a barrister, but also a QC, soon afterwards to be a judge! This for an uncontested and totally straightforward divorce case!

All that having gone through, Sandra and I made preparations to be married. A date was set—July 17. I was broke, of course, with the prospect of QC-sized legal bills and a commitment to maintenance for the boys. I had to find somewhere for us to live, and rents around Heathrow were sky-high. I was going to need a deposit, so the three months leading up to the wedding were spent doing sixteen-hour shifts and crashing out chez Pete the Feet.

I was managing to spend one night a fortnight at the Coleman place, where I was given a great welcome by Sid and Eva, Sandra's parents. Plans were made for a very low-key wedding, to be attended only by close family, and Worthing Register Office was duly booked. The day was a Friday, and I managed to book two weeks off from the previous Monday, during which I found furnished accommodation in Slough, at an ancient building called Upton Court.

There are many theories about Upton Court. The then current house was built around 1325, but the owner (and my landlord), an eccentric old gentleman called Mr. Cobb, told me that a previous house on the site had belonged to Earl Godwin, the father of Harold, the last Saxon King of England. The property certainly appears in the 1086 Domesday Book, so there may well have been some truth in Mr. Cobb's assertion. Nowadays the house, presumably renovated and modernised inside, is the headquarters of the local *Slough Observer* newspaper.

Several of the rooms had been rented out as bedsits. Mine, like the others, did not have a vertical or horizontal plane in it. The ceiling in our sitting room was seven feet at one end and less than six feet at the other! We had a share of a bathroom with another tenant, an engaging young man from Strabane on the border of County Derry with the Irish Republic. As "the Troubles" were in full swing, Warnock Cinnamon (for that was the young man's name) had a wealth of stories about life on the "front line." I know you will forgive me, Warnock, if I have not spelled your surname correctly.

I had an uncle, my mum's brother, who lived in Slough. At the wedding, my parents bless them, asked if they could stay with us at Upton Court. As the only honeymoon we were going to have was a few days in the bedsit, we politely declined, and they stayed a few days with Uncle Willie, so we did see them during the day.

The financial grind eased a bit when Sandra got a job at the Slough Telephone Exchange and I went back to working at Heathrow. There was going to be no chance of getting a CID Aide, as there was a long queue of applicants. The most I could achieve was a quick driving course and a permit that enabled me to crew up one of the three patrol cars at the airport—Kilo Alpha—the airside car, the driving of which required an additional course on air traffic control procedures. The vehicle was as much under their control as that of the police radio.

The landside car was Kilo Papa—Papa standing for "Perimeter." "Kilo Foxtrot" covered the freight and maintenance areas. This was a popular duty for "skivers," as the area offered several refreshment spots and secret "tuck-aways" where the crew could read or listen to radio entertainment and, I dare say, take the opportunity for a snooze on nights.

Things are a lot different now at Heathrow as well as at other, smaller airports. There have been some spectacular robberies in the freight area, the most notorious being the Brink's-MAT bullion robbery of November 1983, and the growth of world terrorism has necessitated a totally different and vastly more professional approach to policing Heathrow.

The Brink's-MAT job was to have a poignant sequel for me in January 1985, but more of that later.

I can say that I was right in at the start of Middle Eastern terrorism as it directly affected the UK.

On the afternoon of September 6, 1970, I had finished my seven to three early and was briefing for four hours' extra duty when all officers in the police station were bundled into a van, rushed out onto the airfield, and taken to a quiet area off the main taxiways. En route we were told it was a full emergency—an aircraft had been hijacked and was on its way into Heathrow. We were to surround the plane after it had been parked. A line of emergency vehicles including ambulances and fire appliances raced across the tarmac and was waiting as the aircraft came to a halt.

It was a Boeing 707 of EL AL, the Israeli airline. A Metropolitan police vehicle also arrived. As the engines switched off, my group was deployed around the aircraft and steps were brought up to the door, which opened outwards. I was not in a position to see what happened after that, but I believe armed Met officers went aboard first, followed by two ambulance crews.

The would-be hijackers—a Nicaraguan called Patrick Arguello and a Palestinian woman named Leila Khaled—were taken off injured and departed by ambulance, accompanied by Met officers. Arguello died in hospital and Khaled was taken into custody.

The flight had been from Tel Aviv to New York and had stopped at Amsterdam en route, where the hijackers had boarded. After takeoff, the terrorists had showed their hand but were thwarted because the pilot, being warned of the situation by the crew, put the aircraft into a deep dive, throwing the attackers off balance. Passengers attacked Khaled and an Israeli air marshal shot Arguello.

With my colleagues, I stood guard over the aircraft while it was emptied of passengers and crew and taken apart by Scenes of Crime officers. That gave me something to talk about when I finally got home late that evening.

The company at Heathrow Police Station, as it has been on all my postings, was composed of generally good guys. Gary Smith and Trevor Turley got back from Bruche at the end of June and found themselves on my shift, and Sandra and I went out with them and their women a few times. There were other larger-than-life characters around, but what made it absolutely different from Hove was the widespread nature of the guys' accommodation. Hardly anyone lived near the airport, and many had over an hour's travelling to and from work. One PC lived so far from Heathrow that when he transferred to Gatwick he did not move house, as he was now much closer to his workplace!

Despite working all the hours I could and considering Sandra's wages, the goal of getting a deposit to put down on a house never seemed to get any closer as prices were rising faster than I could save.

Then fortune smiled on me again.

# CHAPTER 9

## Stansted Airport: A Quiet Life in Essex Countryside

In the autumn of 1970, a light suddenly appeared at the end of my personal tunnel when a decision was made on high that Stansted, in Essex, should become the location of London's third airport. Quite apart from the furore and protests this decision ignited in rural Essex and Hertfordshire, it became obvious that more police would be required at Stansted other than the sergeant and four who were currently stationed there.

It was made known that the BAAC needed, as a start, an extra six PCs and an inspector. It was also whispered that anyone volunteering for a posting there would be treated as a "compulsory transferee" and would qualify for considerable assistance in acquiring accommodation.

A little bit of history of the airfield would not go amiss here. During WWII and the ensuing Cold War, Stansted was a bomber base of the US Air Force. At one time during the war, the US had over one hundred bases in East Anglia, but in the late 1960s the three main stations had been Mildenhall, Lakenheath, and Stansted. The heaviest bombers had operated from Stansted, which consequently had the longest runway. At the time of my going there, it was said to be the longest runway in the UK. Research suggests otherwise, but it was unusually long. Around the perimeter were horseshoe-shaped hummocks known as the "shooting-in bays," where returning aircraft used to loose off their unused gunnery ammunition. During the later development of the civil airport at Stansted, these hummocks were levelled. I wonder how much lead could have been recovered from them!

A little bit of research on the area ensued prior to our decision, and Sandra took little persuading that it would be a good move for us. Quaint and quirky though Upton Court was, it was no place for a family and she made no secret of the fact that she wanted us to start one. More research in *Dalton's Weekly* and *Exchange and Mart* showed that property prices in the area were a fraction of what they were around Heathrow and the country environment was in a different class. Accordingly I put in my request.

A week or so later, the personnel superintendent had me in for an interview. Why on earth did I want to move from a busy international airport like Heathrow to a backwater like Stansted? My reply was two-pronged. Firstly the idea of growing up with the airport through all the challenges that offered appealed to me. Secondly I was finding it hard to get a deposit for a property locally and did not want to live more than forty miles from work, my wife wanted to start a family, and in the Stansted area we could afford it. He smiled and shook my hand. "It's a deal."

Just before Christmas 1970, Sandra moved back to her parents and I tidied up the loose ends at Upton Court before joining them.

* * *

In early January 1971, I drove myself up to Stansted. It was a week of frost and fog, and nothing moved on my new patch. I was greeted by Sergeant Jim Miller, who enquired as to where I was staying. I told him I had nothing fixed but hoped he'd help me to get a B and B locally. "No problem," he laughed. "Follow me."

We drove off the airport through the freezing fog, and I had no idea where we were going until he indicated right and we pulled off the road into a car park. Peering through the fog, I could just make out a pub sign for "The Chequers." I joined Jim who indicated to the pub. "Here we are then."

Still steeped in county police tradition, I asked, "Is it okay to stay here?" Of all the taboos in the counties, a policeman found to be living in a pub had a ticket straight to Discipline and Complaints and a hefty boot out of the job.

"Of course it is. They're good friends of mine."

We went inside to a very small, snug, and intimate public bar, where I was introduced to the landlord, Nobby, and his wife, Doris. Nobby was a small, dark-haired man, perhaps in his forties, and Doris a bubbly, blonde lady of approximately the same age.

They asked how long I wanted the room for, and I replied, "If the price is right, until I can buy a property in the area."

Doris replied, "12 shillings a night B and B, less if you can help out occasionally in the pub." I looked at Jim and he smiled and nodded. I shook hands on the deal and was shown up some steep and rickety stairs to a small, spotless room, really old-fashioned as befitted this lovely old pub. Jim said, "Mine's a pint and I'll see you at the airport in the morning—9 o'clock."

I rang Sandra to give her the news, and she was delighted. I was going to pay 12 shillings a night—£4 4s a week (£4.20 a week)—and the BAA was going to give me £3 10s a night for accommodation and meals (£24.50 a week). I was sure I could fit lunch in fairly cheaply. As it turned out, Doris insisted on giving me a lunch box at no extra charge, as helping out behind the bar in a homely little pub like The Chequers was so easy after my Limehouse experiences.

The clientele comprised around 60 percent local residents. The remainder consisted of passing trade off the A11 London to Norwich road, beside which stood the pub. The name of the village was Ugley, which as you might imagine caused a certain amount of mirth among nonresidents.

Work at Stansted was, initially at least, practically nonexistent, and I was able to spend a fair amount of time house hunting. The "police station" was a shack on the entrance road into the airport, which had no scheduled flights apart from one daily flight to and from Palma, Majorca, run by the long-defunct Channel Airways.

The old stager PCs who had been at Stansted already—John Graves, John Lindow, Roger Lawrence, and Ray Cole—gave my fellow newcomers and myself a warm welcome, and were extremely helpful with their opinions on various locations around the place for house hunting.

A smart, new police station was planned and, in fact, built within weeks and a dog handler's course arranged for Roger. Our new inspector was named Arthur Mason and was due to start fairly soon when the new station was complete. However, the progress of London (Stansted) Airport was totally mired down in the traditional British planning laws. It was fair to say that its police presence was expanding faster than the airport was.

Within a month, I had found a flat in the nearby Hertfordshire town of Bishop's Stortford, only ten minutes from the airport. It was a two-bedroomed apartment with a little boxroom on the first floor of a small, modern purpose-built block. Sandra came up for the day, looked the flat over, and approved. I put the offer in and she was very happy, especially when I told her the next part of the "compulsory transfer" benefits. I was to have all the costs of removal paid in full, including all legal and survey costs, and, best of all, the BAA would give me, as an interest-free loan over ten years, the 10 percent deposit I needed on the flat.

The cost of the flat was £4,500—the interest-free loan was £450, to be repaid at the rate of £3 5s per four-weekly period, taken directly from my wages. The repayments on the flat were £360 a year or £30 per month, £10 a month less than the rent on the Upton Court bedsit and less than my new airport allowance, which was based on the rent allowance paid to Essex police in whose area we operated! Overtime was not to be had at the Heathrow rate, but who needed it? Many times since then have I blessed the BAA for lifting me out of the grind for the first time in my life.

Sandra came north in early March 1971 and liked the flat a lot, although seeing the Essex countryside over the next few weeks, she longed for us to get a cottage. She loved The Chequers and the area around it. We became regulars there as it was about three miles from the flat, and we made some good friends among the locals.

Nobby, the landlord had been informed he had a terminal illness and had arranged for Doris to be taken out by a local businessman—a builder and undertaker called Jim. The deal was that Nobby would get a first-class funeral for free, and his widow would be well looked after! As it turned out, I discovered some years later that Nobby actually outlived Jim!

Another regular with whom I became friendly was a big, happy-go-lucky man with an Abraham Lincoln beard. He was a local handyman and builder, Colin Camp by name. He confided that he was snowed under with work, and when he found I was handy at painting and decorating, he asked me to help him out occasionally.

I was happy to do this as, not long after her arrival, Sandra found that she was pregnant and, although I was no longer in financial mire, a little extra income would be useful with the new arrival in mind. Sandra herself had found a temporary job at Bishop's Stortford Telephone Exchange, rather than be lonely on her own at the flat. As her pregnancy progressed, she gave that job up. Our firstborn, Joanne Eleanore, was born at the Herts and Essex Hospital, Bishop's Stortford, on December 22.

As it happened, Roger Lawrence's wife was in the same maternity ward, and our children were born on the same day. Roger and I and those from the police station who were not on duty, plus a local Stansted village PC, Peter Suckling, got uproariously drunk in The Chequers, ably supported by many of the local customers. Even after throwing in at least one round "on the house," Nobby declared it his most profitable night ever!

Within a few days of Sandra and Jo coming home, my parents arrived from Penicuik, eager to see their first granddaughter—they already had four grandsons. I took my dad up to The Chequers, although he was completely teetotal, and introduced him to the locals. He got on particularly well with an old fellow his own age, called George Camp. George spoke with the thickest rural Essex accent ever and my dad with a broad Penicuik one. Both were keen gardeners and had a long discussion about the subject, although I don't believe either understood a word the other said!

Police work at Stansted showed no sign of increasing. Occasionally on a late Friday or Saturday evening, some local lads would decide to come up and have a jolly around the place in their pride and joy cars. One of my ex-Heathrow colleagues, Larry Arthur, was quite adept at finding little bits of cannabis on these youths, so it was not entirely blank, but there was very little in the way of real police work to be done.

The usual thing on nights was to do a complete check of the perimeter, sometimes two, always at a different time each night and varying between clockwise and anti-clockwise, and that could take a couple of hours. On late shifts, there was a fair amount of socialising at the fire station. This had the advantage of getting quicker notice from the control tower of anything happening, and also the fire service guys were an extremely sociable lot. I became quite friendly off-duty with a couple of them.

One of the airport duty managers had once been an airport fireman, and he often turned up at the fire station. We also became friendly with him as he lived with his family in the same street as we did in Bishop's Stortford.

Sandra was quite happy looking after Jo, and we had taken in a student from the local teacher training college to supplement the income; but suddenly Colin Camp and his wife, Rosemary, decided out of the blue that they wanted to move to Looe, in Cornwall. Colin asked if I'd like to put in an offer on their cottage, which was only a few minutes' walk from The Chequers.

By a huge slice of coincidental luck, the railway had just introduced a fast train from Cambridge to Liverpool Street in the heart of the City of London, with Bishop's Stortford being the penultimate stop, and overnight the value of our flat went up by 50 percent. I got a quick valuation of the flat and the cottage from the estate agent son of Sergeant Cowell of Stansted village police station.

The figures were very favourable. I offered Colin the full valuation for the cottage and put the flat on the market at just above its estimated value. The first caller snapped it up at the asking price, and Sandra and I became the proud owners of Boundary Cottage, Quendon, with our fees covered more than adequately by the price difference!

Our student finished college a few days before the move, and on the appointed day I loaded all our belongings into a hired van and ran them out to Quendon. We encountered a slight problem in that a friend of Colin's, the other named driver on the van hire, had called off sick. He had been supposed to drive the van down to Cornwall, and then stop off overnight with friends near Plymouth before returning the van the following day.

Colin, of course, had to drive his heavily loaded estate car to Looe, and the only solution was for me to drive the van there and back. We had to empty the van of our things, move them into the cottage, and then load Colin's belongings from the lawn into the van, have a quick snack, and drive off, leaving Sandra to cope with the baby and the furniture in the cottage.

It got more complicated in Looe when I discovered that the street where the Camps' new dwelling was located was too narrow to drive the van down, and everything had to be lugged by hand for about fifty yards. I remember very well the drive home along the M4 motorway, where I had to go off twice to have short naps, as I was on the point of falling asleep at the wheel.

Boundary Cottage was a lovely place with a large garden, and as Jo grew into a toddler she loved to roam around the garden.

Babe in the Wood.  Jo at Quendon amongst the bluebells aged 17 months.

There was one spine-chilling moment, though. The Cottage was at the side of a very busy road—the main A11 from London to Norwich, and one day Sandra and I looked at each other. "Where's Jo?" Panic! Someone had left the front door open for a second, and Jo had crawled out. We found her sitting on the kerb with thirty-ton trucks hurtling past about three feet away.

My boys, Stephen and Gregor, came up for a holiday and also loved the area, although they said they missed the sea.

My boys, Stephen (L) and Gregor, just before I lost them to Australia.
Compare with photo in final chapter, taken 26 years later!

Although Stansted showed no signs of getting any bigger, our inspector, Arthur Mason, had arrived. A broad Cockney, who had served both in the Royal Navy and the army, he found it frustrating trying to motivate our small force. We found it just as difficult to motivate ourselves, and I took to bringing my Labrador puppy in on nights so that I could train him with Roger Lawrence's dog. This training was very successful, and I have applied the system to my subsequent dogs.

One night we finished our training routine and returned to the police station for refreshments. My Lab, Joss, must have crept off without my noticing.

In the morning, I was awakened by a phone call from Inspector Mason.

"Did you bring your dog into the nick last night?"

"Yes, guv'nor. You know I am training him up."

"Well, you aren't training him very well, son. He crapped under my desk and I only found out when I put my foot in it!"

Bless Arthur. An apology and a pint soon sorted that out, plus a few new carpet tiles from stores.

In the autumn of 1972, the force realised that I had put in rather a lot of intelligence from the airport, due in no small way to my friendship with the Mets Special Branch man attached there, one Alistair Mountain.

Several men with dodgy reputations were using the airport to fly out at intervals to Spain. Channel Airways had started a twice-weekly flight to Malaga.

I was invited to attend a basic CID course at the Metropolitan Police Detective Training School, beginning in November.

Before I went, Sandra announced that she was pregnant again. I reckoned to be back from the course before the pregnancy got serious. Sandra decided to stay with her parents for the duration of the course, especially as it included Jo's birthday and Christmas. I found a reliable and decent air hostess—Jo Sleeman from Channel Airways—who could house-sit for us while we were away

The course was hard work but very rewarding. There were 105 students from all over the UK. I stayed at the police section house at Tooting with four others, all from outside the Met area—Dave Beach from Birmingham, Harry Sleeman (not related to the air hostess) from Devon, Dave Ellis from Cheshire, and Terry Holmes from Bedfordshire. We had an invariable system of studying. From 6:00 p.m. until 9:00 p.m. Monday to Thursday, all five of us would get together and throw questions around. At 9:00 p.m., we'd go for a pint or two, and at 11:00 we'd be tucked up in bed. The five of us took the first five places in the final exam.

Metropolitan Police Detective Training School, February 1973.
Yours truly fourth from right in back row, sporting magnificent facial hair!

The other notable thing about the course was that it got me back into rugby. There was a sports session every Wednesday afternoon. One of the Met Special Branch DCs on the course—Bill Emerton—was a useful rugby player for Streatham and Croydon RFC and soon organised sixteen of the male course members into a makeshift team. We played a total of five games on Wednesday afternoons, usually against Met subdivision sides and usually got a good drubbing before, by some miracle, we won the final game at Barnet. When I got back to Stansted, I joined Bishop's Stortford Rugby Club and played most Saturdays for their fourth XV as a competent (at that level) blind-side flanker. The team was known as "The Chindits." In the season I joined, it was undefeated, putting over a thousand points on the board in the process, and conceding fewer than 150.

After the final class every Friday, I made my way to the Coleman house to spend the weekend with Sandra and Jo.

At the end of the course, I brought them back to Quendon, and then there came a bombshell.

Sandra miscarried.

It was a traumatic time, and I knew straightaway that she was longing to return to Sussex.

My run of luck continued. The BAAC CID chief came to Stansted to see me. He spoke of my performance on the CID course and confessed that plans to start a detective section at Stansted had been put on ice, due to the slower-than-expected expansion of the airport. Rather a waste of my talents, he opined.

I asked what he had in mind. He told me there were two CID vacancies coming up in the BAAC—one at Belfast, the other at Gatwick.

I hemmed and hawed a bit, even though my heart was pounding. I did not want to appear to be too keen.

"If I were to transfer, what would the conditions be?"

He smiled. "You'd want a compulsory transfer, is that right?"

I nodded.

"Not a problem, but this time we'd meet only the costs of removal and the fees, not another interest-free loan." He'd done his homework.

I told him I'd have to consult with Sandra, although I knew what her response would be. He told me he'd wait at the airport while I went home if I preferred that to phoning.

The result was as I'd expected. Sandra loved the house and the area, but in those days she could not drive, so was stuck at home because public transport was practically nonexistent. She missed her parents, and the miscarriage had been the last straw.

I went back to see the detective superintendent, and it was fixed that I'd go to Gatwick. I'd report there in just over one month.

I put the cottage on the market straightaway. We had a very interesting inquiry almost immediately.

Answering a knock on the door, I was confronted by an old lady in a shawl.

In a broad Essex accent, she asked, "You sellin' your house?"

"Yes."

"How much you want?"

"Twelve and a half thousand pounds."

"I'll take it."

"Don't you want to see round?"

"No. Bin here afore."

"Okay, I better give you my solicitor's details, and I'll need yours too."

"Ain't 'avin' that."

"What?"

"Lawyers. Can't stand 'em. It's cash in your hand. Take it or leave it."

"It doesn't work like that. There are deeds and things."

"Twelve and half. You want it or not?"

"I'd love it, but the law says you need to do certain things."

"Fergit it, then. I'll come back Monday for your answer. Twelve and half and nothin' to pay out. Think on it."

I told the local Stansted PC, Peter Suckling, about the conversation, and he identified the caller straightaway as Mrs. Smith, the local gypsy queen. He said she probably had a lot more cash than £12,500 buried in her yard, which was patrolled by a couple of bloodthirsty Rottweilers.

Anyway, it fell through, of course, but not before I'd wound my neighbours up by telling them I'd had a cash offer from the gypsy queen.

"You wouldn't do that to us, would you?"

"Would you do it to me?"

Downcast eyes. Then I reminded them of the positives. "You'd have an inexhaustible supply of clothes pegs, your pots and pans would be repaired, and your knives sharpened on the spot, and, oh, the smell of barbecued hedgehog drifting over the garden fence on a nice summer evening."

They were not amused.

It didn't matter. I got my full asking price within a week and, at the same price, bought a house in Southwick, not far from Sandra's parents. The fees were all found by the BAAC, so no increase in the mortgage was necessary. On the downside, it was twenty-five miles to drive to work instead of just three.

There's a postscript on Mrs. Smith. She died a few years later, and, by all accounts, her funeral was the North Essex event of the year, with hundreds of gypsies descending on Quendon in Mercedes cars, horse-drawn carriages, transit vans, and various beaten-up pickup trucks. There were reports of a gang of big blokes digging her yard up to a depth of three feet over the next week. I'd like to think they found what they were digging for.

# CHAPTER 10

## Gatwick Airport: Transfer to a Larger Airport and Detective Work

I actually started at Gatwick while we were waiting for the house deals to go through, and we were living with Sandra's parents again in the meantime.

I made friends quickly at my latest posting, and when the conveyancing was completed, I hired a van and took two of my new colleagues—John Watkins and Geoffrey Britten—up to Quendon to move everything out.

It was a Saturday, and, as it turned out, it was just as well I took John and Geoffrey up with me. It probably saved me a lot of time and anxiety. Here's why.

On the very day of the move, an armed robbery was carried out at the little branch bank in the airport. The bandits were masked, of course, and carried what the cashier believed were handguns. Only one of the robbers spoke, and he had, said the cashier, an Irish accent.

News of the robbery filtered through to Gatwick, and I heard about it on my return after a week's moving-in leave. John Watkins pointed out that we had been in Quendon at the precise moment of the robbery. Although I had planned to drop in and see the guys at the airport, we had fallen behind with the move and had gone nowhere nearer to the airport than the A11 south. I thought no more about it. Police inquiries of the time came to nothing, and the whole event receded into the background.

Many months later, I received a phone call at work from John Graves at Stansted. There had been an arrest in the case of the bank robbery! A lady had been arrested in Spain trying to pass traveller's cheques that had been part of the proceeds of the crime.

"Guess what," said John. "She's the wife of one of the airport firemen!" He went on to name a fireman with whom I had become particularly friendly. "He's been nicked too."

I named the duty officer. "Is he involved?"

John replied, "He hasn't been nicked, but I bet his bum is twitching. We never knew if anyone else was involved, apart from the pair who did the job."

There was a pause, and then, "Weren't you around here that day?"

I admit my blood froze for a second. "Yes, I was moving from Quendon, but we were running late and went nowhere near the airport. I was with two PCs from Gatwick."

John advised me to get in touch with the investigating officer from Harlow CID before they got in touch with me. He named the detective.

By this time, of course, I was on Gatwick CID and immediately informed my DS, Adam Christie. Neither John Watkins nor Geoffrey Britten was on duty, and Adam advised me not to contact them, but to let Essex CID talk to them first.

As it turned out, we all made independent statements of our movements on the day in question as did my former neighbour, Mr. Last, whom I had teased about the gypsy queen. He had helped with emptying the cottage, and the new owner had seen us arrive with an empty van and leave with a full one, either side of the time of the robbery.

Both the duty manager and the fireman were weighed off with ten years' imprisonment. If there had been a "getaway driver," he was never caught.

It took four weeks from the time of my arrival at Gatwick to be confirmed as a detective constable, while the incumbent DC worked off his notice.

During my spell in uniform at Gatwick, I found myself on a section consisting of a very sociable bunch and made friends easily. The two guys who had helped with the removal, John and Geoffrey, were just two of them.

Shortly after my arrival, the Airport Authority announced that it would like to increase the number of interpreters available to them. The level of skill was not high—well below court standards—but was intended to take care of a situation involving non-English speakers long enough to get an idea of what it was about and pass it on from there. All that was required was that any applicants should pass a brief airport and passenger-related conversation test. The Authority even offered to pay for foreign language lessons to get one up to that standard. All BAA staff were included, not just the police.

I passed the French test without too much fuss and, tongue in cheek, applied to do a course in Dutch. This was at the behest of John Watkins, who spent a lot of time in Holland in those days and wanted someone to do the course with him. There were regular flights into

Gatwick from a smaller Dutch Airline, perhaps Transavia, and, strangely enough, we had recently had to deal with a Dutch passenger who was much the worse for drink and who refused to speak English.

To my surprise, the Authority agreed to pay for the course for John and me, and we were introduced to Mijneer De Bruin, our tutor.

I took to the language straightaway, finding the pronunciation system agreeably close to my native Penicuik dialect. I have used my knowledge of the language many times since on trips to Holland and Belgium.

There was an amusing incident a few years later, when I was travelling on the London Underground and two young Dutch girls were discussing the physique of a male fellow traveller and, very explicitly, how they would like to handle him. As I passed them on my way off the train, I complemented them in Dutch on their taste in men. I wished I had had a camera!

In late 1973, I had an unwanted decision to make. Sheila had remarried, to a likeable and good-looking man called John Golding. They now had a daughter, Julie. John was a printer by trade and had had the offer of a very well paid job in Australia, with approved immigration status and a subsidised sea passage to Sydney. Would I give my permission to allow Sheila and him to take the boys out of the country? Without my permission, they could not go.

This was not easy. I knew that if they went out and stayed there, it could be years before I could see the boys again. On the other hand, the jobs situation in the UK was not good, with rising unemployment and doubts about the long-term economic future of the country. (I know—nothing much has changed in the last nearly forty years!)

How could I face the guilt if I did not allow them, and the boys especially, to have a brighter future? I acceded to the request, and on the day of their departure I travelled down to Southampton to see them off, finding when I got there that the time I had been given was not their check-in time, but the time for the actual departure of the ship. They were already aboard, and all Sandra and I could do was to wave at the tiny dots at the rail of the ship, hoping they were two of the tiny faces and could see us. On returning to Sandra's sister Janet's house near Fareham, where we had left Jo, I was very upset.

After a very short time in Sydney, Sheila and John split up. I heard of this through Marion Blundell, mother of our former babysitter Corinne. Sheila had kept in touch with Marion.

I phoned the telephone number given to me by Mrs. Blundell, and £18 of conversation later Sheila had convinced me that everything was all right. At least, what she said was that she did not want or need my help. The finances had been taken care of, and they would not be coming back.

Shortly afterwards I lost touch. Sheila had moved and did not want me to have the address. She had instructed Marion Blundell not to let me have it. It was to be nearly twenty-five years before I saw the boys again.

One day—March 14, 1974—I arrived home from work to find the house was empty. Our next-door neighbour rushed out. "Sandra's gone into labour!" she told me. "I've got Joanne here."

I rang the maternity unit at Southlands Hospital and was astonished to find that I had another daughter. Hannah had been delivered minutes after Sandra's arrival in the unit. The speed of this delivery was in sharp contrast to the long labour endured by Sandra prior to Jo's arrival!

* * *

The mid-1970s were years when the legal abortion system came into full swing in the UK, and girls wishing to terminate unwanted pregnancies were able to do so if two medical practitioners were in agreement that it was in the girl's interests.

This did not appear to present any problems—the two doctors could work from the same premises, even the clinic involved, and be seen within minutes of each other, if not at the same time. Soon the word got around in the less liberal countries of Europe that the service was easily available in the UK, and girls began to arrive at Gatwick and other UK airports from predominantly Catholic countries like France, Spain, and Ireland.

Mostly these girls had appointments at legitimate clinics and came with directions of how to get there using public transport, but in their psychological state they were still prey for unscrupulous illegal taxi and minicab drivers.

The main clinics were in London and Brighton. Whenever we identified such girls, we would try to ensure they got on public transport with full directions at the other end.

However, there were a few who had flown over with only the name of a clinic and no appointment, having been desperate to keep the real reason for their journey a secret from family, and so avoiding incriminating correspondence. These kids, for that's what the majority were, presented much more of a problem, and, unless they were legal minors, there was not much to be done within the strict guidance of the law.

However, we tried to do our best for them, in some cases actually getting them to wait in the terminal until we were off duty before delivering them to the clinics ourselves.

I found one distraught Breton girl from Nantes, Virginie, aged eighteen, who had already been intercepted by a minicab tout. My French skills came in handy, but it was in blunt Anglo-Saxon that I told the tout where his future lay.

As it was close to the time for going off duty, I drove her to the clinic, which fortunately was in the Seven Dials area of Brighton, practically on my direct route home. I waited to ensure she was okay but found that she could not be fitted in for two days.

I took her home, where Sandra looked after her, and then I got her to the clinic on the appointed day, collected her afterwards, and returned her to Gatwick.

A week or two later, we got a very nice thank you card from her, together with a plea not to reply to it, not that I could have anyway as I didn't have her address.

Some months later, another letter arrived with the same plea, enclosing a wedding photograph!

It was about then that I decided we had a family of just the right size and did not want to create any more. Accordingly I took surgical steps to ensure that there would be no more babies and underwent a vasectomy at a hospital close to my home.

The operation took place on a Thursday morning, and on the following Saturday afternoon, I turned out for the police second fifteen at Burgess Hill. Getting out of my kit after the match, I discovered my stitches in my jockstrap! I was probably quite pale for a bit, but there were no ill effects!

On to CID then, and the run of work there was generally confined to thefts of and from baggage, cars in car parks being broken into or stolen, and the usual crop of opportunist thieves lurking around in the terminal building at busy periods. In those days, Gatwick was a small enough operation for these petty offenders to be easily identified by uniform patrol and shown the door, but occasionally one would slip through the net.

As at Heathrow, there was an ongoing problem with baggage loaders. I'm happy that at Gatwick it was very much a minority involvement, and with a bit of intelligence it was possible to build up a pattern when certain loaders were working together. With help from HM Customs and the nearby Crawley or Horley CID, we carried out a few raids when we recovered some property and evidence and neatly knocked the problem on the head, at least for several months.

A good source of this intelligence had been the Wingspan Club, the social club for Caledonian Airways, in the maintenance area of Gatwick. Adam was already an associate member there, as was my fellow DC, Ken Apps, so it was not difficult for me to join. The Caley chief engineer, a fellow Scot called Jimmy Keith, was very keen to have more police contact, as the maintenance workshops had some high-value parts and materials in stores.

I was in the Wingspan late one Saturday morning when a bunch of boisterous blokes gathered, and I discovered that they were the British Caledonian rugby team. I revealed my interest in the game and was promptly invited along to watch that afternoon's match. The fact that the team got together for a couple of pints before the game led me to believe they were on or about my standard!

All the club committee was on the playing pitch during the match, so I ended up running touch and going back to the club afterwards, where I paid my membership fee to the rugby section and was told I'd be playing the following week.

The fixture was at Newick, where they played totally committed agricultural rugby involving the careful negotiation of strategically placed cowpats. The cattle were obviously Newick fans!

I played nearly every Saturday after that, my duties easily being arranged to fit. The Wingspan Rugby Club had tours arranged, and I went on two to France and one to South Wales. Unfortunately I missed out on the tour to the Seychelles, as I had run out of leave, owing to the arrival of daughter number two—Hannah Claire—a few months earlier.

In contrast to Joanne's, Hannah's arrival was express delivery. Sandra did not even have time to inform me that she was in labour before she was whisked into Southlands Hospital at Shoreham-by-Sea, and by the time I got home that day, I was a father of another gorgeous little girl.

By then, of course, we had moved into our pleasant semidetached house in the Fishersgate district of Southwick, then a town in its own right, but now part of Adur District, together with Shoreham, Lancing, Sompting, and Coombes. My family now felt rounded and complete.

Business went on as usual at the airport, and most of the CID work was pretty routine.

John Watkins came on to CID as an aide. He got the whiff of a decent and different case, which at first the bosses were not interested in pursuing, as only the most minor of a series of offences by the same man had been committed at Gatwick.

This is how it happened. I'm going to change all but one of the names as life has moved on. Also the most vulnerable victim in the case has probably set her life in order and would not like to be reminded of an unfortunate chapter in her life, provided of course that anyone reads this! Her parents, if still around, most certainly do not want to be reminded.

The first victim was a girl in her mid-twenties, of a nice personality, which was not immediately apparent, being hidden beneath a demure and prim exterior. Her father was a retired army officer, her mother devoted to her husband and daughter. Let's call the daughter Louise and the father Major Albert Devonshire.

One day Louise met a young man who must previously have featured in her most memorable dreams. He was dark and swarthily handsome and appeared to have connections in the very best circles. I will use the name he called himself, as it will by now have been long discarded and known only to him.

He introduced himself as the Hon. Jefrey Jess Le Vance De Roath. He was cultured and beautifully spoken and bore a remarkable resemblance to the now notorious Lord "Lucky" Lucan.

When I first actually met "De Roath," I was almost convinced that we had captured Lucan, one of the most wanted men in the world following the murder of a maid and the attempted murder of his wife at a select apartment in the very best part of London. In fact, De Roath was from the wrong side of the tracks in Bristol and had been in custody as a youth offender. He'd done exceptionally well to develop his aura of culture, and it was a crying shame that he put his skills to the use he did.

"Louise" introduced De Roath to her parents, who were completely charmed by the man and happily gave their blessings to their daughter becoming his wife. De Roath also persuaded "Major Devonshire" to part with a considerable sum of money that he promised to invest for him.

De Roath and "Louise" lived the high life around London on the major's money, and when that had gone De Roath embarked on a series of frauds on the major High Street banks.

His luck inevitably started to run out, and he decided to take flight with "Louise" to Argentina, with whom, incidentally, Britain has no extradition treaty.

They arrived at Gatwick, where De Roath purchased first-class tickets using a cheque of the purest rubber, and informed British Caledonian that his purpose in travelling to Buenos Aires was to take up a position as an attaché at the British Embassy there.

Accordingly he was fast-tracked via the VIP lounge and given priority boarding onto the aircraft. During the flight, he and "Louise" were pampered and fussed over in the first-class section. Much later, when I interviewed a couple of the cabin crew, I found that his first action on arriving in Argentina had been to complain about the stewardesses!

So the criminal career of Jefrey Jess Le Vance de Roath in this country ended at Gatwick with the commission of two offences. He passed a fraudulent cheque (there were, of course, no funds in the account to cover it) and the obtaining of services by deception—the use of the VIP lounge and fast track to the aircraft. Not a lot in the context of his previous career, but John convinced our bosses that we should collate everything, as the final offences had been committed on us. The Mets and Devon and Cornwall were only too happy to let us.

John made contact with the South American desk of the Foreign Office and was informed that there was no chance of getting De Roath back. As I said, there was no extradition treaty with Argentina.

The case stalled, and eventually John, his period as CID Aide over, returned to uniform.

A few weeks later, I began to finalise everything, having put a "wanted" notice out on De Roath. I rang the Foreign Office, giving the extension number obtained by John. A very cultured voice answered, "Carruthers, FO?" I'm not about to drop the real name!

I told Carruthers that I was just wrapping the case up, but did he have any information about De Roath? Yes, he did, having been informed via the Argentine Immigration of an address. "Not a damn thing we can do about it, old boy."

However, he asked me to fill him in on De Roath. I gave him a fairly detailed description right down to the Old Etonian tie.

"What?" inquired Carruthers FO. "The man's an OE?"

"No," I replied. "He's an ex–Approved School boy from Bristol."

"And he's passing himself off as OE? The damned swine! Leave these matters with me."

I hung up, annotated the file, and put it away.

Some weeks later, I received a telephone call. "Ah, Constable Neil, Carruthers here, FO. I think you'll find that De Roath chappie is on a flight to Gatwick." He gave the flight number. "His lady is with him."

"Why is he coming back?" I asked.

"Damned if I know, old boy. Nothing to do with me. I just handle the information."

I called John Watkins, who was on two rest days. Did he want to be the one making the arrest?

"Try stopping me. I'll work my rest day for free."

I called Major Devonshire with the news that his daughter was on her way back. He replied that he was setting off immediately from his home two hundred miles away.

So it happened that when we boarded the flight upon its docking at Gatwick, John Watkins "felt De Roath's collar." I arrested Louise, of necessity, but at the police station, after making a statement, she was immediately bailed, tearfully, into the care of her grateful parents upon their arrival at the airport.

De Roath made a voluntary statement "under caution," running to some twenty pages, each of which he happily signed. The duty solicitor, Mike Bailey, represented him, a man I had always found to be totally straight. We charged him with a sample three or four offences, including one of the two at Gatwick, and put him before the magistrates in the morning. He was duly remanded in custody for seven days.

A week later, he appeared again. In the interval, he had fired Mike Bailey and engaged none other than Sir David Napley, the doyen of criminal lawyers. Sir David applied for bail with conditions and the magistrates, obviously overawed by the top man's reputation, and the argument that he had obviously returned voluntarily from Argentina, which could not possibly be refuted, granted it, to everyone's utter astonishment.

That was "good-bye, Jefrey," for he failed to turn up for the next hearing and a warrant was issued for his arrest. It was to be some time before we met again.

It was Louise who told me how Jefrey had come to return "voluntarily." They had run out of money in Buenos Aires, and someone approached Jefrey offering him a job in the Falkland Islands.

She had no idea where the money for the airfare came from, but they travelled to Port Stanley, where Jefrey, now being on British soil, was immediately arrested and escorted back to Buenos Aires, where he and Louise were put on the flight to Gatwick.

\* \* \*

On a wider scene, things were about to change again. Airports were becoming increasingly dangerous places. Across the globe, there were hijacks, complete and attempted, and attacks by terrorist groups on airports themselves. Incidents of the type that I had experienced at Heathrow in 1970 were becoming uncomfortably commonplace.

The first recorded European hijack took place over Lisbon in 1961, when the six hijackers involved wanted only to drop anti-government leaflets over the city.

The first serious hijack of a long-distance flight was of an EL AL Israeli aircraft from Rome to Tel Aviv in July 1968, when the plane was diverted to Algiers, and over five weeks of negotiations were necessary before the passengers, crew, and offenders were released.

The year 1970 ushered in a rash of them. The US, Israel, Japan, India, USSR, Canada, Germany, and Finland were all victims of attacks. One of these was, of course, that of September 6, 1970, involving EL AL, when I'd had a tiny peripheral role in its resolution at Heathrow.

The crime seemed to perpetuate itself around the world, the high profile and value of intercontinental air travel having an irresistible appeal for terrorist organisations, eventually culminating in the full horror of September 11, 2001.

Of course, to carry out a hijack, the perpetrators must board aircraft, and the only places they can do so are airports.

Quite apart from hijackings, terrorist attacks on airports themselves became a problem in the early 1970s. On May 30, 1972, a three-man team from the Japanese Red Army faction, supported by the Palestine Liberation front, made a random attack using automatic weapons and hand grenades on the crowded terminal at Lod Airport, in Tel Aviv. Twenty-six innocent passengers were killed and seventy-eight injured.

The inevitable effect of all this terrorist activity on the British Airports Authority Constabulary was the winding up of the force. BAAC simply did not have the means, manpower, or training to be able to tackle events like these.

The Policing of Airports Act of 1974 handed the responsibility for policing Heathrow over to the Metropolitan Police. This left the (then) small number of officers at Gatwick, Stansted, Belfast, and Edinburgh as too small a splintered rump to be any kind of efficient unit.

Inevitably the forces in whose territory they stood took over the policing of these airports. Stansted went to Essex Police, and Edinburgh to the Lothian and Borders Police. The Royal Ulster Constabulary took Belfast.

Gatwick was slightly different. The airport perimeter had been like a pimple on the borders of Surrey, and in mid-1974 this salient was straightened out by the simple expedient of moving Gatwick into Sussex.

In the spring of 1975, Sussex Police took over the Gatwick Division of the British Airports Authority. Prior to the takeover, the Sussex chief constable, the ebullient George Terry, later Sir George, held a meeting in which he gave reassurances to all those officers who had left Home Office forces, sometimes, like me, under some sort of cloud.

The clock, he said, for everyone had been reset to midnight, and all sheets were now pristine clean.

Mr. Terry had been my chief constable in East Sussex prior to its amalgamation into Sussex Police, when command of the combined force fell to the West Sussex chief, Mr. T.C. Williams. Mr. Terry had taken over from Mr. Williams shortly before this meeting. He was as good as his word, although not every officer at Gatwick was happy with the change.

My fellow DC—Ken Apps—left to set up his own security firm and, the last I heard, was doing well. Four or five PCs left to join the BTP, the British Transport Police, still a non–Home Office force to this day.

On April 1, 1975, I stopped being DC 315 Neil and found that I was DC AN043, one number up from my previous Sussex identity.

Overnight the staffing doubled. In CID, where we had run with a detective sergeant and two DCs, we found ourselves with a detective inspector, two sergeants, and four DCs. The workload did not increase, so I found myself scratching around for something to do.

The real crunch came on my first Sussex payday, when my wage cheque was less than half of what it had been under the BAAC.

It went without saying that overtime vanished. We had still been on airport allowance, based on the Surrey rent allowance. That was slashed by 25 percent to the Sussex rate. I had been in the habit, whenever possible, of doing inquiries out and about on the way to or from work, thereby managing to claim a bit of mileage allowance for the distances driven on duty, as well as the associated overtime. That stopped, so I had to meet the full cost of driving the fifty miles a day to and from work. My car was a thirsty Hillman Super Minx, doing twenty miles to the gallon and even with petrol at 50p a gallon—

that's 11p a litre—I soon realised that I could not keep it up. I put in a request for a transfer, specifically to Hove, where I was still familiar with the territory. I knew that if all else failed I could follow the others into the BTP and be based at Brighton Railway Station.

An inspector came down from HQ and interviewed me. I was quite straight that my request was purely on financial grounds relating to the costs of travel and that, with my young family and a fairly new mortgage, a house move was out of the question. I didn't get Hove—I hadn't really expected to—but was posted to Worthing. This was almost as good as it was only seven miles from Fishersgate, with excellent bus and train contacts if required.

It was with some regret that I said good-bye to my Gatwick friends and also to my British Caledonian rugby teammates, as it had been made clear that I would not get time off to play for anyone other than the police!

Nowadays, nobody in Sussex gets time off even to play for the force, and the fact that the Sussex Police now runs only one team, which is languishing in the very basement of the English rugby pyramid, says it all.

# CHAPTER 11

## Worthing First Time Around: Back in Sussex Police, a Few Cases and Promotion

I went in to Worthing Police Station on a rest day before transferring, to find out what I would be doing and discovered that, initially at least, I would be back in uniform pending an opening in CID. This meant a trip to Lewes and the clothing store, as all the uniform I had was BAAC.

Sgt. Myall was still there and was predictably scathing about the quality of the stuff I'd brought in and the fact that all the holes for badges and numbers were in "the wrong place."

I was pleased to see that Sussex had now adopted the clip-on tie that had been such a system shock to Superintendent Cummings at Nutfield Training Centre a few years previously!

Arriving at Worthing, I discovered that I would be on "C" shift—the same as I had been at Hove, starting at 1:45 p.m. next day—the rest of that day being given over to some familiarisation and an interview with the divisional commander—Chief Superintendent Kevin Somers.

Now, the formidable Mr. Somers was a pillar of the local Roman Catholic community and a prominent figure in the Knights of St. Columba—as far as I know, the RC equivalent of Freemasons. He was a large fleshy man with a jovial expression and a strong Southern Irish accent. His sister was, reputedly, a senior sister in a convent, so you get the drift. The conversation with the chief super went like this.

Chief Super: Welcome to Worthing, Constable Neil. Take a seat.

Me: Thank you, sir.

Chief Super: I see you are a family man and you have two small daughters.

Me: That's right, sir. I also have two sons.

Chief Super (peering at the personnel file): Oh, yes, I see. Why are they not on your Airport Authority papers?

Me: That's because they are in Australia with my ex-wife.

Chief Super: Ex-wife? You mean you're divorced?

Me: Yes, sir.

Mr. Somers's expression changed from jovial to stern. He stood up abruptly. "Well, that will be all, Constable. I wish you well at Worthing."

I was to discover, talking to some of the veteran cops at Worthing, that Mr. Somers was something of a throwback to when Shoreham and points west were in the West Sussex force. That force had been much under the discreet influence of the Duke of Norfolk, the most senior Catholic layman in the land, and a resident of Arundel Castle, just down the road. Chief Constables had consequently been invariably Roman Catholic.

I was also to discover at Worthing that a call to a burglary in a "nice" part of the town was invariably either a "How's Kevin job," or a "How's Keith job." Keith was Detective Superintendent Keith Cantle, in charge of Divisional CID and a leading light in the local

Freemasons. On admission to such houses, one was wise to take a quick look around for manifestations of either loyalty and proceed accordingly!

After a couple of weeks, I was put into CID for "a trial period." This was just one step up from an aide. I found that work at Worthing was surprisingly brisk, there being a not-insignificant hard core of regular offenders in the town.

I was soon given a permanent appointment, and I am convinced to this day that the result that got me the job was probably the most minor crime I ever investigated.

A boy had the lamp stolen from his cycle in the bike shed at school. He had told his father he had no idea who the thief was. Daddy had insisted it be recorded as a crime. Daddy was Detective Superintendent Keith Cantle! It was with barely concealed glee that my new detective inspector, Gordon Harrison, handed the investigation over to the rookie in the camp—me.

I went along to the school just before classes ended for the day and identified the bike in the shed. When the pupils turned out, I spoke to young Cantle. I could tell immediately that he knew who had taken the lamp but for some reason had been scared to tell his father. I got the name out of him. A boy had been bullying young Cantle and had actually demanded the lamp from him with fairly explicit schoolboy threats. I went home with Master Cantle and got a statement in front of his mother.

The next day I took the offender home and interviewed him too, also in front of his mother. He admitted the offence, and I reported him.

Statistically this was a triumph, as the crime was no longer a simple "theft from a bicycle" but the much more impressive one of blackmail, otherwise known as "demanding with menaces." The offender was cautioned and that was that, except that Detective Inspector Harrison called me in. "You're a jammy bugger, but we need all the jammy buggers we can get. Consider yourself permanent."

Gordon Harrison was not universally liked, being a bit too much of a forthright Yorkshireman for some Southern tastes, but I always got on extremely well with him and never found myself without his unstinting backing.

Okay, I'm biased. He wrote my staff assessment in 1977, which contributed hugely to my promotion to sergeant.

Gordon had been a very good Rugby League player and had played at Wembley in the Challenge Cup final for Hull FC against Wigan in 1959.

To play League at that level, you have to be pretty hard. I remember the occasion of an informal football match between Worthing CID and Uniform. I played on the wing, and at one point in the game I turned the fullback and headed for goal, only to be put up in the air by the man I'd just beaten. When I got up and turned round, Gordon had the unfortunate fullback by the collar of his shirt, feet almost off the ground, growling, "Do that again, son and I'll bloody have you!" By a quirk of fate, when I finished my service back at Worthing, my uniformed inspector was Gordon's son, Stuart, locally born but cut somewhat from the same cloth!

Financially, this was a bad time. Police wages had fallen way behind other occupations, to the extent that when Jo started at Fishersgate First School, she qualified for free school meals, not that we allowed that indignity to happen, as it was only a two-minute walk for her to come home for lunch.

Paid overtime was not to be had. There was a "detective allowance," but one had to work a minimum of extra hours to qualify for it and, when you got it, it amounted to less than 5p per hour! It all went on beer, as it was expected that each DC made regular visits to pubs designated as "his" for the purposes of showing one's face and picking up intelligence. Also it was wise to go to some of these pubs in pairs, which meant a minimum of two drinks purchased.

The other two DCs on my section were Dave Deal and John Adams. Dave was a small, neat man with a twinkling sense of humour. John was big—and I mean *big*. He was a touch over six feet tall, with a hugely broad chest and shoulders, and he was a very useful rugby prop forward. In tight corners, he would have been my companion of choice every time.

Very sadly, Dave and John are no longer with us and are missed by all that knew them.

My detective sergeant was Ivor Webb, a very useful cricketer and a regular in the Force cricket XI. Ivor took me into Sussex County Ground one day for a bit of net practice, and I had the privilege of not only bowling at the England Cricket team captain, Tony Greig, but also nicking a bail off with one that didn't turn, even though I had wanted it to.

"Well disguised," said Tony Greig.

"Thank you, Mr. Greig," said I, trying not to blush.

Ivor is now a life member of Sussex County Cricket Club, a well-deserved present upon his retirement from regular and "civvy" police service in 2008. I went to his leaving "do," and it was wonderful bumping into so many people I remembered over forty-odd years in and out of the job.

Incoming telephone calls could be a problem at that time, as the Worthing CID contained DCs Mill, Deal, Neil, O'Neill, and Neale Clarke. Not good news on a crackly line! I think it was Portsmouth that had DCs Hitchcock, Hipcock, and Hedgecock, so conversations between the two offices could be a bit of a lottery.

Most of the workload dealt with by Worthing DCs tended to be minor burglaries and thefts. In those days, every, and I do mean *every*, reported burglary got personal attention by at least a DC and a Scenes of Crime officer. There was an early DC who came in at 7:00 a.m., usually to interview prisoners held overnight on criminal matters, but if there was an outstanding burglary, the prisoners had to wait.

This was, of course, before the Police and Criminal Evidence Act of 1984, the introduction of which effectively meant that the prisoners now get priority over the burgled householders.

Briefing or "morning prayers" was at 9:00 a.m. when the detective inspector or delegated detective sergeant would run over events of the last twenty-four hours and allocate new crimes to DCs, besides listening to bleats from the CID clerks about overdue files or illegible handwriting. DSs or DCs would give any update to cases currently running, and the collator would chip in with any hot intelligence.

Immediately after "prayers," any burglaries not handled by the early DC were attended straightaway. Burglaries to dwelling houses took top priority, followed by factories or shops, and finally burglaries at unattended buildings.

How different it is today, when the best the householder may expect is to talk to a clerk and be given a "crime number" for his insurance claim. It is not unusual now to read of cases where police have not attended a "live" burglary, that is to say, one where the offender is believed to be still on the premises. In the 1970s, and before, "burglary in progress" shouts meant patrol and traffic cars descending on the address in minutes, if not seconds, with a dog and handler close behind.

A few more unusual cases came my way during my time on Worthing CID. There was the matter of a South African gentleman, purporting to be an Israeli graduate of an Australian university, complete with false papers, who got a job as a departmental head in a prestigious boys' fee-paying school in the town.

The informant had been the headmaster of the school, who was also its owner. Peter (I won't give his surname for reasons as before) found he was buttoned up tight and was charged with obtaining a pecuniary advantage by deception. He obviously knew that the headmaster had been the informant, because after he was given a suspended sentence, he asked to see me and made a statement implicating the headmaster in indecency against the boys in his charge. He named names of boys offended against.

In view of the headmaster's stature in local society, and the fact that it may have been a "How's Keith" job, it was investigated by an officer of a rank more considerable than mine.

The headmaster was never charged, but the school closed down almost overnight and he left the area in a bit of a hurry.

Then there was Lennie, a "Sahf Londoner" from somewhere around Peckham. In June 1977, Lennie stole a maroon Mercedes car from a golf club in Dulwich, having taken the keys from its owner's coat in the clubhouse. The car had a custom gold stripe down its sides, so it was very memorable to anyone who saw it.

He then embarked on a grand golf tour inasmuch as he visited upwards of fifteen golf clubs between South London, Rustington, Worthing, Brighton, and Newhaven as well as a bowls club at

Saltdean. His MO was to walk nonchalantly into clubhouses and search coats, looking not only for something with the owner's address on it, but also for house keys. Wallets came in handy too, of course. He then called at several addresses, always knocking on the doors. He didn't have a lot of luck in that in almost every case someone was at home. When challenged he always said something about the golf club that the householder was at. In most cases, he left empty-handed, although he did enter some unattended homes. In each case where he had been seen, of course, the householder had a perfect description, and as Lennie, no doubt to impress, always left the Mercedes where it could be seen, an unusual number of complainants noted down the index number and distinct description. One of the householders actually thought about ringing the police, and the number was circulated to all patrols.

A unit in Newhaven spotted the car going in the opposite direction, but by the time the officer turned around, the Mercedes had vanished. Stops were put on all four roads out of Newhaven but it seemed the car had evaporated into thin air.

A short time later, a farmer on the top of the South Downs reported seeing a maroon Mercedes being driven across one of his fields and phoned the information in, as it was spooking his sheep.

Soon after that, a resident of the small hamlet of Firle under the north side of the Downs informed police control that his Morris 1100 car had just been stolen.

There is only one road out of Firle, and at the end of that there are only two choices—towards Lewes or in the direction of Eastbourne. Lennie chose Lewes and got stopped and arrested at the Beddingham turnoff. DS John Dicker and I collected him from Lewes Police Station.

At first he denied everything except the theft of the car from Firle, despite the huge amount of evidence. He insisted that he had never been in a Mercedes, despite assurances that at least five people could identify him.

Meanwhile, the scenes of crimes officer (SOCO) who had been sent from Lewes to examine the Mercedes that the farmer had found with its sump ripped out by a boulder—radioed in with news of the damage. The interview had progressed to a long silence to let Lennie have a think or two. Out of the blue, he blurted, "Will I be stuck on for the damage to the Merc?" As we had told him only that the patrol car in Newhaven had lost him and had not mentioned him going off-road, John Dicker's laugh made him realise he'd dropped himself in it. That saved the time and trouble of identity parades, although in the end that would not have mattered as his fingerprints were all over the Mercedes.

Gerald came from Liverpool. He was out of work and bored with life, so he decided to try British Rail and travel the country. He went down to a Liverpool main line station, where he examined cars in the all-day car park. Examined from the inside, I mean. Eventually his search bore fruit in the shape of a Barclaycard. I was later surprised to learn from Barclaycard Security how many motorists had a company credit card just to be used for petrol and who kept it in the car at all times!

Using the Barclaycard, he bought a single ticket to Manchester, where he did a round of the shops, buying a large suitcase and a few quality items of clothing before checking in at a half-decent hotel, using the card, of course. He was no doubt banking that the owner of the card would not be filling up that evening.

In the morning, he dumped the card, went to a Manchester mainline station and repeated the trick, this time going on to Leeds. From

Leeds he went on to Peterborough, then to London, and finally to Worthing, by which time he was the owner of two large, heavy suitcases, which he checked in at a local hotel.

He made his way down to Worthing's main shopping precinct, Montague Street, where he went into a Jones Shoes shop, picking a very expensive pair of shoes. The shopworker obviously possessed a very good nose for a criminal, because while Gerald was choosing shoes, the assistant went into the back shop and rang the police station.

Gerald's luck had run out because when the call went out on radio, John Adams and I were only a few yards away, parking up in Montague Place. While I went in to talk to Gerald, John quite literally filled the doorway, and Gerald came quite peacefully. He was dealt with locally and got a nice eighteen-month holiday near the seaside in Lewes.

One afternoon in 1977, I got a call from the local benefits office, or DHSS, as it was then called. They had someone in claiming benefits and suspected that he was trying to defraud them. The office was just across the road, and a colleague and I walked over, where we found Willie Martin in the company of one of the local clerks. She put the allegation to Willie in our presence. He nodded his head and said, "Guilty as charged, sir," in a broad Belfast accent. We took him back to the police station, where he made a full confession.

Now, apart from his broad accent, Willie had a shock of carroty hair and a face full of freckles. He was wearing a sleeveless vest, and his arms and what we could see of his chest were covered in tattoos, many with Ulster Loyalist themes like "No surrender," "Remember the Boyne," and one that was obscenely insulting to the Pope. In fact, his descriptive form had to have two supplementary pages describing his tattoos!

He made a full statement of confession, which went something like this. He had arrived in Brighton on his first trip out of Belfast, where things had been becoming uncomfortable. He had no job to go to and little money after paying a month's rent on a bedsit. He had gone to a pub on his first evening and had struck up a conversation with a man who advised him how to make false claims on the DHSS. First he had to go to the local Brighton Office and put in a claim giving his real name and address. He would get an "emergency" Giro cheque, and later more money would be posted to his address.

He should then go to other offices in the area, where he could give a false name and state he needed an emergency award as he had just arrived in the town and had to find a place to live. They would then give him more money to get by on, and he could then go on to the next town and repeat the process and so on.

Willie carried out the first part of the plan. "Jeez, it was so easy," he confided.

Afterwards he caught a bus to Worthing, and when he was called in to see the Social Security clerk, he was told he'd have to sign a form with his details. The girl asked for his name. "Jeez," said Willie, "I'd to think fast, so I had."

"My name? Oh, yes, it's Giovanni Martini."

The clerk then rang the police station!

I charged Willie with "attempted criminal deception," and he was kept in for court in the morning. I typed a summary of the case and judged exactly where to finish the first page. "The defendant was asked his name and replied . . ." Page two started "Giovanni Martini."

"Police were called, and he was arrested and later charged with the offence now before the court. After caution he replied, 'Sure that girl was awful clever to guess it was a false name.'"

I was in court in the morning when Willie was put in the dock, resplendent in red hair, vest, and tattoos. When the clerk asked him to verify his name, he replied, "Oh, aye, that's me all right." The clerk asked him how he pleaded, and Willie said, "Oh, hell aye, I'm guilty, so I am."

The court inspector then read out the facts. At the end of page one, he paused while he turned the page and instantly collapsed in laughter, which he turned into a totally unconvincing, spluttering cough. When he had recovered and composed himself, he repeated the end of page one and managed to gasp "Giovanni Martini!" Even the magistrates found it difficult to control themselves, and Willie turned to me. "Hey, what's so funny?"

Forgive me, but opportunities for humour can be few and far between in the world of crime detection!

The next memorable case was the reemergence of Jefrey Jess Le Vance De Roath, who had been living on his wits in a crime spree, mainly fraud of course, around the country. He was arrested in Newcastle upon Tyne on a straightforward "stop check" and brought to Shepherd's Bush Police Station by two Geordie officers, who were going on to another Mets station to collect and take another offender back to their manor. The arresting officer had left a statement giving De Roath's reply under caution at the time of his arrest: "Please don't hand me over to DC Neil. He'll beat me up!"

John Adams and I drove up to Shepherd's Bush to collect him. I'd kept the crime file in my locker at Worthing, as it was in BAAC format and the new regime at Gatwick had not known what to do with it. As we went into the custody area, I could see De Roath's face, pale and peering through the cell flap. I couldn't resist it. I made a sign of cutting my throat as I smiled at him.

The custody sergeant told us to go and get a cup of tea, as De Roath had just been given lunch. When we returned, the sergeant was roaring with laughter. "You can't have him yet. He's just eaten his knife and fork!"

They were plastic, of course, and he had broken them up into small pieces and swallowed them. The police surgeon was called and pronounced him fit to travel. "It'll take a few hours for anything to happen, and they will probably pass right through. They might strain him a bit, so get him checked again when you arrive at your destination."

I drove back to Crawley with De Roath squashed in the back with John. He was kept there overnight and put up before the magistrates in the morning, complaining that he had had to eat his breakfast of scrambled egg with his fingers as we would not provide him with a knife or fork!

I returned to Crawley in the morning for the court appearance before handing everything over to prosecuting solicitors. I saw no more of De Roath until he appeared at Lewes Crown Court some time later. He'd fired Sir David Napley and, not surprisingly, was consequently having difficulty getting representation. He ended up defending himself, with a well-known Brighton solicitor sitting behind him. I had to call all our witnesses as he denied everything.

When I gave my evidence, he attacked me as having seduced his wife and put words into his mouth, despite his lengthy statement of admission. The *News of the World* loved him. "The Lord of the Lies" was their headline with a long account of how he alleged I'd fitted him up in order to get my wicked way with his wife. After paragraphs of this drivel, the final sentence was, "DC Neil denies these allegations." Thank you, *News of the World*. That sure put the record straight.

His defence was that he had been in the SAS in Yemen and had carried out some very dangerous forays in enemy territory, for which he had been awarded an ungazetted Military Cross. This was all a plot by the government and MI5, using me as a pawn in the game to discredit him, as they thought he would blow the whistle on some very illegal activities. There was, he said, no point in trying to verify his defence with the War Office, as they would deny everything.

He was convicted, of course, and sent down for two years. About four years later, when I was with Regional Crime Squad, my unit was enjoying a tea break in a café in Hooley, on the A23 in Surrey, when a road gang came in for refreshments. I heard one of them regaling his mates in a fruity voice with derring-do tales of his undercover work in the SAS.

I did not turn and look at him. I did not need to, and I did not want him to see me, even though he would probably not have recognised me with long hair and scruffy clothes, as opposed to my CID suit and tie. When I went to leave the café, I recognised Jefrey straightaway. I was teamed up that day with Dave Deal, who suggested going back and winding him up!

Back at Worthing, in the spring of 1977, I got my annual assessment from John Dicker, who was now my DS, and Gordon Harrison, who was just about to move on promotion. Both suggested I should apply for promotion to sergeant, as I had passed the exam while I was at Gatwick. I went along with it, and there was a succession of "boards" who were impressed enough to put me on to the final trial by ordeal—a chief constable's board.

This consisted of the aforementioned chief, George Terry, a chief superintendent called Nicholas Jelf, whom I'd encountered a few times in not the best of circumstances, and someone from personnel.

Before going before the board, everyone had advised me, "If the chief asks if you are prepared to move, tell him you are. If he then offers you a promotion and you don't want to go there, turn it down. He can't say you are not worth promoting, and he'll offer you somewhere else."

I sat in front of this austere assembly. George Terry said, "Mr. Neil, you used to be at Hove, then you turned up at Gatwick. What happened in between?"

I told him the straight truth, hiding nothing. The chief then said, "Okay, Mr. Neil. Are you prepared to move house on promotion?"

I thought of all the advice given, but George Terry was staring right through me and was, I decided, not a man to be lied to.

"I'm not, sir. I have a young family and a fairly recent mortgage. My first daughter recently started at school. My wife is close to her parents, so I'm sorry. The answer is no, sir." I got mentally prepared to get up and leave the room, especially seeing the disbelieving look of horror on Chief Supt. Jelf's face.

"I see," grated the chief. "If I offer you the superintendent's job at Crawley, you will turn me down, eh?"

"No, I won't, sir, thank you very much. I accept. On his money, I can afford to travel."

There was a moment of silence as Chief Supt. Jelf and the personnel man buried their faces in their hands, and then George Terry threw his head back and roared with laughter, the other two very quickly following suit. "Very, very good, Mr. Neil. How does Brighton Uniform suit you?"

"Thank you, sir. Yes."

"Off with you then. You'll get a notice in the next few days."

So it was that I became PS AN043 Neil of Brighton Police.

# CHAPTER 12

## Brighton Uniform Patrol: A Brand New Sergeant Arrives at Brighton

Three weeks before my arrival at Brighton, I'd had occasion to obtain a statement from a railway employee who had witnessed some offence or another in Worthing. Due to his duties, it involved seeing him at around midnight at Brighton Station. I finished the job and drove off south in Queen's Road, towards the coast road.

Halfway between the station and the seafront is the Clock Tower junction, where traffic lights control five converging roads. It was well after 1:00 a.m., and the lights were red as I approached them.

I stopped at the white line and waited, and after several minutes, they were still red. I reversed to and fro a few times to try to trip them, but they stayed stubbornly on red. Eventually, seeing no traffic in any direction, I drove slowly over the junction into West Street.

A dark figure bearing a torch leapt from a shop doorway a few yards down. It was a police constable, and he held his hand up to stop me.

I pulled over and opened the driver's window. The officer stuck his head partly through. "You just went through a red light, didn't you?"

Yes," I replied, "but the lights are…"

"Don't mess with me. You went through a red light. Yes or no." He poked his head a little further through the window so that his nose was close to mine.

"Yes."

"You're a c***! You know that? Go through red lights, and you'll get yourself nicked. Now clear off." He pulled his head back out of the window.

I always made a point, if stopped, never to reveal that I was "in the job." Doing so was definitely a two-edged sword. You never knew what grudges the stopping officer might be nurturing. Also the car was a CID mini, the only tomato-coloured one in Sussex Police, and the radio had been silent throughout. I made a mental note of the PCs number, only revealing here that it started with a "B."

I started at Brighton, C1 Division on August 1, 1977, doing a nine-to-five for admin purposes. I discovered that, once again, I was to be on "C" section, or "C column" as it was known in local Brighton parlance. The section was on nights, so my first meeting with them was on the Tuesday evening.

I got in slightly early to introduce myself to the section inspector, Brian Belton, a tall, slim, good-looking, and very humourous man. The other sergeant that night was Graham Lindfield, a very active and capable supervisor, with a fearsome piratical beard. The third sergeant was on leave, due to return the following night. He was Ron Chillingworth, whom I had met on a number of occasions, as he had been on CID prior to promotion.

In the briefing room, the section sat around a long table. Brian Belton introduced me and named the PCs sitting round the table. At the far end, a PC seemed to be sitting with his face half-covered. I recognised the number, and Brian introduced him: "This is PC T***** B****," before continuing around the table. I noted that there were no female constables present.

I gave a short summary of my career, before saying, "You should know that I am a c***. This is on the authority, no less, of someone sitting in this room. No doubt he will identify himself to you after the briefing and explain why he has that opinion of me.

"Now we are going to get on very well, but you should know that I am quite insistent on courtesy to normal members of the public and even to most offenders. I am also quite hot on safety. For instance, I would never stick my head through a driver's open window when the engine was running. What would happen if he suddenly accelerated away?"

After the briefing, Brian Belton asked me what all that had been about. I related my experience of the previous month. He laughed aloud. "What a lovely come-uppance!"

I saw the PC before he went out. I shook his hand and said, "I guess we are quits now." I never had any problems with him after that.

Here is a quick résumé of how Brighton was policed in 1977. Until 1969 it had its own independent police force, distinguished by the fact that in summer months the uniform included white helmets. Many old "borough" men had kept their helmets, and all of them regretted their passing.

The town was still divided into two divisions, only now they were called "subdivisions." I was allocated to C1 subdivision, which was divided from C2 by Ditchling Road and Grand Parade down to the Palace Pier. To the west, the subdivision boundary was the border with Hove and to the north the borough boundary with East Sussex on the A23 London Road.

The subdivision was, of course, further subdivided into beats, and each sergeant was responsible for a number of those beats. The policy in those days was that a PC was assigned on almost a permanent basis to a specific beat. I have always believed this to be a good way of policing as the residents and traders on each beat know the four PCs that patrol it and the PCs know them.

Each beat had a police box either on it or closely adjacent—some boxes serving several beats. Paperwork for beat officers could be delivered, completed, and collected there so that the PCs did not have to take time going into the police station. All the boxes had basic facilities for making tea and coffee.

Both subdivisions had three double-manned patrol cars, which most beat men aspired to, giving them an incentive to be efficient officers. One advantage of being on C1 was that the administration of the police station and custody suite fell to C2, which meant that, apart from overseeing paperwork, sergeants could get "out and about" at some point every day and could supervise and advise "on the ground." The control room was also the responsibility of C2 subdivision.

Wednesday and Thursday were taken up with familiarisation—of the men and of the territory, going to various incidents and seeing how each man dealt with it and familiarising myself with the various characters to be found out and about in the subdivision at odd times of the night. Brighton was then, and still is now, a twenty-four-hour city.

During refreshment break on the Thursday night, Brian Belton informed me that I would be in charge of the mobile unit, better known locally as "the heavy mob" on Friday and Saturday between 10:00 p.m. and 2:00 a.m. He told me to find out all about the duty from Graham Lindfield.

The job involved being in charge of a Land Rover with a driver and six PCs—probably the biggest guys on D Column—the section on the 2–10 shift. These seven—drawn from both subdivisions—worked 6:00 p.m. to 2:00 a.m. on those days and were usually, leave and other absences permitting, the same seven guys every four weeks that the duty came up for the section involved.

The Land Rover and crew were to attend every incident of rowdy and violent behaviour in the town—usually in the centre, but it was not unknown for the unit to attend one of the housing estate pubs dotted around the edge of town. Such incidents were not at all uncommon, particularly in or just outside certain notorious pubs, more usually at closing time or just after.

In those days, pubs stopped serving drinks at 11:00 p.m. and had to clear the bars by 11:30, so it was not at all unusual for the pavements outside these pubs to be suddenly thronged with drunken, often violent young men. Some moved on to the many nightclubs around the centre, while others started to make their often quarrelsome ways home.

There was usually a lull around 12:30 a.m., when most had dispersed on foot or by taxi. Then after 1:00 a.m. the nightclubs began to chuck out and the problems recurred, sometimes inflamed by bouncers hired for their physical presence and brutality rather than their brains. Thankfully times have changed, and door attendants, as they are now called, have to undergo training and have a code of conduct and a licence to protect. Saturday was a repeat of Friday, except that the problem was frequently exacerbated by the presence of "stag parties" often from out of town and as far away as Portsmouth or London.

It was 10:00 p.m. on Friday, and the team was already waiting to go out when I emerged from the briefing. The driver, Phil, was a PC I knew quite well from rugby, when his propensity for punching opposition players had cost the Force XV a lot of points over the years. Sadly, he died young—sadly, because I knew that when he was "unplugged" he was a gentle and amusing big man. "Plugged in," Phil could be a beast.

"Never mind," I thought. "The driver never leaves the vehicle unattended, for obvious reasons." Graham Lindfield had explained that rule. I did not know the other six men, but not one of them was under around six foot two inches—one was, he confided, six foot eight! All were equally impressive measured around the body!

The first "shout" was to a report of a disturbance in a bar on West Street, just south of the Clock Tower junction. We had just left the police station, and within two minutes Phil roared up and stopped outside the bar. The vehicle had not completely stopped when the back door shot open and the six big guys leaped out of the back and into the bar before I'd even got out. I followed them in just in time to see a six-versus-four brawl in full swing. The six were "my guys" and the four were violent drunks.

I had to shout to make myself heard, asking the manager if the four men were those responsible for the disturbance. He nodded. I yelled to the PCs to get cuffs on the four and get them out into the Land Rover. I pitched in to help one of the PCs who was having a one-on-one struggle and, after a violent interlude out in the street, eventually got all four into the vehicle and back to the police station.

They were all booked into the cells as "section 5 arrests," that section being of the Public Order Act of 1936—using threatening, abusive, or insulting behaviour whereby a breach of the peace is or is likely to be occasioned. This, I learned, was the standard charge for people arrested in Brighton as a result of disturbances, unless someone was seriously hurt or property damaged and evidence was available to back any allegation up.

As soon as the four had been booked in, I got Phil to drive to a nearby police box and got everyone to go inside. I made it plain that whenever I was the "heavy mob" sergeant and we were called to an incident, I would be first out of the vehicle. Two or more of the crew, depending on the seriousness of the report, or the first impression of the incident on arrival, would back me up, and I was not going to have policemen brawling in the spit and sawdust of a pub floor.

I could see the guys muttering among themselves until Phil, the driver, spoke up. "You want to listen to him. He's a good guy in a tight spot."

Phil was referring to rugby, a rather different kettle of fish, but never mind—he had the respect of the crew and now, by association, so did I.

The next call was to a fight near the clock tower. Phil pulled up. Two guys were rolling around on the pavement, no more able to punch each other than to stand up straight. I went out and called three of the crew. We got them in the back of the Land Rover, and, incredibly, they were brothers who lived with their parents in a street near Seven Dials. I told Phil to take them home, and I handed them over to their angry mother. I could sense the crew's approval. No paperwork other than a notebook entry!

I don't remember much else about that weekend, other than that there were a few incidents around the town. On Sunday night, Brian Belton took me to one side. "I've been talking to "Inspector X," the D column inspector from C2. He says his officers were very impressed with you on the mobile unit. It will upset Graham (Lindfield) if I take him off it, but you and he can do it alternate weekends." I didn't tell him that I would have been happy for Graham to do it every weekend!

Football fans could be another problem in the town centre, sometimes even on a Friday night, especially when London or South Coast teams were visiting Brighton and Hove Albion.

At the end of the 1976–1977 season, Tottenham Hotspur was relegated to the Second Division and Brighton was promoted from the Third. Millwall, Charlton, Southampton, and Crystal Palace were all in this division too, all clubs with serious local rivalry with Brighton fans, so there were going to be some lively Friday and Saturday nights during the season.

The liveliest, though, was the Friday evening before the Tottenham game, which took place on April 15, 1978. Both Brighton and Spurs were in contention for promotion to the top division—eventually Tottenham went up and Brighton lost out on goal difference.

That spring I was in the habit of riding my bicycle to and from work. Cycling along Western Road and past the clock tower, I rode past dozens of groups of rowdies and several fights in progress.

On arriving at the police station, I realised that the sections had been depleted to make more men available for policing the football ground and the area around it the following afternoon. It was later estimated that three thousand Spurs fans had arrived during the Friday evening and had been tanking up.

I cannot remember who was mobile unit sergeant (except it was not I), but apart from the Land Rover and six, between us C1 and C2 had fourteen officers to handle the baying mob. The 2–10 shift PCs were retained on duty to bolster our numbers.

For every ten Spurs fans, there was one boozed up Brightonian aching to fight. I changed quickly from my cycling gear and without even briefing I grabbed a car, thrust a young PC into it, and then spent the next four hours going to and from the police station ferrying prisoners, or breaking up fights.

At one point, I found a PC isolated, truncheon drawn, facing a mob of two dozen or so yobs. I drove straight at them with sirens and blue light on, scattering them and then herding them with the car to the landward end of the Palace Pier.

There had been numerous serious injuries, including stabbings, and in the back of the car during this incident was a witness to one of those—a Tottenham man. He said, "My God, is it always like this in Brighton?" I said, "Pretty much."

Eventually we received more help from places like Burgess Hill, Lewes, and Hove, and the place was more or less contained by 3:00 a.m. with the cells filled sometimes four apiece and some offenders taken to Hove and Shoreham to be lodged.

The following day, Brighton beat Spurs, and I guess the North London fans were either too cheesed off, or too knackered to stay. Either way Saturday night was a comparative haven of peace and quiet.

Shortly after arriving at Brighton, I received the result of the exam for promotion to inspector, and to loud cheers from the section I announced at briefing that I had passed with something to spare. Neither Graham nor Ron had passed his promotion exam, and when Brian Belton next went on leave, I was asked to do the duties of acting inspector.

I can't say I enjoyed it as there was too much deskbound work. The next time he went on leave, I had been put on to other duties and I did not return to the section for eighteen months. By then I was not needed for "acting," as both Graham Lindfield and Ron Chillingworth passed the inspector exam at the next sitting, and of course both held seniority over me.

Ron meantime was in charge of the plainclothes unit, mostly referred to as the vice squad. It was a small unit of four PCs and a sergeant, and the colloquial name will give a pointer as to the sort of work involved. It was a maximum six-month attachment, the thinking being that any longer on the unit would corrupt officers.

When Ron's period in charge expired, the chief superintendent, Norman Cooper, sent for me and offered me the job. It was explained that, because of the delicacy of some of the work I would answer directly to him, or if he was absent, to his deputy, Superintendent Cyril Leeves.

So it was that I left the section for what turned out to be eighteen months, and I did not return until December 1979. What happened in that time is the subject of the next chapter.

On my return, two things were in the process of happening. The first was that Brian Belton was leaving on promotion to chief inspector, and his replacement was to be John Bishop.

I knew John quite well through rugby, at which he could have been a class player had he had a mind to it. He was a big man, just over six feet tall, with a huge chest and shoulders combined with a low centre of gravity. At our standard of rugby, John, playing at centre three-quarter, was very difficult to bring down.

He also had a party trick of taking a beer bottle in each hand, then going facedown on the floor supported by his toes and the beer bottles, then walking the beer bottles out in front of him until he was fully extended. That bit is hard enough. Try it and see. What he did next was to walk himself back, which meant at one point his full, considerable weight was supported by one beer bottle-holding hand.

I went back on nights on December 18. John obviously had a lot of admin to get through on that Monday and did not appear. He started with us on Tuesday, December 18, and I introduced him to the troops at briefing. Afterwards Graham took him out for a look around the town, and I was attending to whatever it was I had to attend to when an urgent message came over the radio.

"Receiving reports of a train crash between Preston Park tunnel and Clayton Tunnel. Fire Brigade and ambulance attending." This was followed by an unnecessary request for Inspector Bishop to make his way to the scene to set up an incident post, because the reply from John was, "We already are on our way." They had obviously got it off the force-wide channel in the car before Brighton had a chance to circulate it.

The site of the crash was quickly established as Sweet Hill Bridge, on our ground but only just. It was a couple of hundred yards south of the boundary with Burgess Hill subdivision and could be reached only by a track leading off the A23 Brighton to London road opposite the Braypool Sports Ground. Plenty of units were attending, so I took myself off to the control room to give any assistance I could and to make sure we were in touch with all our beat men to rope them in if required.

It had been a very nasty crash and three people died. I sent a couple of vans out to the scene to bring in any uninjured witnesses, so that we got statements from them as soon after the event as possible.

I had a statement team ready on their arrival, but a radio message from John Bishop said that in view of my recent experiences I should personally interview one witness, a certain Miss Warner. How the man could be so tongue-in-cheek at the time of the most trying ordeal a brand new inspector could have on his first couple of hours on the job speaks volumes for John.

As instructed, I found Miss Warner, who transpired to be one of the dream girls of the day for all red-blooded men. She was Jane Warner, a renowned beauty model and a regular of the celebrated page three of *The Sun*. What a lovely girl she was, too. She was truly beautiful, even out of makeup, and remarkably composed after having had the fright of her young life.

It took me about an hour to take the statement, during which time just about every young PC on the section, and some considerably older, popped their heads round the door to have a look. Miss Warner took it all in her stride. I got someone reliable to run her home afterwards.

The Wednesday following the rail crash—December 27—I reported for duty on the 2–10 shift. There was a message for me to see Det. Chief Inspector Tony Mathews at 9:30 a.m. the next day. Tony was in charge of the Brighton office of No. 6 Regional Crime Squad.

The meeting was to offer me a three-year attachment to his squad. He did not have to ask me twice. It was a very welcome forty-first birthday present. Tony had been a detective sergeant at Hove when I did my ill-fated CID Aide there eleven years earlier, and I'd had a lot of time for him then.

I knew that the Regional Crime Squad dealt only with serious criminals. Putting "crims" off the streets had been the major reason for joining the job in the first place. I was to start on January 2. I was not to don uniform again for six years. I had a bit of regret about leaving a great group of men and women who always looked after each other if the spot got tight.

# CHAPTER 13

## 'The Vice Squad' - The Seamier Side of Brighton Life

The Plainclothes Unit, known by everyone except Police HQ as the vice squad, operated from a small office on the ground floor of Brighton Police Station. It consisted of a sergeant and four PCs drawn from the area extending from Newhaven in the east to Lewes in the north and Hove to the west.

The four PCs were in pairs, each pair posted for six months. Two of the PCs were exchanged for new men every three months, offering the best continuity of manpower.

Ron Chillingworth met me at the unit office at 9:00 a.m. on the first morning and introduced me to the two officers who had been with the unit for three months. They were PCs Mike Fagan from Lewes and Robbie Fuller from Brighton C2 subdivision. The two new PCs were Steve Lewis, also from C2, and Barry Jeffcoat from Hove.

None of the PCs had any CID experience, which is why someone like me, with such a background, was put in charge. The procedures of the job often involved putting crime files together—good practice for the PCs, who often hoped to get on to CID in their careers.

Learning the ropes was entirely "hands-on." There was no course at the Ivory Tower to prepare the PCs or me for what lay ahead.

At 10:00 a.m., I had to see Chief Superintendent Norman Cooper, to whom I would report directly. Mr. Cooper was a legendary figure in Brighton, where he had served his entire career. He was a big man in every sense—broad-shouldered and chested, with piercing brown eyes and great beetling black eyebrows. This was all complimented by a powerful growling voice, which had an amazing range and resonance. Nobody who found himself on the receiving end of a Norman Cooper "rocket" ever forgot the experience. I know I didn't! More of that later.

Also present was Superintendent Cyril Leeves, Mr. Cooper's 2IC, who would be my direct boss in any absences of the chief super. Mr. Leeves was almost an opposite character to Norman Cooper, on the face of it. He was quiet, thoughtful, and soft-spoken, but it was not long until I realised that he was the perfect foil for Norman Cooper's ebullience.

The main topic at this interview was the delicacy of the tasks I might encounter. The areas of responsibility included offences of indecency, which not infrequently seemed to involve persons of some prominence in society or the "arts."

A case quoted to me was of a man holding a position of some authority in the Houses of Parliament. (Not an MP or a Peer, I hasten to add.) This worthy person had been found to have a strong attraction towards young boys, and enough evidence had been found to substantiate an allegation of indecent assault on one youngster, but not enough to prosecute, because the parents of the boy involved had been unwilling to support the action. The matter had gone, via Chief Superintendent Cooper, to higher places, and the man involved had been quietly retired. He subsequently moved away from the Brighton area.

The plainclothes officers kept a very discreet card index of every matter coming to their particular attention. It was never intended that the index be used in evidence, but it was a valuable source of intelligence for CID and others investigating serious sexual crimes.

Shortly after I finished my spell on the unit, a decree came from on high that this index must be destroyed, and my successor dutifully incinerated the lot.

Not long afterwards, there was a case of abduction and horrific sexual assault on a very young boy. That index would have been an obvious starting point in investigating that case, as everyone was sure that, if the offenders had been local men, enough clues were in there to have pointed the finger at them. I can understand the pressures behind the actions of the "powers that be," but it is just one example of many of practical coppers trying to do their jobs with hands tied behind backs.

Nowadays, with advances in DNA science, many "cold" cases are being reexamined, with perpetrators being charged and convicted many years after the original crimes. I would like to think that this case might become one of them. The card index would also have been a valuable tool in investigations like the "Babes in the Wood" murders of two little girls in 1986, in Moulsecoomb Wild Park on the edge of Brighton, a case that is still officially "unsolved."

Briefly, to keep the memory of these little girls alive, if for no other reason, there follows a brief résumé of the facts.

On October 9, 1986, two little girls, Nicola Fellows and her friend Karen Hadaway, both aged nine, were reported missing from their homes on the Moulsecoomb estate on the northeast edge of Brighton. A search was organised, and their bodies were discovered in a wooded area close by, called Wild Park. They had been strangled and sexually assaulted. Moulsecoomb is a far from affluent part of Brighton, which, like so many similar areas, has a strong sense of community, and the crime caused total outrage. Police reaction was proportional, and it was not long before a local twenty-year-old man was arrested and charged with the murders. He was duly tried and was acquitted. On February 4, 1990, a seven-year-old girl was abducted from the Whitehawk area, one similar in many ways to Moulsecoomb. By a miracle, the near-dead body of this child was discovered in a local beauty spot, and her life was saved. The same man, now aged twenty-three, was arrested and charged with abduction and attempted murder. This time he was convicted and sentenced to a minimum of fourteen years' imprisonment. At the time of his conviction, the law barring "double jeopardy" still applied in England, so that he could not be retried for the murders of the two Moulsecoomb girls. In 2005 the law was changed to allow for such a retrial if significant new evidence were to be found. The police have already had one try at a retrial, which was rejected by the High Court in September 2006. For the sake of the memory of the two little girls, I hope all the time that more new evidence comes to light.

* * *

Prostitution was another area that the unit took an interest in. Prostitution became illegal only if the girls involved "solicited" on the streets or public places. Although Brighton had, and still has, a large population of prostitutes, there were hardly any instances of street solicitation. The girls operated from home, or "massage parlours," advertising their businesses either by cards left in telephone kiosks or newsagents' windows, or in discreet, small ads in the local press.

So long as these girls operated alone and in private, they were, quite rightly, not harassed by us. However, we were interested in others connected to them. Management of a brothel was an offence, a brothel being defined as premises where two or more girls operated for purposes of prostitution. "Living on the proceeds of immoral earnings" also attracted our attention, and persons falling into that category of offenders were normally "pimps." Unlike many other towns and cities in the country, not many "pimps" appeared to be involved.

Something the unit did do was to make courtesy calls on "working girls." This was a two-way thing. We could reassure the girls that if they were worried about anything to do with clients, we could take a look at them and warn them off if it was prudent so to do. Due to the inherent dangers of their profession, these girls could frequently detect warning signs not visible to others. The visits could sometimes lead to the identification of any pimps, although it was very unusual for a girl to point the finger, and, as I said, pimps were not a big problem in our area.

We did have one delivered to us by his girl. He made the unfortunate mistake of using more violence on the girl than usual. We had a tearful phone call from "Nanette" demanding we "do something about it like you promised."

While the case was still "hot," we got a statement of complaint from "Nanette," leaving any reference to prostitution out. She also gave us details of a joint bank account into which she paid money several times a week. She produced a statement showing that as fast as she paid it in, it was withdrawn at a London branch of the bank. These were in the days before "cashpoints" were available universally, but even if they had been, it was not physically possible for "Nanette" always to be in London to draw the money.

We obtained a statement about the prostitution aspect, with which we obtained a warrant for the pimp's address, and this enabled us to get a witness statement from the bank concerned. Unfortunately, the pimp's address was temporary, and he had made himself scarce.

Almost immediately, "Nanette" disappeared, only to turn up in Hastings as a victim of domestic violence. She had asked Hastings police to get in touch with me, and the upshot was that we arrested her pimp, "Freddie," in Hastings blind drunk in her flat.

"Nanette" was not his only "girl," as we found another five operating around the South London area, each with a joint bank account with Freddie, who, we estimated, had been making about £3,000 a week—very good money in 1978!

"Freddie" went down for eighteen months for "living off." "Nanette" quickly withdrew her statement regarding the assault and promptly vanished, never to be seen again.

At the start of my attachment to the unit, a big slice of our time was taken up by regular visits to Brighton's public toilets. Until then I had never heard of "cottaging."

This is a practice whereby men gathered at public lavatories for the purposes of sexual connection with each other. There might be two men together, there might be more. I once came across a "daisy chain" of ten!

There were six main toilets, or "cottages," in Brighton, usually tucked away a bit out of sight, or poorly lit, or both. Our job initially involved going to each of these places once or maybe twice and clearing the participants out, having obtained names and addresses. This did not stop the problem but might have slowed it down.

One day I got a summons from on high to see the chief super. He was not in a good mood!

"The people in the public toilets, you know who I mean, what are you doing about it?"

"As instructed, guv'nor," I replied, "moving them on and taking names and addresses."

"Well," growled Norman, "that just isn't enough."

He had a letter on his desk, and I could see it had a "House of Commons" heading. There was a "Headquarters" rubber stamp, plus a signature and handwritten note that I seemed to identify as the work of the chief constable. Oops, obviously someone influential had paid a visit to a notorious public toilet in Brighton.

"I want them nicked, starting now."

"Okay, sir," I replied. "How do you want them charged? Indecent exposure? Indecent assault?"

He frowned. "Unless they commit indecent assault on an unwilling person, such as yourself, do them for conduct liable to cause a breach of the peace."

I didn't like it too much, but you didn't lightly disobey Norman Cooper, and the order was lawful and valid.

For a week, the toilets were "purged," and the problem fell away for a few months. About twenty men of various ages found themselves in front of the magistrates, a unique and shameful experience for most of them. All pleaded "guilty," although one prominent man—an orchestral conductor whose temporary "partner" had been a bus conductor—threatened to contest the case. His solicitor, perusing the police case and aware of the presence of the local press, advised him that a guilty plea might be a smart career move!

In January 1979, when IRA activity was at its height, a long-distance coach was making its way from London to Edinburgh and was on the A1 in North Yorkshire, when a call was received at New Scotland Yard informing them that there was a bomb on it. As the caller had a broad Ulster accent, gave an IRA code word, and told the controller that the bomb would go off close to the big army base at Catterick, a full alert went out, and the coach was stopped in driving snow in the middle of the night.

The happy bunch of passengers was turfed out of the bus to wait a safe distance away, while the bomb squad was called out and a replacement coach despatched from a nearby town. Each passenger had to identify his own baggage (suicide bombers were practically unheard of then and in any case were not associated with the IRA).

After about three hours, the passengers went on their way and the bomb squad got on with the job of practically dismantling the coach. One of the passengers from the coach, one Melvin Kingston, approached a North Yorkshire officer and told him he knew who had telephoned the warning. He gave him the name of Timothy Powers and a Brighton address.

The telephone call was traced to a kiosk in St. George's Road, in the Kemp Town district of Brighton, only two hundred metres from Powers's address. The informant was taken to Harrogate Police Station, where he gave a statement.

He, a young man by the name of Melvin Kingston, and the suspect, Timothy Powers, were part of the gay scene in Brighton and were rivals for the affection of a certain well-known Scottish comedian who was living in Edinburgh. The comedian had decided that

Kingston was the boy for him and had dispensed with Powers, inviting his rival to a weekend with him in the Scottish capital.

Prior to his leaving, Kingston and Powers had a blazing row at the Pool Valley coach station in Brighton. The ruckus culminated in Powers screaming that he, Kingston, would never get to Edinburgh alive.

After a discussion between North Yorkshire Constabulary and the Met Bomb Squad, Sussex Police was contacted and requested that we trace and arrest Powers, who could be interviewed by Special Branch and then await collection by North Yorkshire officers. As the circumstances of the offence fell loosely into the category with which my unit dealt, I was summoned before Chief Supt. Cooper first thing in the morning and given the job of arresting Powers. I should have thought the offence had been committed in Brighton with the phone call, but who was I to argue? It was a different task, and welcome at that.

With Steve Lewis, I went round to Powers's address, a bed-sitter in Sudeley Place, Kemp Town. There was no reply, and one of his neighbours told us he would be at work. After his regular day's work, he was a barman in one of the pubs in the town centre until nearly midnight. The neighbour did not know which pub, but gave us a pretty good description of Powers.

Starting about 7:00 p.m., Steve and I began to check the pubs, starting with those known to be gay-friendly. In fact the premises we found him in at nearly 11:00 p.m. had no connection with gays and was some way over on the Hove side of town. He knew why we were looking for him and made an instant admission, coming along with no problems.

Back at the police station, he requested to be allowed a phone call to Gerry Fitt, then the leader of the SDLP in Ulster!

Of course I checked this with Special Branch, and apart from noting it on his custody sheet, I was told he could make the call. Powers had Mr., later Lord, Fitt's phone number in his diary and insisted Mr. Fitt would take the call, even at two in the morning. I rang it and heard the unmistakable tone of Gerry Fitt's voice. I identified myself and told him we had one Timothy Powers in custody, who insisted he would take the call even at that late hour.

"Aye, put him on," was the reply, and they had a brief and apparently amicable discussion. Afterwards Mr. Fitt insisted on speaking to me.

"He's told me what it's about and I've advised him. If he needs a surety for bail, you can tell the court I will be happy to stand it."

Obviously I was intrigued about the connection between the two, and Powers told me he had been a party worker for the SDLP in Belfast. Mr. Fitt was obviously a busy man—it later transpired that at the time he had been brokering secret talks between the British government and the IRA.

A few months later, he had been instrumental in bringing that same government down, thereby facilitating the election of Margaret Thatcher, of whom more later. Yet he spared time in the middle of the night to talk to an ordinary barman. Oh, and before anyone jumps to the wrong conclusion, Gerry Fitt was definitely not gay!

While waiting for the North Yorkshire escort to arrive, Powers was interviewed at length by Special Branch behind very tightly closed doors. SB told me he had been very cooperative, and we could release him into the custody of the escort, which arrived at around 7:00 p.m.

The North Yorks guys were big and bearded and would, amongst the gay population, be described as "bears." They were also hungry, thirsty, and in plainclothes. They found the circumstances of the case quite incomprehensible and way beyond their experiences. Love (or lust) between same-sex couples was well out of their imaginations or remit.

Steve and I decided to show them a bit of the gay scene and took them to a certain pub on the seafront that served food with the beer. The barman fell instantly in love with the bigger and more "bearish" of the two and simpered over him, insisting on bringing the food and shandies to our table, rolling his eyes at him, and remarking, "I bet you've got such a lovely manly body," and similar chat-up lines.

I told the PC he could probably take the barman back to Harrogate too and explained why. "Bloody 'ell," he growled, "get me out of here!"

Powers was eventually dealt with at Magistrates' Court in North Yorkshire and copped a fine and suspended sentence.

A day or so later, we were plunged into an inquiry that was to take all our time for some months and that, in the "enlightened" world of the twenty-first century, would never even get off the ground.

In those days, the Metropolitan Police had a branch known as "Obscene Publications," which was also in the middle of a long inquiry into an organisation known as the "Paedophile Information Exchange," or PIE.

This unit had information that a flat in Hove was the nerve centre of an organised pornography operation. Then, as now, porn was divided into two broad categories. Soft porn involved pictures or movies of unclad girls or couples, perhaps in totally suggestive poses but with no sexual penetration.

Hard porn or hard-core was a step beyond with actual activities of sexual intercourse and everything associated—male on female, male on male, or groups.

Nowadays all this kind of stuff is available on the Internet, either free or at a price, and nobody outside religious pressure groups bats even a part of an eyelid except, of course, where children are involved.

Depending on your country or state's laws, a child for the purposes of porn can be under twenty-one, under eighteen, or under sixteen.

At the turn of 1978 and 1979, attitudes were not so liberal and even recognised sex shops could not legitimately sell "hard-core."

So it was when two members of the Metropolitan Police Obscene Publications Squad arrived at Brighton bearing exhibits and other evidence pointing at the Hove flat's use for the production of hard-core. I got all the team together and placed them around the building, and then I took the Met lads to Hove Magistrates' Court, where we obtained a search warrant for the flat.

We took the foregoing precaution because although 99.999 percent of magistrates are completely honest, you don't want to be the one who gets a bent one and finds that the property has been cleaned out before you get there!

We obtained entry to the flat with no problem and were confronted by piles of evidence in the shape of magazines, films, sheets of negatives, unprocessed film, and enough documentation to keep us busy for weeks. We had to arrange a van and a pile of empty boxes to take all the stuff away. The owner of the flat was present and stated that he was looking after everything for someone else. Apart from that, he declined to make any comment.

I have not seen his name in print since the termination of the case, so I will take it that he has been living a different life, and, for the purposes of the story, I shall call him Peter Gifford. I arrested him and took him to Hove Police Station, where he declined to be interviewed. He was bailed to return to the police station in a month, when I hoped, vainly as it transpired, to be able to charge him with a holding offence under the Obscene Publications Act.

On return to Brighton Police Station, I had a quick conference with Supt. David Tomlinson and the Mets lads. Mr. Tomlinson arranged a secure cupboard for the storage of the exhibits while we processed them prior to inquiries getting under way, and on his advice we quickly consulted a diary kept meticulously by Gifford and arranged interviews with a number of local people whose details appeared there. He also arranged a local PC—Ron Harvey, known as Squadron Leader because of his luxuriant moustache and RAF background—to join the team as exhibits officer.

This was before the days of computers being used for anything other than Commercial Branch work, and everything was going to be painstakingly logged and cross-referenced and labeled. To simplify labeling, Steve Lewis was said to have made all the seizures at Hove, so all the exhibits found there were numbered from SJL/001 upwards.

There is time here for a quick word about Ron Harvey. During a conversation about hobbies, Ron told me he liked to play the classical organ. I asked if he played stuff like Reginald Dixon's "Oh I do like to be beside the seaside," or was he more a St. Saens organist?

"I'll show you," he replied. He took me to Brighton's cathedral-sized St. Peter's Church and produced a key, which let us in. He then sat at the magnificent organ, worked a couple of switches, dug some sheet music out from somewhere, and launched into a wonderful rendition of Bach's Toccata and Fugue in D Minor.

I was, for once, speechless. I discovered that Ron had actually given organ recitals in many revered locations and on BBC Radio 3. This only goes to show that if you scratch the surface of the average PC Plod, you might be surprised at what you unearth.

Of the first four interviewees who lived locally, none had heard of the raid and had had no chance to concoct any kind of story with Gifford. As it turned out, he did not contact any of the potential witnesses, as he did not have a backup record of names and phone numbers from his diary!

In the course of the inquiry, we traced more than one hundred witnesses, none of whom gave any serious problems. However, the inquiry gave at least two of the witnesses problems of their own.

Gifford had teamed up with a renowned pornographer, now dead and nameless here, and his wife. Together they had a reciprocal arrangement with a Swedish porn publisher to use their facilities in Stockholm, provided Gifford and his partners provided the girls. We traced a number of girls, the youngest of whom was sixteen years of age, who had gone to Stockholm with Gifford. The sixteen-year-old had gone with parental consent and was of legal age in the UK and Sweden. She will remain nameless, as I understand she still lives around Brighton. She was a very beautiful young girl, whom the Crown Prosecution Service representative confessed he could fall seriously in love with!

A second girl, Ghislaine from London, insisted that she had been taken to Stockholm under false pretences that she would be modelling for magazines. She said she had been threatened that she would be abandoned in Sweden with no money if she did not comply with the plot, which involved some twelve men dressed as the Swedish national ice hockey team. Naturally, this girl became a main plank in our case until it became known, at the last minute in the Crown Court, that she had gone willingly but had concocted the coercion part, as she believed her mother would kill her if she knew the truth. It had been her mother, accompanying her to court, who had insisted she confront us with the facts.

The third girl to cause a problem was a thirty-five-year-old mother of two from Nottingham. Margie, as I shall call her, bore a very striking likeness to Marilyn Monroe and was identified, as were so many, by cross-references on Gifford's sheets of negatives with the names in his diary. She had aspirations to being a model, although, of course, her age was very much against her. But like many of Gifford's girls, she had answered an advertisement for "glamour models" placed by Gifford in her local newspaper.

She had agreed to come to Brighton for a photo shoot, which started with Gifford photographing her solo—clothed and unclothed, in poses that were from innocent through to lascivious.

He had then introduced her to a young man, a student at the local university, and she was shot with the boy in "soft" and "hard-core" pictures. She was paid the daily rate and returned home.

She told her husband she had been doing fashion shoots for catalogues.

Soon afterwards Gifford was in touch with her, inviting her to go with him to make movies in Sweden. She went willingly, telling her husband it was another rung on the modelling ladder. She was shot firstly in stills, wearing what she was to wear in the movie but gradually removing it bit by bit until she was nude.

She then performed "hard" for the movie before returning with Gifford to the UK. He promised to send her money on to her but never did. Because of this, when we contacted her, she was quite willing to cooperate. After liaising with Nottingham Police, Steve and I made an appointment to see her at a time when her husband would be out at work.

Accordingly we arrived outside her house in a decent part of Nottingham at the appointed hour. Margie was waiting at the garden gate. "You can't come in. My husband has taken a sick day off work." I said we could see her at Nottingham Police Station later. "Oh, no, he'll want to come along. He knows someone is coming to see me about the Sweden trip, but he doesn't know about the porn stuff."

I said, "Look, we've come all the way up from Brighton to see you. I promise you I could take a statement, and your husband won't know what it's all about. Alternatively we could arrest you under the Obscene Publications Act and get a statement down the road." This was a bluff, but the poor girl was not to know that, and she led us into the front room.

She despatched her husband to make a pot of tea, and while he was out of the room I quickly summarised what was to be in the statement and sorted some pictures out, some fairly innocent fashion-type shots, others not quite so innocent! While he was in the kitchen, I quickly showed Margie some of the more salacious photos and scribbled down the exhibit numbers—SJL/106, SJL/107, and so on. By the time the husband had returned, I was ready to put the heading on the statement—her name, address, phone number, and so on.

With hubby listening intently, I went through the introduction as how she had responded to advertisements and had come to Brighton for a fashion shoot. I showed her a photo of her in an elegant maroon cocktail dress. "Did Mr. Gifford take this?" "Yes, he did," she replied. I showed the photo to hubby. He nodded.

"Yes, she's very photogenic, isn't she," he said. I put the exhibit number of that photo in the statement and pulled out another, in a different outfit. I showed this to the husband. "And did he also take this? I have another copy." I showed the "other copy," to Margie, who nodded. "Yes."

The interview continued like this, with the husband seeing only what I wanted him to see, but Margie seeing and identifying the real thing.

When we got to the end of the statement and asked her to sign each page, my heart was in my mouth. Would the husband want to read what I had written, which bore little resemblance to what I had said I was writing, but which was a graphic account of what had happened to Margie in Brighton and Stockholm?

When Steve and I left, hubby was very happy that Gifford, whom he believed was no more than a con man, was getting justice. Margie was a quivering heap of beautiful relief when we bade her farewell at her garden gate, and the first stop for Steve and me was the nearest pub!

There were many more witnesses throughout the country, and also we were able to identify a number of locations that had featured in shoots.

When we had amassed enough evidence, we handed the case over to the director of public prosecutions for guidance to what else had to be done. We stayed on the unit pending interviews with Gifford, the professional pornographer, his wife, and another lady who had been involved in setting things up.

It was during this inquiry that I became the recipient of one of Norman Cooper's legendary "bollockings."

As part of the case, I had circulated details to all forces for attention of departments dealing with vice. This was really a "fishing expedition" to see if Gifford turned up in any of their inquiries.

One day I got a telephone call from a sergeant in the Bournemouth Vice Squad. He had a professional photographer in his area who had a lot of information about my man and his activities in the Dorset town. What was more, this potential witness, Eric Black, was willing to come to Brighton with some exhibits and provide whatever statement was required.

When he arrived, Steve Lewis and I met him and took him to an interview room, where we spent two hours getting the statement. The matter was conducted on first-name terms, as the man seemed naturally outgoing and friendly. At the end of it, we took him to the top floor canteen and treated him to a Brighton Police lunch before he went on his way. He never was used as a witness, although some of his information proved to be very valuable.

A few weeks later, I was summoned to Norman Cooper's office. The chief super sat at his desk glowering at some papers. I felt a sense of foreboding when he did not, as he usually did, invite me to sit down. He looked up at me, his eyes piercing from beneath his beetling eyebrows. "Who's this Eric Black?" He flicked the paper across the desk at me. I saw that it was headed "Dorset Police," and a vision of Eric Black came immediately to mind. I told Mr. Cooper who he was and my involvement with him. The chief super rose slowly to his feet and launched into a tirade, which started loud and just got louder, like Ron Harvey operating a crescendo pedal on the pipe organ.

It seemed that Bournemouth Vice Squad had done a raid on a busy brothel in the town, where some six or seven girls were, as Mr. Cooper put it, "Flogging their mutton." "Guess who's running this operation, Sarge?"

He didn't wait for my reply. "Yes, your bleeding mate Eric Black!" he bellowed.

He paused for a rare breath and I interjected quickly, "Sorry, sir, but what's this got to do with me?"

He threw a photocopied page across the desk. I picked it up. Whoops! It was a copy of the address page from a diary. One of the entries read, "Allan Neil, Steve Lewis, 01273 606744." That was the then phone number of Brighton Police Station.

The tirade continued about how careful you have to be dealing with people in your line of work and what if the *News of the World* had got hold of this information. "Brighton Vice Cop and the Pimp! Bleedin' hell, I can just see it!" After what seemed a lifetime, Mr. Cooper subsided into his chair and indicated that I should sit down.

He smiled. "How's the inquiry going then? You're doing a great job on it." My stripping was over, and it was as though it had not happened. That was the trademark of a Norman Cooper "bollocking." Once it was over, it was over, but you never forgot it, ever.

At the end of the court case, I realised that two miracles had happened. Firstly we had taken charge of more than sixty thousand individual potential exhibits and had not lost or mislaid a single one. Secondly, I picked up a commendation, as did everyone else on the inquiry. I'd always wanted one of these.

Meanwhile Mike Fagan and Robbie Fuller had been replaced at the end of their six-month attachments. PC Rory Lee from Newhaven and

PC Mick Gregory, an ex-Mets PC now working at Brighton, came in. Almost immediately we picked up another interesting if worrying case.

Malcolm Pyrah was a very successful show jumper in the equestrian world. He also ran a photographic processing company in Hemel Hempstead. It was the kind of business that derived its main income from cassette films that were bought "process paid" in the shops and sent to him in the envelopes supplied.

In autumn 1979, I was summoned to see Supt. Leeves, who pushed a couple of photographic prints across his desk. My first thought was that it was more to do with Gifford, but on looking I could see that they were much more amateur. They depicted a young girl in a school uniform engaged in an obvious sexual act with the photographer, whose face was not visible, unlike his external male genitalia, which were.

Mr. Leeves showed me a letter, written on headed notepaper and signed by Malcolm Pyrah. The letter had found its way to Mr. Leeves via force headquarters and Shoreham subdivision, before being forwarded for attention of the Vice Unit.

Mr. Pyrah's company had a huge throughput of films to be developed and printed in sophisticated machines before being sent back in the form of prints and negatives to the people submitting them. About one in every two hundred films was checked for quality control, and, unfortunately for the photographer, this had been one of them.

Copies of the relevant paperwork came with the letter, which showed the customer to be one Barry B***** of an address in Shoreham. I agreed with Mr. Leeves that the girl looked no more than twelve years of age and that I could probably identify her from the school uniform, the badge of which was clearly visible and, after tweaking by HQ Photographic, would probably be eminently readable.

"Okay," said Mr. Leeves. "Get on with it then."

I took the new PC, Mick, with me, and we ran the negatives up to HQ Photographic before going straight on to Hemel Hempstead and getting a statement from Mr. Pyrah. He was able to identify the photographs for the court.

Meanwhile, by sheer coincidence, Barry Jeffcoat was following some information up that a taxi driver in Hove was giving underage schoolgirls money in return for taking part in sexual acts with him. Our two inquiries came together with the identification of the same offender.

We picked the tweaked photos up from HQ next day and could easily identify the school uniform. Barry and I went to the school and saw the headmaster in private, showing him the photos, covering up all but the girl's face. He was able to name the girl straightaway, but called the form mistress in to confirm it.

The girl, she said, was twelve years old and had a slight, if temporary, disability problem, which necessitated her travelling to and from school by taxi. She named the taxi company and gave us the girl's address, revealing that she was not in school that day, owing to some hospital appointment or another.

She lived on a council estate in Hove, and Barry and I travelled down to Hove Police Station to enlist the help of a WPC, as a female child was involved. The rest of the team went on standby close to the taxi office.

We'll call the girl Della, as that contains no clues as to her real name. Her mother answered the door. Yes, Della was at home. She was up in her room. The WPC went with Mum to get her, and they came hurrying down the stairs straightaway.

"She's done a bunk out of her window." Her bedroom was right over the front porch of the house, and she had obviously spotted the uniformed WPC, probably thinking she was in a bit of bother.

We left the WPC to explain to Mum what it was all about and did a quick search of the area. Della had, however, gone very quickly to ground, and time was obviously now important. Would she get in touch with Barry B?

Obviously the taxi driver who took Della to and from school would be a suspect. I called Hove Police Station and told them to post Della as a "misper," a missing person, and to get a full description by radio from the WPC at the home address.

I also asked the others to go round to the taxi company and get a full list of their drivers, without letting them know what it was about. Meanwhile, Barry Jeffcoat and I made our way to Barry B******'s address.

There was no taxi outside, so we sat up and waited. Meanwhile the other came on air with the list of drivers. I asked them simply if there was somebody called B****** on the list.

Bingo! They had a B. B****** of the address we were sitting outside. We reckoned he was probably on the school run by now, and we had time to get in to Hove Magistrates' Court and get a search warrant. Luckily we caught the last magistrate just before he went home, and by producing the photos and telling what we had found out, we got the warrant with no difficulty.

Barry B****** returned at about 5:00 p.m., obviously for his tea, before going out on his evening jobs.

We executed the warrant and found ample evidence of his activities, not only with Della, but also with other youngsters.

We arrested him and took him to Shoreham Police Station, where the case was taken off our hands by the detective inspector who, when the case came to Crown Court, was commended for his vigilance. Neither Barry nor I nor anyone else on our team got even a mention. Typical!

Della came to no more harm. She was found that evening at a friend's house and taken home. We had asked Mum to be understanding as a girl of that age could so easily be taken in by a man like B****** in his mid-thirties.

The judge took B******'s offences so seriously that he sent him down for twelve years.

In December 1979, as detailed in the previous chapter, I returned to uniform patrol, and then into the Regional Crime Squad.

The Gifford case eventually reached the Crown Court around the following April, and, apart from having to forget Ghislaine as a witness and having a fight in court to protect Margie's identity, we obtained convictions all round.

As I said, that case would not even get a foot off the ground in the twenty-first century, but that was then. Has the world progressed? Make up your own mind.

# CHAPTER 14

## Regional Crime Squad: Targeting Serious Crime and Criminals

Tony Mathews had been a detective sergeant during my unfortunate CID Aide at Hove ten years earlier. Now he was the detective chief inspector in charge of the Brighton branch of No. 6 Regional Crime Squad.

I had had a lot of time for Tony during our brief Hove acquaintance. I found him straight and nonpolitical with a very quiet manner. I was to find later that the Tony Mathews to be found before 9:00 a.m. was Mr. Hyde to the Dr. Jekyll that existed after that hour!

The interview for the job was brief. My record was open on the desk, and I got the impression that it was to find out if I was willing to work some pretty long and unsocial hours and be able to put up with long periods of surveillance and inactivity. "There's no trial period," said Detective Inspector Chris Page, the 2IC. "You're either in or you're not in." I indicated that I was in.

Now it is best to set out a brief résumé of the Regional Crime Squad as it was in the late 1970s and early 1980s. It has since undergone some sweeping changes. All the RCS units were merged into the

National Crime Squad in 1998, and then on April 1, 2006 this was renamed and rejigged into the Serious Organised Crime Agency.

This is a large and complicated operation in which not only police officers are involved. All I will do here is point anyone interested in the direction of its Web site, www.soca.gov.uk.

When I was a member, each region of the police forces of England and Wales had its Crime Squad. The southeastern area was Region 6 and comprised Surrey, Hampshire, Sussex, and Kent. Our unit operated from Brighton, and there were other offices at Southampton, Walton on Thames in Surrey, and Aylesford in Kent.

Each office consisted of a DCI, a DI, six DSs, and seven DCs. Each DS was semipermanently teamed with his own DC. The odd number of DCs was because one of them was the motorcyclist on surveillance jobs. My first partner was DC Paul Flowers, and when he returned to his division, my old colleague from Worthing, Dave Deal, took his place.

Before being let loose as part of a two-man team, each member was obliged to attend a surveillance course at Maidstone, Kent HQ. The next course was to be in two weeks' time, and until then I was teamed up with DS Lennie Wheeler. I soon saw why the course was essential.

On day one, we were involved in a fast-moving surveillance operation on a team of active high-end burglars, and the day was a whirl of speeding, unmarked cars, cryptic radio traffic that I could scarcely understand, and swift unannounced changes of plan. The day had started with briefing at 8:00 a.m. and being "on the plot" by nine.

The "target" had been "housed" by an earlier-starting team, meaning that proof had been obtained that he had been at his home address overnight and was still at home. "On the plot" meant that each crew took up a strategic position so that when the "target" moved off he could be followed in an approved manner in any direction.

The early starting crew was in an "OP" or observation post, from which they had a clear view of the premises and could observe any comings and goings. Everything was "logged" as it happened—important, because the logs were frequently used as evidence, as much by the defence as by the prosecution.

The saying was that the "OP" had "eyeball" at the start. If and when the "target" moved off, the first of the following cars became "eyeball," and all radio traffic was initiated by that crew or, strictly with their permission, anyone with something important to convey. Just like it is on television, the team in the "OP" had binoculars and cameras. Unlike TV anything with a reflective surface stayed well back from the window and observers made sure that their faces did not get too close to the glass.

You never, ever, moved curtains to look! The kind of villain with whom we were dealing was frequently well versed in anti-surveillance routines. They were very often extremely violent too, and before going on the surveillance course, I had to attend a week of firearms training at HQ in order to qualify to carry arms. I found that I was no Wyatt Earp, but I was proficient enough to get my certificate.

Off to Maidstone, then. The tone was set for the week by the fact that as soon as you checked in and put your bags in your room, you went off to The Bell pub in the village of Coxheath, some five kilometres south of Kent HQ.

This pub became our unofficial headquarters where we would meet after a day's frantic training to debrief and unwind. The cars used on the course were drawn from the various offices of No. 6 RCS—the vehicles used on live operations.

Early in the course, we were tipped off by instructors not to ask awkward questions or get in the way of Tony Mathews before 9:00 a.m. "Bear with a sore head" does not begin to describe him before that magic hour, we were warned!

Cars were crewed two up when they set off at the start of the exercise and when they set off from The Bell back to Kent HQ, meaning one of each pair had to stick to one pint!

Debriefs were serious stuff, but at the end of them a party atmosphere soon took over, with singsongs and silly party games. "Mine Host" of The Bell made the RCS guys very welcome, as each two-week course brought with it a very welcome source of trade, and the local clientele joined in with the fun when it got going!

One old lady "regular" confided that it reminded her of when the flying boys used to come in during the war in operational breaks, usually caused by fog or low cloud bases. West Malling fighter station had been just a couple of miles away.

The main purpose of the course was, of course, to learn how to observe without being seen, both in motion and in static situations. I won't go into this in detail as I don't know how much the systems have changed thirty years on, so would not want to "blow anything out."

I do admit to being alternately amused and infuriated by programmes like *The Bill*, when "a tail" is undertaken using just one car, which is invariably the vehicle immediately following the "target." When the villains stop, the surveillance car often stops just across the road. The criminals never look around; the surveillance officers, wearing "civvy" jackets over their uniforms, sit up in their car, with one talking into his handheld radio while the other winds his window down and takes photographs using a camera with a huge lens! The crooks then inevitably walk into a building, and the police follow and always catch them in flagrante delicto.

Sorry, fans, it just does not happen like that, but then *The Bill* is, at most, two hours long, so you couldn't expect three weeks' worth of sixteen-hour-day surveillance to fit in, nor could you expect them to pay for eleven surveillance officers, five cars, and a motorbike!

At the end of the course, it was back to the Brighton office as a fully operational member of the squad. This does not necessarily mean we worked in the Brighton area. In fact this seldom happened as the offices were fully interchangeable—everyone in England and Wales did the same training and used the same methods. Working in your own patch meant a heightened risk of your face being recognised—back to *The Bill*, where Sun Hill bobbies follow Sun Hill villains and are never "clocked"!

A lot of work was done in the Metropolitan Police area, where we were generally assisted by C11 Branch, which covered intelligence and surveillance and used the same surveillance system as we did. In addition it had a dedicated covert observations team trained to find and remain in concealment as an "OP."

These positions were often known as "CROPs"—an army term meaning "concealed rural observation posts." The skills in this were considerable and had been developed by the armed services as forward artillery and intelligence points. The skills used also applied to snipers, and, like snipers, the observers had to be able to remain still for long hours on end. When the "target" and the mobile surveillance team moved away, the CROP stayed live, and that was when the observer was able to relax, get some rest, and maybe grab a bite to eat.

During the latter part of my time with the RCS—in 1982—we carried out a number of surveillance jobs around the Paddock Wood area of Kent. These operations were in conjunction with C11, as the targets were London villains who had been successful enough to buy large houses in the area.

One of the C11 team was DC John Fordham, a CROP specialist who, on January 26, 1985, was killed by one of the notorious Brink's-MAT robbery mob, Kenneth James Noye, leading to one of the most odious miscarriages of justice ever.

John had been in the process of setting up a CROP in the garden of Noye's substantial house in West Kingsdown when Noye's guard dogs detected him. When challenged, the unarmed John tried to walk away, but Noye stabbed him ten times in the back. At his trial, he was acquitted on the grounds of self-defence.

In 1986 Noye was imprisoned for fourteen years for his part in the Brink's MAT robbery, but was released in 1994. In 2000 he was convicted of the murder of Stephen Cameron, in what was initially described as a "road-rage" killing. It later transpired that Cameron might have owed Noye money for drugs. Noye has been linked to several other murders, which have remained "undetected."

I don't recall if our target in the 1982 operation was Noye, but it was in the right area and would undoubtedly have been someone known to him.

To digress for a moment, there is certainly money to be made from crime. Noye is currently trying to appeal against his sentence, and his lawyer is one Giovanni di Stefano, whose other clients have been Saddam Hussein, Tariq Aziz, and Ali al-Majid (Chemical Ali) of the murderous Iraqi regime.

On his books, there has also been Patrick Holland, who was found guilty of the kidnap and murder of the Ulster reporter Victoria Guerin. Jeremy Bamber, convicted of killing his adoptive parents and sister and her twin children in Essex, was also a client, as was Nicholas van Hoogstraten, the Sussex millionaire criminal.

John Gilligan, said to be Dublin's biggest drugs baron and suspect in the death of the aforesaid Victoria Guerin, is on his client list, which continues with Charles Bronson, aka Michael Gordon Peterson, Britain's most violent prison inmate. He has also represented Ronald Arthur Biggs, one of the Great Train Robbers, and Ian Strachan, convicted of attempting to blackmail the Royal Family on sex and drugs allegations.

You will be surprised to read that di Stefano has made billionaire ranking on his legal expeditions. Oh, if only working for the good of society carried a fraction of the same rewards.

I was involved in numerous short jobs, like the Kent lot, but my time was more taken up with one particular RCS job known as Operation Bentley.

This began with an insomniac man in East Sussex taking his dog for a walk at 3:00 a.m. on a night with a full moon in early 1981. As he walked down a footpath near the little village of Bodle Street Green, just outside Heathfield, he saw two men in the middle of a ploughed field apparently engaged in digging.

He watched, as the men appeared to bury something before walking to a vehicle on the opposite side of the field. The vehicle was driven past the end of the footpath where the witness stood, and he was able to make a partial note of the index number.

He made a mental note of the spot where they were digging before going home. In the morning, he telephoned his local PC, saying he thought he had witnessed someone burying a body.

Either the PC was switched on enough, or the informant was someone whom the officer knew was trustworthy, or both, but he raised a forensic team and the local CID before going to the field and having the informant direct them to the spot. The long and short of it was that they dug up a box containing a large amount of currency.

The partial car number was run through the police computer, and several possibles were identified. There were fingerprints in the box, and it was not long before the vehicle's owner was identified and confirmed.

Owing to the amount of money involved—tens of thousands of pounds—and the identification of the fingerprints, RCS was brought in straightaway and commenced surveillance on the car owner, who lived in Pevensey, on the East Sussex coast.

Other channels of intelligence became involved, and it was apparent we were dealing with a major operation in the importation and distribution of cocaine.

I spent many hours in the "eyeball" position near Norman's Bay railway station, from where, using powerful binoculars, I had a clear view across the Pevensey marshes to the target's house over a mile away. There was only one way out of the road in which he lived—into Pevensey Bay village—and whenever he emerged from it, he had a tail of five RCS cars and a motorbike discreetly behind him armed with cameras. Time and again he led us to another suspect in the supply and distribution chains, and the case was built up, a brick at a time.

Eventually we had seventy-one targets at as many addresses in London and the southern home counties, and at 5:00 a.m. one morning, assisted by all the other No. 6 RCS offices, C11, and the Flying Squad, we struck.

My "target" was a totally innocuous middle-aged man called Albert Y., who lived in Tottenham. He had been a courier taking cash out to Brazil, where he liaised with the Colombian part of the operation, handing the cash over and taking possession of the cocaine.

They had it all worked out. At certain times, they could guarantee the drugs getting through friendly Brazilian checks and onto the plane to Lisbon, where, again, certain "guarantees" were in place.

The drugs were transferred to a motor vehicle, which was driven from Lisbon either to a minor port in Normandy, to be placed in a small vessel, or if conditions were felt to be satisfactory, driven to a Channel port and brought into the country on a ferry.

At the time, Portugal was not associated with drug smuggling, and the gang had got away with it. No doubt if Albert had been arrested in transit he would have been abandoned as a "mule" and left to his fate. He told Dave Deal and me that the money made it worth the risk. He had no criminal record, so would probably have copped a friendly sentence.

Dave and I interviewed Albert at length, and he came over as a very nice guy in his middle age just taking a chance on getting out of the rut.

The main dealer in the affair actually escaped through a toilet window, and the whole operation was jeopardised for a few days. Then he made an unwise telephone call from a hotel, which was one of dozens asked to look out for a certain number being dialled.

The Pevensey connection was arrested at his home, and a search revealed about £300,000 hidden under floorboards.

Another participant that Dave and I arrested was one Mohammed Anwar, a Moroccan national who insisted that he could not speak English. He was part of a connection that brought cannabis into the country as part of a trade deal with the cocaine and had been living for six or seven years in Amsterdam. I think he was totally flabbergasted when I questioned him in Dutch, so that he actually answered the questions.

The amusing sequel was when I was in court as prosecution witness in the case and related my questions and his answers in English. As they do so often, the defence barrister demanded to see what was written in my pocket book. I handed it over obediently.

"But this is gibberish," he cried.

"No, it isn't," I said. "It's Dutch. Mr. Anwar and I spoke in Dutch, and as required I have recorded the conversation verbatim. I am a qualified Dutch interpreter." My fingers were crossed to the point of cramp as I said that, but the judge and barrister let it go.

All the "Operation Bentley" defendants were convicted with the single exception of Albert Y., who was as guilty as it gets, but who was such a likeable guy I did not grudge him his moment of good fortune. I guess the jury must have liked him too!

Just after Bentley, I was placed on a surveillance instructor's course at Maidstone. This was much the same as my previous surveillance course, but went deeper into the reasons for our methods and threw in a bit of instructional theory. It meant I would be instructing on forthcoming surveillance courses.

When I got back to the squad, DC Peter Hardy had replaced Dave Deal as my partner. Peter was a great detective and first-class copper but was fundamentally opposed in character to Dave Deal. Where Dave had been quiet and diffident, Peter was gauche and aggressive.

One form of policing is not necessarily better than the other, and it suited both of them to be as they were. While Dave never needed encouragement to get on with the job, Peter had sometimes to be held back or reigned in. He always enjoyed trying to get his sergeants to the point of discomfort one way or another.

To give an example, one day a job meant he and I had to travel to Ramsgate Police Station. Why, I don't remember. I drove there, and the general rule was that if one member of the crew drove to a destination any distance away, the other would drive back. At Ramsgate we found the police station in a state of mourning. A policewoman had been killed in a crash on the notorious A299 Thanet Way. Several people opined that it was the most dangerous stretch of road in the country.

We finished our task, and Peter got behind the wheel. I eased in beside him. He turned to me and growled, "Thanet Way? You think I'm scared of the Thanet Bloody Way?"

"Uh-oh," I thought, "here comes another Peter Hardy wind-up," and prepared for a fast drive to Maidstone and Brighton. I knew that if I showed any signs of being nervous or worried, it would only make Peter worse. I reached over to the back seat and picked up Peter's *Daily Telegraph*, which I spread open before belting myself in and, putting my feet up on the glove compartment, I made a show of nonchalant reading.

As we pulled into Maidstone HQ and my nerves began to un-shred, Peter turned to me.

"Do you always read the paper upside down, Sarge?"

Tony Mathews's attachment on the RCS ended around this time, and his replacement was DCI John Rees, a short, broad Welshman with thick black hair and piercing dark eyes. He was another good detective with bags of energy and a one-track desire to get things done. However, the chemistry between him and me was not always right, and we clashed on a few points, culminating in my being called into his office and informed that if I carried on the way I was going, he'd rip my career to shreds.

I confided to Peter Hardy that he might be getting a new sergeant soon, and he must have spoken to someone in the Force Operational Support, because a few days later I was approached by Detective Inspector Tony Randle and invited to join his team.

Tony was in charge of a unit known as the "commandos," a title I found a bit gung-ho. His unit was not national like the RCS and dealt almost exclusively with local matters. What it did is outlined in the next chapter. Tony gave me few days to think his offer over.

A move was going to mean a drop in income, as there was nothing like as much overtime involved. Two things swayed me; firstly I would have more time with my family and maybe catch up on a lot of DIY, but secondly and mainly, I knew John Rees wanted me out and John had a habit of getting what he wanted.

I had no problem with that. It was his operation, and he had the right to run it the way he wanted. However, I knew that if I didn't use a bit of initiative, I would more than likely be bumped out into a uniform job at God knows what station.

I called Tony to accept the offer and then told Mr. Rees.

"Are you mad?" was his reaction. "Nobody applies to come off the Crime Squad."

I think he was slightly miffed that I had preempted him, but we parted on reasonably good terms, and he has been friendly towards me whenever we have met since.

# CHAPTER 15

## The Commandos: Surveillance and Close Protection

So it was that one morning in early 1983 I reported to DI Tony Randle in his small office in Brighton Police Station.

Tony was a dapper man, dressed like all his unit in casual clothes, but three leagues smarter than the rest of us. He was a local man, very enthusiastic about "his" unit and "his" lads. He had built the commandos up from scratch and had adapted the RCS surveillance techniques to suit his remit, to the extent that, although I was qualified to teach surveillance to the Regional Crime Squad, he felt I should do a refresher in his methods at our Lewes HQ.

Apart from surveillance, the commandos also undertook "close protection" jobs on persons whose positions or profiles put them at risk of lethal attack. The theories and practice of close protection was the subject of an intense three-week course organised by the Royal Corps of Military Police, based in Chichester, with some input from the SAS Regiment from Hereford.

A lot of work was carried out in conjunction with the Drugs Squad and the DHSS Fraud Unit. A few of the officers in the unit had been trained in CROPs (concealed rural observation posts), and, finally, some short-term undercover work could also be undertaken.

In comparison with the RCS, the commando area of operation was very much just countywide, and we left the county only on live "follows" and then only with permission from Tony Randle, or if he was not available, from Operational Support at HQ. If the "follow" was "hot" enough, in the opinion of the senior officer on it, "retrospective permission" could be obtained.

This was designed to mollify the sensitivities of powers at be in neighbouring forces and beyond, when out-of-force officers were operating in their areas. This "retrospective permission" could not always be guaranteed, though, as I was to find out later!

When I started on the unit, there were three offices, at Brighton, Horsham, and Hailsham—known as Central, North, and East. There had once been a West office based at Littlehampton, but its personnel had been split between Horsham and Brighton prior to my arrival. Shortly after my arrival, the Hailsham office was amalgamated with Brighton.

We had our own language over the radio, using mostly code words, and each member had a nickname. Examples were that Tony Randle was known as "Squirrel," Brian Sole—a Horsham DS—was "Riss," and I was "Abo" deriving from my reputation on the Crime Squad of being first out of a car if a foot-follow was needed. Abo = Aborigine = "walkabout." Good, eh?

After doing the refresher surveillance course, the next part of the learning curve was to learn the fundamentals of "close protection." This is basically "bodyguard" training.

Tony Randle organised a course based at headquarters, which proved to be just about the most intense and physical I had ever done. As stated earlier, the course was run by the military police, and there was a lot of fitness stuff in it. The personnel taking the course were drawn not only from the commandos, but also from the Armed Response Team—what is called SWAT elsewhere in the world.

An assault course, army style, was laid down at a disused quarry at Beddingham. At the start of the course, just getting round it was an achievement, but by the end we were diving for cover and letting off shots at targets. There were two girls on the course, and they had to do it too! No "ladies' tees" on that course!

There was classroom theory work and also fieldwork, where you would walk your "VIP." SAS guys in plainclothes might pose as assassins or alternatively ordinary members of the public who might be acting oddly, as they often do. This was to alert one into spotting telltale signs that can tell one the difference when, if the situation were "for real," you might have less than one second to make your mind up and act.

We were taught special driving techniques, such as how to deal with following or pursuing vehicles, roadblocks, and ambushes, and how to get your car out, with its precious cargo in one piece.

Shooting practice was a large part of the course, using a variety of offensive and defensive weapons, not only on the range, but also in rough terrain, suitably protected against stray shots escaping from the confines of the quarry that we used.

After a final exam, we were ready to be let loose on the unsuspecting public and their vulnerable VIPs.

Almost all the close protection performed by me after the course was on controversial political figures. At a Labour Party conference in Brighton, four of us had a job that was just a little different in that the protected "VIP" was not to know he was under protection. He was Gerry Adams, the Sinn Fein leader who was in town for a meeting. He was not to know because he could have made it seem that he was not being protected, but was being watched. I had to smile at that as MI5 or one of the security services probably *was* watching him.

Another VIP whom we had to protect without being seen by him was the Duke of Edinburgh, when he visited Stanmer Park, Brighton to participate in carriage races. The duke used to "flame out" if he caught a policeman anywhere near him.

I was fortunate enough to be sent on two aerial reconnaissance courses, designed to teach me how to carry out surveillance from the air. These courses were held at RAF Abingdon in Oxfordshire, the base of the Oxford University Flying Squadron. The officers running the squadron were all regulars.

Everything looks so much different from up there, and each one-week course consisted of serious map-reading and a succession of tasks, such as "seek and find" searches with RAF personnel acting as "targets." The aircraft used were Bristol Bulldog two-seaters, where the observer sat alongside the pilot, on his right.

On my first course, the police officers, mostly sergeants drawn from seven different forces were, for some reason, all housed in the officers' mess. Stewards served all meals at table.

The first time I was served, the steward kept addressing me as "sir"; I pointed to my sergeant's shoulder chevrons and said, "Call me sergeant."

The steward's nose went up in the air, and he retorted, "In this mess, sir, everyone is addressed as 'sir,' sir."

The course went smoothly, and I felt I had learned quite a lot. So, apparently, did the RAF, for on the basis of their report on me I was sent back for a more advanced course a few months later. On the second course, the sergeants were housed in the sergeants' mess, which I actually much preferred. The food was buffet style, the amount unrestricted, and if you went out into Abingdon or Oxford in the evening, there was a buffet of tea and sandwiches available until midnight.

My pilot on the second course was a Welsh Flight Lieutenant called Viv. I cannot remember his surname. Like all the pilots, he was a QFI (Qualified Flying Instructor) and he showed me the basics of flying a small plane. By the end of the week, I was taking off, flying around when exercises were over, and landing the aircraft.

After the final exercise of the course, Viv told me that his sport was aerobatics and if I liked he could show me his fifteen-minute routine. My brain said "no," but my mouth said "yes."

After making sure I had nothing that could fall out of my pocket, off he went. The next quarter of an hour was possibly the most frightening and exhilarating of my life. Viv performed barrel rolls, stall turns, loop-the-loops. He made the plane fall out of the sky like a tumbling leaf. He demonstrated negative gravity, as in space, and "multiple G" manoeuvres, ending up with what he called the "Prince of Wales Feathers," when the plane went vertically up until it reached its stalling point, fell backwards, then went up twice more, firstly to the left, then to the right.

At tea in the mess later, just before setting off home, a sergeant from air traffic control told me he was surprised I wanted food after Viv's stunt!

In 1983 the unit received information that a professional burglar had recently been released on parole from a ten-year sentence and had been "housed" in Brighton by the Probation Service. All the indications from his part history in various parts of the country pointed to his continuing his professional activities as soon as released. His name was William Vass. No compunction about giving his name as I have certain knowledge that he carried on his usual ways until very recently.

We set up surveillance on him, and soon he had led us to a number of addresses in the Sussex area. Some he was undoubtedly "casing" for possible burglaries, but one or two were obviously social visits, which we noted as possible drop-offs for stolen goods.

Finally we observed him putting bags in the back of the little Fiat car that he had acquired and tailed him to a tiny village in rural West Sussex, where he drove into the driveway of a thatched cottage that he had already visited on a "casing" trip. One of the team got a view from a field and saw him emerge from the rear of the cottage, carrying one of his bags. He drove off, followed by the team with the exception of one pair, DC Graham Davies and myself. I ran round to the back of the cottage while Graham confirmed there was nobody at home. Sure enough, a leaded glass window was broken and wide open, and there were scuffmarks from footwear on the windowsill.

We passed the information on and had William "pulled" by a traffic car, just as he entered Hove. In the boot, they found enough to arrest him for "going equipped"—a torch, two big bags, rubber gloves, and a small rubber hammer of the type used to drive tent pegs into the ground. There was no "swag" though.

This was obviously disappointing, and Tony Randle instructed Graham Davies and me to interview him at Hove. We told him that a local resident had seen his car emerge from the driveway and had rung police with its index number.

We had better things in mind for William, so we bailed him to go to Steyning Police Station two weeks ahead. We later found that when he got to the back of the cottage he was too late, as someone had beaten him to it and the cottage had already been burgled! He had obviously made no attempt to enter, possibly fearing that the original burglar might still be inside!

The operation on William was continued, obviously without Graham and me, who had been compromised, and as the team had been reduced we got permission to fit a tracker to the Fiat.

A few days later, with the surveillance in full swing, I was riding my bicycle homewards in North Street, Brighton when I saw the Fiat stopped at the lights. I rode over, said hello, and told William I was on my way home and we all had the afternoon off, as it was our office dinner that evening.

Obviously encouraged, William set off westwards, followed at a safe distance by the team. He drove all the way into Gloucestershire, where, at dead of night, he was seen to break into the home of the lord lieutenant. After lying low until the traffic picked up, he set off eastwards, and the team had him "pulled" again, this time by Gloucestershire traffic officers. In the Fiat were two big new bags full of high-quality silverware, later identified as being the property of the lord lieutenant.

Several warrants were then obtained to search houses that William had visited "socially."

I had the job, with others, of searching a house off Nevill Avenue, Hove. Nothing was found in the house, but in the garden, which resembled Passchendaele in 1917, I found a line of perfectly formed little wooden cloches, covered in clear plastic. Inside each cloche I found several cannabis plants, which had been carefully nurtured. Each seed had been sown in a small peat pot, and as they had grown the plants were transferred into larger and larger peat pots.

I arrested the householder and took him to Hove, where he gave a "no comment" interview. Crown Prosecuting Service decided to take the case to court, and the defendant elected to go to Crown Court.

Amazingly, by today's standards, CPS decided to go ahead with the case. I mention this job as I ended up falling foul of the judge in court.

I started to describe the cloches and their contents and immediately the defence counsel succeeded in persuading the judge to get the jury out of the court. I started to give the evidence, so the judge could, well, judge it.

Defence counsel immediately demanded to know my qualifications for describing the cloches and plants. I told the court I had been gardening since I was a small boy and could answer any question about these plants.

Defence counsel demanded to know if I had a degree or diploma in horticulture or if I was a member of the Royal Horticultural Society.

"No," I replied, "but why don't you ask the questions and see what you think of my answers?"

The judge turned to me and demanded that, as I was unqualified to comment on the condition of the plants, I would not put any evidence regarding the condition of the garden or its contents.

This was silly, I thought. "Your Honour, does that mean that I cannot describe a defendant as 'scruffy' because I do not have tailoring qualifications?"

I swear the judge's face went through all the colours between sallow and beetroot, before he addressed me with a terse sentence containing the word "contempt."

The fact that the defendant was acquitted is neither here nor there, and I tell this little tale only to illustrate what a fine line police witnesses must tread when giving evidence.

* * *

In the last week or so of school holidays 1983, Sandra, the girls, and I went on a wonderful trip to Normandy in our VW camper van. We camped in an orchard near the town of Pont l'Eveque. The owner of the orchard made his own cider and Calvados (apple brandy) and was a very sociable guy. There were lots of other children there—of many European nationalities—and I was happy to see the girls get on so well with all of them, language no problem!

The night before our departure, the whole site was treated to "Pot au feu avec le mouton et aux herbes" (excuse my French!). This involved the cooking in a cauldron over a log fire of most of a sheep in a rich herby sauce, accompanied by sparkling cider and then Calvados. It was brilliant. We returned to the site a few years later, but, although the orchard was still there, all the camping facilities had been withdrawn.

Sadly, on returning from the trip I found that my father, who had been house sitting for us with Mum, was ill. He insisted on returning to Penicuik, however, and a few days later we got a call that he was now very sick.

Joanne was staying with friends by prior arrangement, but Sandra, Hannah, and I drove north in the camper. Dad seemed to recover a bit, though, and I drove back south, as it was time for the girls to go back to school.

Almost immediately I had to return to Penicuik, this time flying up, as Dad had a serious relapse and had been taken into the Royal Infirmary in Edinburgh. Tony Randle kindly gave me an advance on the next year's annual leave on top of a week's compassionate.

I was shocked to the core when I saw Dad in the infirmary. In only a few days, it was as though he had shrunk, and he was very weak and pale. He had been diagnosed with untreatable cancer of the pancreas and, as it turned out, had less than forty-eight hours to live.

I stayed with him most of that time, being relieved by relatives to go for some food, and I was right with him when he breathed his last at around 2:30 in the morning. I was pretty inconsolable, not just because I'd lost my lovely dad, but because I had seen so little of him since joining up in 1966.

The young doctor who certified his death told me he had not heard a word of complaint from my dad in the time he had been in the ward, although he must have been in dreadful pain at times. It was so typical of Dad. He would not have wanted to feel he was a burden on the medical staff.

I walked home to Penicuik, crying my eyes out all the way to the Burgh boundary and declining two offers of lifts before I composed myself to tell my mum and sisters the news.

Dad's funeral was amazing. It was held at Mortonhall crematorium, on the southern edge of Edinburgh, about six miles from Penicuik.

Bear in mind the social status of the deceased. He was a disabled ex-miner and mill labourer with little or no education. He had worked latterly in the most menial of jobs—a street sweeper. He had been a council tenant for thirty years and, apart from organising the Hearts Supporters Club, Penicuik Branch, had held no official position, other than as an elder of the Kirk.

The undertaker had hired the larger of the two chapels at Mortonhall but, as a long-time friend of my father, had anticipated that they might need more room. The crematorium rigged up some loudspeakers outside for the overflow from the chapel. As it turned out, more than thirty mourners took advantage of that facility.

I had never met the minister, the Reverend Ronald Sewell, but he paid a fitting tribute to my dad, and afterwards he sounded most sincere when he told me I had lost a fine father.

Outside the chapel, shaking hands and kissing cheeks, old Mrs. Wallace said it all when she stood back and looked at me. "Ye ken, ah've never seen a polisman greet afore an' ah'll likely ne'er see't again, but manny ah kin unnerstaun it. Yer faither wiz a richt gidyin!" The translation is at the end of this chapter.

Well, Dad, if you are up there looking down (I know you won't be down there looking up!), you'll have seen my progress, or lack of it since 1983, and the problems and vicissitudes. I hope I have handled them to your approval. I've tried not to complain too much, as you would never have. We are all as proud of you now as we have always been.

\* \* \*

Back to work, then, and an early job was a bit of undercover. It was only for one night, but it was scary.

There had been a murder in the east of the county. It had been among the criminal element, and, as is usual in such cases, information was thin. The detective superintendent of the area—Bill Clements—had had a tip that a certain gypsy had something to say but could not possibly come to a police station to pass it, nor could he meet up with any officer in a pub or elsewhere. No, the officer getting the information would have to go to his gypsy site and sit with him long enough to allay suspicion before he would pass the information.

Tony Randle was contacted, and I was given the task of turning up at the site in an already condemned old banger—no tax disc, and apart from being secretly insured, obviously totally illegal. I already had long hair and a few days' stubble and had to dress in a manner that would fit in. I chose torn jeans and a grubby T-shirt with a cannabis logo on it. The car had poaching gear in the back—rabbit snares and ferret nets—and I left it unlocked at the gate to the site.

If anyone asked, I was a friend of the informant's from Barlinnie Prison, Glasgow, where he had served a sentence ten years earlier. My best Scottish accent and the likelihood that no one else on the site had been in Barlinnie at the time made my cover story plausible.

Against all force orders, my warrant card stayed at home. Imagine my fate, not to mention the would-be informant's, if that had been found in my possession!

The informant and his girl had a young baby and had obviously not realised that dirty nappies should be disposed of outside. They also heated their caravan with paraffin, kept the windows shut, and smoked nonstop. The site was patrolled by about six assorted Dobermans, Rottweilers, and Alsatians, and the first thing the informant told me was that I had better come up with what he wanted or it might not be easy to get me off the site.

What he wanted was to be let off two drunk-driving charges. What he had, he said, was the identity of the murderer and proof linking him with the crime.

In the end, after intense negotiations, it was agreed that when the informant attended court in Hastings on his drunk driving charge, he should hand over his information. The case would be adjourned while the information was assessed and investigated. If it looked good, the charges against him would be dropped "on a technicality."

I heard later that it all fell through. The informant was convicted of drunk driving, and as far as I know the murderer is still at large. More than that I cannot say, except that it was scant reward for the scariest night I have ever spent anywhere.

The spring of 1984 produced a really good job that was, like so much, never acknowledged. It was my own fault, really, because, unlike a certain Shoreham detective inspector mentioned in a previous chapter, I never tried to "spin up" my part in things.

Two large credit card companies were experiencing numbers of cards being fraudulently used. Inquiries by the companies' internal security departments revealed that these cards had not been delivered to their recipients. These days were long before the development of "chip and pin," or telephone activation, so unsigned cards were particularly valuable as the thief simply signed them in his own hand.

In-house surveillance by the Royal Mail pointed to two sorting office staff as being the initial thieves. Neither's description tallied with that of the regular offenders, one of whom was a blonde female and the other a very tall, heavy male with a noticeably large, square head. Early arrest of the two postmen would result in the likelihood of other offenders never being identified, so further inquiries and surveillance of the postmen outside Royal Mail premises were put in place.

The inquiries led to an address in Southend on Sea, which was quickly searched on warrant by Essex Police. The bird had unfortunately flown, although her family was still there. The most important find at the address was a letter from the female suspect to her mother.

There was no address or phone number on it, but the text and postmark indicated that the girl had gone to Penarth in South Wales, where she was looking for a job as a barmaid. It was signed "Julie," and had been postmarked two days earlier.

All this happened early on a Saturday morning. Graham Davies and I had gone into the office to await the news, and on receiving it I immediately tried ringing for permission to go to Penarth to follow it up. I did not feel that we could leave it until after the weekend in case the girl rang home. She might even have rung home since the Essex raid. Mobile phones were rare in those days.

Permission had to come from the superintendent at Operational Support, but he was not answering his home telephone, nor had he left an alternative number where he could be contacted. Tony Randle could not be contacted either. I decided that Graham and I should set off for Penarth and get retrospective permission later.

I arranged for the ops room inspector to contact his opposite number in South Wales to let him know we would be on their ground, and gave the index number and call sign of the observation van, in which we would be travelling. This vehicle was one that we used when keeping an eye on a static target or premises. The observer(s) sat in the back out of sight, and it was equipped with radio that could be used from that position.

We left Brighton at around 9:00 a.m. and reached Penarth just after 1:15 p.m. We had decided en route that we would try pubs in Penarth radiating out from the town centre, but while heading there we passed a pub that had its own car park at the front. Parked in there was a car with a Southend on Sea index number.

It seemed a good place to start, so we parked across the road and went in. It was nearly empty. Graham sat down and I went to the bar. The barmaid emerged from the other bar. She was blonde and in her twenties. I ordered halves and started a conversation with her. Her accent was noticeably home counties.

I said, "You're not from round here, are you?"

"No," she replied. "I'm from Essex."

"I used to live in Essex. Which part are you from?"

"Southend."

"I used to live at the other end of the county near a village called Ugley. My name's Allan."

"Oh, hi. I've heard of Ugley. My name's Julie."

I took the beers back to the table and told Graham we had, incredibly, found our target. We sipped our beer, keeping an eye open in case Julie left.

Pubs shut at 3:00 p.m. in those days, so we dragged the time out with another half and a sandwich before leaving just before 3:00.

We manoeuvred the van so that we could see the car park yet be able to move off in either direction.

Julie came out around 3:15, and my guess was right. She got into the car with the Southend number plate and drove off with us following at a discreet distance. At one point, she stopped unexpectedly and we had to drive on past—not an advisable move when there are no other vehicles in the "tail."

Fortunately, she had not been suspicious, but had stopped at a post box to pop a letter into it.

Eventually she led us to a housing estate and stopped outside a semidetached dwelling. We managed to park up unobtrusively and were elated when, no more than ten minutes later, she reemerged in the company of a tall, heavy man with a noticeably large, square head!

We had been trying, since entering South Wales, to contact their ops room on the radio, without success. We decided to run with it and see what happened. At least, if we lost them, we had an address that South Wales could deal with.

The car drove off with Julie at the wheel. This was promising, as the man would probably have been more likely to watch the rear in the driver's mirror.

We managed to stay with them all the way to the Severn Bridge, where we decided to turn back and ring in to South Wales's Headquarters. Their base being in Penarth, they would obviously be returning there at the end of what we hoped was a shopping expedition. I found a telephone and was put through to their operations inspector.

I explained the situation and, remarkably for a Saturday, was put through to a detective inspector on their regional crime squad, who had just stood down with several of his team from another job. We arranged to meet them at a service station on the M4 on the outskirts of Cardiff, where we briefed them up on all aspects of the job.

They left us with one of their personal radios, and the plan was that they would "plot up" both ends of the Severn Bridge and follow them back to Penarth to ensure they did not drop any property off en route. We were directed to park up close to the address and observe what happened when they returned.

We had a few hours to wait but eventually picked up the RCS "follow" on our borrowed radio. As soon as we sighted the car, we told the "follow" and they backed off while the car parked at the front of the house. Julie went to open the front door, while her companion opened the boot of the car and proceeded to remove a number of bags, some bearing logos of well-known chain stores.

We called the RCS guys in, and they promptly arrested the pair. The boot was crammed with goods purchased from various shops in Bristol. Stuffed in the car's glove compartment were shop receipts, and in the man's wallet and the girl's purse were a number of credit cards, all subsequently established as being undelivered to addressees in the Brighton area.

A search of the house revealed enough goods to cause the RCS guys to call in one of the South Wales Force's vans!

A good quantity of the stuff recovered had been obtained in the South Wales area. That was good news as they could deal with the offenders, covering what they had done in our force area and others in the charges and "TiCs." There was no need to have them transported back to Sussex.

"TiC" is short for "taken into consideration," and is a way of clearing up outstanding matters without charging offenders with a long list of offences. These offences are "taken into consideration" by whoever passes sentence before deciding what to weigh them off with.

Our van had not been compromised, which was also good news, as the male offender was a Brighton man. Nor was there any need for Graham or I to give any evidence, therefore not revealing that he had been subject to Sussex surveillance. You can't do that now as all aspects of police actions in the case must be revealed to the defence. I'm not kidding!

After we stood down, I tried the superintendent's number again. This time he replied, but sounded extremely unhappy that we had taken ourselves off to Wales without his knowledge.

The following Monday, when we returned to work, he had us wait in the office while he came down from the ivory tower and delivered a severe "bollocking." Never mind that we had taken out two substantial offenders and cleared up a lot of crime, and never mind the fact that he was not available when I tried for permission, having omitted to keep ops room advised of a contact number.

We never even got a "well done" out of the job, even though I later found that a senior officer in South Wales wrote to our chief constable expressing his appreciation for our efforts and initiative. I was never shown that letter, but found out about it at my retirement "do."

Thankfully, Graham's career suffered no setbacks, and I was very pleased for him when I learned years later that he had achieved chief superintendent rank in another Welsh force.

Jobs, mostly pretty unmemorable, were never in short supply. One such humdrum assignment produced an unexpected bonus for my mother's side of the family.

In Chapter 1, I mentioned that my Aunt Agnes, wife of "Black Jock" Bryson, had produced ten children of her own and been stepmother to another two. Of the twelve, only one—George—had ever got on the wrong side of the law. This had been when he was eighteen years of age and would have been around 1948.

George had got into a fight with another youth—fists only—and had laid him out so well that the boy had required hospital treatment. George had been arrested and given bail.

George had been so ashamed that he did not even return home, but ran away. He had not been in touch since, and his brothers and sisters did not even know if he was still alive. On a visit to Penicuik, I had met his brother Angus, who was visiting my parents. Angus mentioned that the family would love to know what had happened to

George. I got his date of birth from Angus, and when I went back on duty I did a routine check to see if he was still wanted, or even had a record. The inquiry drew a total blank, even with the Scottish Criminal Record Office.

I rang Angus with this information, and he was relieved that George had stayed out of trouble for thirty-six years. That was that, I thought.

With the type of work we were doing, we frequently came across instances of fraudulent Social Security claims. These were usually handed to the DHSS fraud investigators to follow up.

One summer's day in 1984, we had being doing a job in the Heathfield area, and when we stood down, we decided to debrief in the Blackboys Inn, between Heathfield and Brighton.

In the bar was a man I knew as a Social Security fraud investigator. I established that he was off duty, and in the course of conversation I asked him how easy it was to track someone down given just a name and date of birth. I explained why.

"Well," he replied, "we certainly owe you guys a few favours. Give me his details. No promises, but I'll get back to you."

Get back to me he did, within the week. George Bryson, he told me, was employed as a miner in Sutton Colliery in Nottinghamshire. He was currently off work, following an industrial injury, which was why he was so quickly found. He was claiming sick benefit! I was given an address in Sutton in Ashfield.

I phoned Angus with the news, and the Brysons descended team-handed on Sutton in Ashfield, where they were tearfully reunited with the prodigal brother. Needless to say, I never ever had to buy a round if a Bryson was in any pub at the same time as I was!

\* \* \*

Around this time there was a murder in Hove where the main suspect was an unidentified rating in the Royal Navy. Due to an overheard conversation in a Hove pub around the time of the killing this man was thought to be a Petty Officer or Chief Petty Officer. Detectives were dispatched to various Royal Navy establishments to interview all rating of those ranks who were either stationed at these establishments or whose ships had been in Portsmouth, about 50 miles to the west.

After a couple of weeks the officer in charge of the enquiry felt that the team in Portsmouth might have been doing better and for some reason sent me to take it over. I was asked to take two of the Commando team with me and chose Chris Drew, sadly no longer with us, and Mick Curtis, most definitely still around. Chris and Mick really got stuck into the job and soon we caught up with a backlog of 'actions'.

I mention this mainly because of Mick's crash course in naval terminology. At the end of each day we were invariably entertained in the Chiefs' and POs' messes. The first time this happened we were on board a warship, probably a frigate. By way of conversation, Mick turned to a Chief and remarked 'This is a nice boat, mate.'

The Chief glowered at him. 'This ain't a boat, laddie. This is a ship!'

'Ah, Okay,' said Mick.

Soon afterwards, we were entertained on board a submarine. Again, Mick felt he should encourage conversation. 'Nice ship, this,' he remarked to a PO, who turned to him sharply.

'This is not a ship, son. This is a boat!'

'Ah, a boat. Okay.' Said Mick.

Later again, we found ourselves in the POs' mess on the Royal Yacht 'Britannia'.

Again, Mick was constrained to strike up a chat. 'This is a nice boat, er, ship, mate.' He remarked to the rating next to him.

'Look, mate,' the man replied. 'This ain't a boat OR a ship. This is a yacht. OK?'

'Oh, right,' said Mick. 'I guess I should keep my mouth shut!'

\* \* \*

My armed close protection training was put to use in national conference situations, beginning with the Association of Chief Police Officers (ACPO) conference held in 1983 at Eastbourne.

Among the senior policemen attending were the Metropolitan commissioner, Sir Kenneth Newman, and Sir John Hermon, the chief constable of the Royal Ulster Constabulary. The period was one of the worst during the Ulster "Troubles," and although Sir John had his own protection officers, we were asked to supplement them.

Needless to say, given the ranks of those around us, impeccable behaviour and attention to detail was the order of the day. Along with four DCs, I was given the night duty. On the face of it, that was the easiest shift, as the subjects spent most of it asleep. However, so did the RUC Protection men, so heightened awareness was definitely required.

The week passed without incident, and Sir John sent a very complimentary letter to Sussex HQ. All of us were shown it.

March 5, 1984 was the day the National Miners' Strike began. It ended 363 days later in defeat for the miners and the start of a lingering death for the British coal industry. The strike has been well documented elsewhere from all points of view. As a serving police officer, I could not take any part on either side, nor could I state my views publicly. There are, however, no prizes for guessing where my basic sympathies lay, given my family background.

Happily, very happily indeed, I was not required to carry out any duties connected with the dispute—that is, except one.

The TUC Conference of 1984 was held at Brighton in the first week of September, at the height of the miners' action. Feelings were running dangerously high as the conference also coincided with a strike by dockers in Scotland.

Many important union officials were in Brighton for the event, none more high-profile than Arthur Scargill and Mick McGahey, president and vice-president of the National Union of Mineworkers. The potential threat against both these men was considered to be very high, but neither qualified for any central government protection.

The commando unit of the Sussex Police was handed the task of giving what protection was possible, considering Mr. Scargill's views of and relationship with the police. Mr. McGahey's profile, as perpetuated by the press, was of a tall, dark, perpetually scowling character with beetling black eyebrows, who spoke with a growling Scottish accent.

The operating plan was that when the conference was in session, our troops would be placed strategically around the hall and its environs. Messrs. Scargill and McGahey would be given direct protection at their hotels. My "man" was to be Mick McGahey, who was staying at the Metropole Hotel on Brighton seafront.

On the first evening, Mr. McGahey was in the hotel bar, holding court with a number of others, mostly union officials.

I sat a discreet distance away, where I could observe the door and the group at the bar. I was armed with a revolver, which was tucked away under the armpit of my loose-fitting jacket. As I was sitting alone, with a soft drink supplied by the hotel, I was fairly obvious.

After some time, Mr. McGahey signed for me to go over to him. He put a hand on my shoulder. "I know who ye are and what ye're here for, but there's no need. I'm quite safe with these fellows." He indicated his companions.

"I expect you are, Mr. McGahey, but I have my orders. I promise I won't get in your way, or try to eavesdrop."

He smiled, his features immediately transformed. "Eavesdrop all ye want to. We're no trying to hide anything." He nodded towards his companions and then turned back to me. "That's a Scottish accent. Where are ye from?"

"Penicuik, sir."

"Oh, aye, I ken it well, and please call me Michael."

We did not become bosom pals by any measure, but I had several conversations with Mick McGahey in the course of the week, during which time I told him of my mining background.

"Ye didnae go doon the pit then?"

"No, I worked in the paper mills. They're long closed now." I went on to tell him about my experiences on the railway and my multiple redundancies. "That's why I joined the police."

"I dinnae blame ye. That's why I'm here. Trying to stop the same happening to my miners."

I never spoke to Arthur Scargill, but I ended the week with a totally different view of Mick McGahey than that perpetuated by the press.

The miners' strike brought out some of the best and some of the not so good in policemen who got involved in it. Tales have been told of officers holding the line under attack despite injuries. Other stories tell of policemen waving wads of money in the faces of miners whose families were going hungry living on strike pay.

I experienced one sad incident in Brighton involving a PC who, up until then, I had held in high regard. In surveillance operations, it was usually best practice to have the "target" stopped and arrested by uniformed patrol after having been observed committing a crime. That way, as in the Penarth job, surveillance officers could avoid being compromised in court and elsewhere. This was, of course, before the necessity for "disclosure."

In this particular case, we were on the tail of a youth strongly suspected of breaking into basement flats, of which there are many in Brighton. We watched as he broke into a basement in a back street in Kemp Town. As soon as he was in, we called a patrol car, which arrived as the burglar emerged from the flat. The aforementioned PC promptly arrested the youth.

A few weeks later, the PC approached me, enraged. "You've cost me six hundred quid! The bastard's gone not guilty, and I'm needed at court next week. I should have been going to Yorkshire on strike duty. Don't bother calling me again!"

Sad.

The next party conference to be held in Brighton was that of the ruling Conservative Party.

\* \* \*

Translation—from earlier: "You know, I've never seen a policeman cry before and I'll probably never see it again, but, young man, I can understand it. Your father was a really good man."

# CHAPTER 16

## The Grand Hotel: An Atrocity from Inside the Bombed Hotel

The Tory Party conference took place between Monday, October 8 and Friday, October 12, in the Brighton Centre. That conference and the events during and after it have been exhaustively written about and picked over. I don't want to repeat all that, but would like to provide an insight into some of the aspects that have been ignored, whether deliberately or unintentionally.

Not a hotel bed was to be had in the whole of Brighton, or in some of the towns on the periphery. The most important Party bigwigs, including the prime minister, Mrs. Margaret Thatcher, and the entire Cabinet, together with their various secretaries and satraps and the dedicated Metropolitan Police protection officers, were to stay at the Grand Hotel, on the seafront adjacent to the conference centre.

On October 4, the Thursday prior to the conference, all those with responsibility for security within the Grand Hotel attended a full briefing. These were mostly commando officers with a sprinkling of the Drugs Squad team. The latter would have the responsibility of manning the control room set up within the hotel.

The briefing was led by Detective Inspector Tim O'Connor, who had taken over from Tony Randle on the latter's promotion to DCI in Special Branch. Tony also had an input to the briefing from his new role, and informed us that the "risk assessment" based on the Security Services intelligence and observations had been adjudged "low."

Those of us to be on duty inside the hotel were reminded of the ongoing miners' strike, which, together with the Ulster situation, appeared to be the likely origins of any personal attack on important members of the Tory Party. Such attacks could be lethal, e.g., firearm or knife, or nonlethal, such as egg throwing. Indirect attacks—for instance, explosive devices—were also to be considered, although the apartments to be occupied by the Cabinet had been searched with the aid of sniffer dogs, or so I believed.

Senior members of the government had their own ex-officio protection officers, supplied by the Metropolitan Police, some of high rank, like Superintendents Sillence and Parker, and while my team and I were ultimately responsible for internal security at the hotel, we were obliged to take notice of their advice.

Away from the hotel, the Met Police personnel were augmented by Sussex Special Branch, led by Superintendent Stan Phelps. After subsequent events, I felt in retrospect that it would have been practical to have had the likes of Superintendent Sillence at our briefing to tell us, in his own words, of the likes, dislikes, and idiosyncrasies of the senior Tories, in particular Mrs. Thatcher.

Besides that, I realised later that I had no idea of the drill they would adopt in the event of an attack or emergency. The close protection methods and training of the Mets were "in house" and not undertaken in conjunction with our system, as taught and used by the military police.

Also, at the briefing, it was stressed very firmly that Mrs. Thatcher was not willing to be subjected to anything like the level of security enjoyed by, for example, the US president. It was part of her image, we were informed, to be seen as approachable and available, and all our activities were to be carried out with that in mind.

In addition, the hotel management, led by the general manager, Paul Boswell, did not want the comfort and enjoyment of its guests needlessly interfered with. In deference to all the wants and needs of every party concerned with the conference and the Grand Hotel, it was the job of my team to merge into the background to see, rather than be seen, and yet to be prepared and ready to act according to the needs of the moment.

Coming on duty with me at 11:00 p.m. on Sunday, October 7 were DCs Toby Pratt and John Rist, whom I trusted and had personally chosen, and WDC Tina Frost from the Drugs Squad, who was to be the control room operator. Already on duty were DC Coxhead and WDC Bilson from the Horsham Commando Unit. They were to go off duty at 2:00 a.m., and the rest of us were to be relieved to go home at 7:00 a.m.

Toby, John, and I were armed with revolvers, concealed, of course, beneath our jackets. Tina was unarmed, as were DC Coxhead and WDC Bilson. Outside the hotel, uniformed officers covered the front and rear entrances, as well as the approaches and nearby junctions.

The coverage inside was to be as follows. The first floor landing was to be manned at all times. This was where Mrs. Thatcher and the senior Cabinet members were housed. Mrs. Thatcher occupied a suite, the sitting room of which served as a temporary Cabinet Office. Until 2:00 a.m., the landing was manned by Toby and John in turns, accompanied by one of the unarmed officers. After that time, Toby or John would be on his own, rotated as much as possible every hour.

The foyer, particularly in the vicinity of the lifts, was also covered at all times by Toby or John when not in place on the landing, and the second unarmed officer was posted in the lobby. The control room was manned around the clock and had radio contact with the Sussex Police operations room and the radio control in the Brighton Centre, as well as UHF contact with us.

There was also a "hotline" telephone to the operations room. The control room also contained CCTV monitors, covering various vulnerable areas within the hotel. Sensors under the carpets guarded all the approaches to the suites on the first floor.

As soon as we could that Sunday, we tested the coverage of the CCTV before the arrival of the VIPs. The floor sensors promised to be a nuisance under normal traffic conditions and proved to be of any use only after midnight when foot traffic had died right down.

My main position was in the lobby, though I could "float" as required. Also I had regularly to relieve the armed officer by the lifts so that he could go to the first floor and change places with his colleague. These interchanges had to be performed swiftly, with little time for discussions, to maximise the armed cover downstairs. Food, supplied by the hotel, was taken when the opportunity arose before the departure of the unarmed officers at 2:00 a.m., ensuring that first floor landing was always manned.

Those of us inside the hotel were equipped with covert (hidden) radios, with which we could communicate with the control room, and our weapons were, as stated, concealed.

The only thing to identify us as police was a small enamel badge showing a red rose on a yellow background. I was unhappy about anything identifying us, as any attacker would know whom to eliminate first. That was until I learned that Tim O'Connor and Tony Randle had had a job on their hands persuading the powers that be that it was not a good idea for us to wear brightly coloured armbands or chequered caps that screamed "police"!

Things really got going on Monday the eighth, with the main arrivals of delegates, press, and other functionaries, and when I arrived for duty at 10:45 p.m., the foyer and main bar were crowded with MPs, delegates, lobbyists, journalists, diplomats, TV reporters, political activists, and general hangers-on.

I had never stood in the midst of a gathering of such influential people of high position and power. They were evidently used to having their voices heard and listened to, and the volume of their continuous chatter was deafening.

There were several ways of checking these people out from a discreet distance, such as personal recognition, a person being greeted by someone already cleared, possession of a clearly displayed conference pass, or someone personally known to hotel management. If not satisfied, I could get close and listen to the conversation, talk to them discreetly, or, as happened on a number of occasions, search their bags in a quiet corner. Nobody ever objected seriously to my doing that, although one or two felt they had to make a point, based on their own senses of self-importance and their view of me as a lowly "plod."

I found it to be a problem that nobody ever warned the control room when important VIPs were about to arrive at the hotel, not even in the case of the prime minister. When she came in through the front door, she was always surrounded immediately by well-wishers, and those not around her would rise to their feet and applaud.

If, as happened more than once, I was not near the front door on Mrs. Thatcher's great coming, I had serious problems vetting those crowding around her, bearing in mind her own instructions that I was to be discreet. I noticed the first time this happened that her Met protection officers got very nervous, so I gave all my concentration to the crowds and left them to mind their charge.

On Thursday the eleventh, I had to attend Hove Magistrates' Court to give evidence in a fairly minor drugs case. I had tried to have the case adjourned because of my duties that week. My request was refused, and therefore, on going off duty that morning, I was unable to go to bed.

I duly arrived at the court, and, after sitting around for an hour or so, my case was called. I went into the court to confirm that the plea was to be one of "not guilty." As you might imagine, I was incensed when, at the request of the defence, the case was adjourned without any apparent problem or reference to anyone except the magistrates. I tried to smile and be pleasant to all the lawyers concerned, but I don't think I succeeded. Even the safety and security of the prime minister and her government took second place to the convenience of lawyers.

I got to bed around 1:00 p.m. and was roused shortly after 3:30 p.m. when my children came home from school in their usual exuberant fashion. I was less than chipper when I arrived at the hotel that night and had to concentrate extra hard on doing my job effectively.

That night, the last before the conference was to end, the hotel lobby and bar were crowded with several private parties in full swing before I even got there. The prime minister was absent at a Young Conservatives' Ball, or some similar function. At 1.8 metres—a touch over five feet ten inches—I found it extremely difficult to keep an eye on any part of a swirling crowd containing a large proportion of tall, bulky, well-fed men without bumping and boring through it. Everyone seemed to be in a happy mood, and a great number of them seemed to have had more than one sniff of the barmaid's apron!

The mood in the ground floor of the hotel at that time has been the subject of much anecdote and recollection by far more important persons than I, so I'll fast forward to 2:00 a.m., by which time my team and I should have been provided with refreshments. I had earlier called Miss Arnold, the duty manager, from one of the phones in reception and was assured that food was being prepared right then. I could understand the delay in view of the level of activity on the ground floor, which was still very lively.

Mrs. Thatcher had returned by then and had retired to her suite after first sampling the jollity of the parties in the bar.

Just after 2:50 a.m., I ascertained that food had not yet arrived and tried to ring Miss Arnold from the porter's telephone right by the front door. Her extension was engaged. I called either Toby or John to cover the foyer for me and went to her office. I closed the door behind me and began to ask her what progress had been made with the meals.

At that moment, there was a loud, sharp crack, followed immediately by a deafening roar and the hotel shook. I knew immediately that there had been an explosion and ran to the office door, which I found had jammed. After some kicking and pulling, I got the door open wide enough to squeeze out.

I ran to the foyer, which I found obscured by a huge cloud of dust. The fire alarms were ringing, and water was pouring from a fractured pipe higher up in the hotel. I checked quickly on radio and was relieved when all three of the team answered my call. John or Toby, whoever had been in the foyer, had had the sense immediately to join the other on the first floor landing when the explosion occurred.

The foyer was pandemonium with women screaming and their menfolk shouting out over the strident ringing of the fire alarm, trying to locate them.

It was immediately apparent that the seat of the explosion had been at the front of the hotel, as the revolving doors had vanished under a great pile of rubble.

Yelling at the top of my voice so as to be heard, I shouted for everyone to be calm and to make their way out of the rear of the hotel. Miss Arnold and one of the hotel barmen assisted by getting them to link hands and started to lead them out. The erstwhile revellers were coated in dust, and I realised that I was too. Maybe the chequered baseball cap might not have been such a bad idea, if kept folded out of sight in one's pocket for just this exigency!

I took hold of a nearby man and asked him to help out in getting everyone out of the back door. He was efficient and calm and played a big part in making things as orderly as possible. Years later, when my wife persuaded me to watch the programme *Countdown* on Channel Four, I recognised my helper as its presenter, the late Richard Whiteley!

I ran back to where the front door had been and saw a wraith-like figure coming towards me. In the swirling dust, he seemed to be holding something up to his face, and I saw it flash. In the dusty gloom, it looked awfully like a gun flash, and I drew my revolver. It never got dangerous, though, as it took just a few seconds to realise that the man was pointing a camera.

"What the f*** are you doing with that gun?" he demanded in a squeaky falsetto.

"What do you think you are achieving with that camera, apart from scaring the sh** out of me!" I replied, my heart pounding.

As I could not make contact with anyone outside the entrance, there was obviously nothing I could do at the front and I made my way to the control room, constantly checking that everything was okay with John and Toby.

"All under control, Abo," they replied to each query, twin islands of calm in the chaos.

From the control room, I was able to work with John and Toby and with the ops room to get vehicles, particularly the prime minister's, to the back of the hotel.

I was desperately worried about this escape route—the only one available—as it was overlooked by a dimly lit multistorey car park. I managed to arrange uniformed presence on each floor of it plus a line of policemen all the way from the first floor landing to the back door to escort the VIPs out when the car park had been checked.

A head check of the Cabinet revealed all accounted for except Mr. Norman Tebbitt. What happened to him is well documented elsewhere, as are the heroics of Station Officer Fred Bishop and Blue Watch from Brighton Preston Circus Fire Station. Mrs. Thatcher's movements later that day are also well known.

What is not generally known is that John and Toby had to insist very strongly that Mrs. Thatcher should not be carried down a turntable ladder at the front of the hotel, beautifully illuminated by fire brigade spotlights. Beyond the promenade, the beach and the sea were just inky blackness with no guarantee of the absence of hostile parties waiting out there for an opportunity to finish the job.

Neither is it public knowledge that the same two junior officers dug their heels in to countermand the very senior Mets officers who wanted the prime minister hustled out before proper checks had been made. They also kept the prime minister and her high-powered cabinet fully informed of developments at every stage.

As if that were not enough, they somewhat spared the blushes of a very senior Met police officer who, on being roused by the explosion, had dived from his room stark naked. With only a hand towel to cover his worldly goods, he was stranded when his room door slammed shut, locked, behind him. They obligingly kicked the room door in for the gentleman.

When the dust had quite literally settled, I wrote a report recommending that John and Toby should receive recognition, in the form of a medal, for their conduct on that night. DI Tim O'Connor agreed wholeheartedly and wrote it up accordingly before forwarding it up the ladder. Tim assures me that Det. Superintendent Jack Reece, the man in overall charge of the bombing inquiry, also signed it and recommended its activation.

View of the Grand Hotel, Brighton a few hours after the IRA attack.
My VW camper is arrowed in red. You can't see it but the interior is
full of rubble that smashed through the plastic raisable roof.

Once the VIPs were clear and it was declared safe to enter some of the first-floor suites, I collected and secured various Cabinet papers that were still in the rooms occupied by Mrs. Thatcher and her senior cronies. It did not occur to me to have a look through them for any reference to the miners' strike!

When there was no more for us to do at the hotel, we made our way to Brighton Police Station to offer ourselves for a debrief. Nobody was available to do this, and we contented ourselves by making written statements, with events still vividly fresh in our minds.

I also got someone to go round and wake Sandra before she had a chance to switch the TV on, and to let her know I was okay.

I returned to the scene and made arrangements to have my vehicle removed. It had been parked at the front of the hotel and had taken the full force of masonry blown out by the blast. My insurance claim made interesting reading! "What was the cause of the accident?" "The Grand Hotel fell on it." "Please provide details of the party responsible." "The Provisional Irish Republican Army."

Later, when I was having problems with the insurance claim, I submitted a report to HQ stating that as the vehicle had been placed at the front door as an escape resource, if needed, the force might see its way to paying for at least some of the loss. I got a reply from Assistant Chief Constable Dibley to the effect that, as the vehicle was being used within the terms of its insurance, the matter of reimbursement was "between the Insurance Company and yourself."

Meanwhile, back at the scene, I thought I detected an air of coolness among some of the senior officers who had been called out and to whom I offered my assistance and that of my team.

At 5:00 p.m., I was told by one of them to go home and stay there pending instructions.

Of course, the TV was utterly dominated by the bombing. I got home completely shattered, having had two hours' sleep in the past seventy-four, and had to watch some cretinous Tory MP from somewhere in the Midlands demand that whoever was in charge of security inside the hotel should be put up against a wall and shot. In other words, me.

Nice, that.

There was also a statement from the IRA, directed at the government, addressed to Mrs. Thatcher. It said in part: "Today we were unlucky, but remember we only have to be lucky once." Chilling!

The next day, Saturday, I stayed at home all day, picking things up from TV and local radio. I received in excess of twenty telephone calls from colleagues concerned that I was all right. Strangely, not one of these calls came from anyone above the rank of inspector.

I thought, "Yep. I get the message."

By Sunday my mood was heading for rock bottom. I saw on TV that an incident room had been set up, and pictures showed the three senior detectives in charge. I knew them all pretty well. One was Graham Hill, whom I mentioned in Chapter 6 as having achieved 100 percent, 100 percent, and 99 percent in his final exam at training school in 1966. The second was Geoff Randle, whom I knew, and still do, from rugby. Finally there was Bernie Wells, who had been a detective sergeant at Worthing while I was there in the early 1970s. All were now superintendents.

I rang the incident room and was passed to Bernie.

"Guv'nor," I said, "I'm stuck at home and going off my head. Nobody wants to know me. Do you need anyone else on the incident?"

"Sure," he replied. "Get here for 8:30 tomorrow."

"Will that not cause you a problem? I don't think I'm exactly popular at HQ."

"I'll sort that out, Allan. Just you get here."

I duly turned up for the daily briefing, held in the gym at Brighton Police Station. Bernie told me to sit through it, and he'd talk to me afterwards.

Having spoken to me and worked out my frame of mind, he teamed me up with a little WPC, Suzy Denyer. Suzy had been on my uniform section around 1980, and I had used her on a number of occasions as a "decoy" when I was on the Plain Clothes (Vice) Squad. She was a smashing girl; small, chirpy, dark-haired, and capable of acting any role given to her. Suzy tragically died on January 18 2012, during the writing of this book. R.I.P. Suzy. **You were a one-off.**We were given the job of searching through the registration books and cards of every hotel and boarding house in Brighton and Hove, over the previous six months, with the exception of the Grand Hotel's, which were to be subject of detailed scrutiny. That scrutiny eventually led to the detection and arrest of Patrick Magee for the bombing.

For two solid weeks, Suzy and I ploughed through thousands of pages and cards, looking for anything that did not look quite right, especially if there was the most tenuous of Irish connections. We put several dozen up for further examination, but apart from a couple of inquiries that might have led to early divorces, nothing came of them.

During this time, I had to go to police headquarters to be interviewed by Sir John Hoddinott, the deputy chief constable of Hampshire, a formidable officer who had been charged with conducting an internal inquiry into police conduct before the explosion. I saw him in the company of a real hard case of a detective superintendent and underwent a grilling during which no stone was turned less than three times. It was, though, very fairly conducted.

As I left the office occupied by Mr. Hoddinott, I came face to face with a senior officer with whom I'd worked when he had been of lesser rank. He performed practically a backward somersault to avoid having to speak to me.

I decided to go and see my doctor and get a prescription for leprosy.

Around the same time, the teams digging in the hotel rubble for clues came up with the timer that had been used to detonate the bomb. It proved to be a thirty-day timer, and it was not long before experts were able to prove that it had been set to go off after twenty-four days.

Bernie Wells called me into his office to tell me this personally. "This should make you feel better," he told me. It also meant that Suzy and I could concentrate on registers and cards completed around that time, cutting the work load by 90 percent.

During the third week of the inquiry, I was teamed up with DC Gordon Thompson, normally with the Commercial (Fraud) Branch. We were provided with a car and despatched on inquiries as far afield as Gloucester, Staffordshire, and Leicester, finding overnight accommodation where we could and ringing in with reports and for instructions twice daily. Gordon proved to be very skilful at negotiating deals with hotels so that, although the limit the Police Authority would reimburse was miserly, we always managed to stay in half-decent hotels.

The people we were sent to interview had all been residents in the Grand at the time the bomb had been planted. None gave rise to any suspicion, but neither could they offer anything in the way of evidence or clues.

We were now into November, and the police promotion boards were in full swing. I had been recommended for promotion to inspector and, I may say against my better judgement, had been prevailed upon to apply for a "board."

Two days before my appointment, Gordon and I were in Leicester and interviewed a gentleman whose company produced training videos for all sorts of purposes. I believe the company had some connection with the actor and comedian John Cleese. After taking a statement, I told the interviewee that I was going before a promotion selection board in a few days and asked if they did a video to show how I could conduct myself at the interview.

No, he didn't, although I was welcome to watch one instructing people how to interview people with a view to hiring them. I expressed my interest, and the amusing video was full of "do's and don'ts" for people running such interviews.

Do's: Call him in on time and leave a gap between candidates as insurance for this.

Make sure the candidate is comfortable. Avoid sitting at a higher level than he does.

Find out as much as you can about the interviewee. Is he married? Does he have a family?

If you must call him by his Christian name and he has multiple names, find out which he likes to be known by. If you can't find out, ask him.

Make sure he knows you are interested in him.

Give him the opportunity to have his say.

Make sure at the end of the interview he knows he has had a fair crack of the whip.

Don'ts: Don't leave him hanging about before his interview.

Don't rustle papers around on the desk. You should know already enough about him so you shouldn't need to do this.

Avoid hostile questions such as, "What makes you think you're the best man for the job?"

Well, it wasn't advice aimed at me, but I could bear it in mind.

Accordingly, I turned up for my promotion board, which was being held in what used to be Chief Superintendent Norman Cooper's office. It was due for 11:20 a.m., and I got there just before 11:00. Two other sergeants were already waiting in the anteroom, which was ominous. One by one, they were called in through the connecting door with the secretary's office. Just after 12:15 I was summoned, by which time two others had joined the queue.

The board, consisting of three senior officers, sat on a dais, their backs to the window. I was directed to a seat at a lower level. The office faced south, and a low autumnal sun dazzled me through the window.

The assistant chief constable heading the board opened a blue folder and flicked through the contents.

"Well, William," he said. "What makes you think we should pick you and not another sergeant?"

His head was a blur in the dazzle. I asked if he would mind if I moved my chair a little. He waved a hand in the air, which I took as a "yes," and scraped the chair into the shade.

"Well, then, are you going to answer my question?"

I replied that perhaps I was not the best judge of that, but in the file in front of him were details of all my experience since joining and my record as a sergeant.

"Hmph!" he said, apparently less than impressed.

I noticed that the superintendent sitting on his left seemed to be concentrating on something behind his ACC. I followed his gaze and realised he was watching a window cleaner lowering himself in a cradle from another wing of the police station roof.

The superintendent on the ACC's right then asked what I thought of the circular recently issued by the chief constable concerning the running of the force.

I replied that I had no views as I had not had the opportunity to read it.

All three seemed aghast! "What? You haven't read the chief's circular?" I explained that I had been working long hours away from home on the bomb Inquiry. With a look of incredulity on his face, the ACC scribbled something on a pad.

He asked if I had any questions. I had one or two like, "Why am I here wasting my time and yours when I should be out catching the bomber?" but I thought it prudent on that occasion to keep them to myself.

He leaned his elbow on the desk as a gesture of finality. "Thank you, sergeant." I got up and walked out as indicated via the door that led to the corridor and not through the secretary's office.

As I passed the door of the anteroom, three seconds after leaving the interview, I heard the superintendent's voice. "Next please."

"Well," I thought, "that's what I call a really fair crack of the whip!"

If I felt badly treated, I was probably not alone. It transpired that nobody who was at all involved in the police operation at the Grand Hotel was promoted until three years had expired.

There was one interesting exception. The man who had been in overall charge, Chief Superintendent Charles Pollard, was soon afterwards promoted to the rank of assistant chief constable of the Thames Valley Police. What was it that US President Harry S. Truman said? I believe it was "The buck stops here." That particular buck obviously did not make the distance!

Back to the inquiry, then, and the breakthrough was quite unexpected. All the registration cards from the hotel from the salient dates had gone for detailed forensic examination. Three and a half weeks before the blast, a man calling himself Roy Walsh had checked in and been allocated the exact room where the bomb had been planted. His registration card was examined and a thumbprint found where he had steadied the card while signing it.

That thumbprint belonged to a man called Patrick Magee, who had been convicted years ago as a juvenile in Norwich for stealing a bicycle. He had moved to Belfast shortly after that. That's how close he came to never being caught.

The address given was fictitious, although it existed, and the full force of the inquiry now concentrated itself on finding him.

The rest is public knowledge. Magee was convicted in September 1986 and received a sentence of thirty-five years, being released less than thirteen years later, in 1999 for reasons of political expediency. If his early freedom has saved the lives of many in Northern Ireland, so be it. The guy was within five seconds of killing me, but I bear him no personal ill will. Many millions have died throughout history, victims of other men's beliefs.

After Magee's arrest, the inquiry gradually ran down. I returned to the commando unit, and life returned to normal.

In June 1985, I took some annual leave and we went camping in the Vale of Belvoir, where the girls could ride horses. I was listening to the radio when the Queen's Birthday Honours list was announced. A whole succession of people was mentioned who had been connected to the Grand Hotel bombing. I had no quarrel with any of them, firemen, doctors, nurses, and so on.

What bothered me was that no policeman was mentioned.

As I said earlier, I had nominated Toby Pratt and John Rist for awards to recognise their outstanding conduct just after the explosion. This recommendation had been signed up all the way to the top. When no commendations appeared for them in the Force Routine Orders, I had not worried, as I believed they would be honoured in the Birthday Honours list.

I drove into Grantham, ironically Margaret Thatcher's birthplace, and bought the *Times*. There was the list, and, sure enough, there was no Sussex policeman on it.

I drove back to the campsite and, amidst family protests, broke camp and headed south. The next day I presented myself at police headquarters and asked to see the chief constable as a matter of urgency.

My request was refused, and when I expressed my opinion that it was urgent and could not await my returning to duty, and that the reason for the request was to find out why John and Toby had been cold-shouldered, I was told, in no uncertain manner, to get lost.

There were several ears attached to senior officers when I opined, quite forcefully I suppose, that the chief constable had proved himself to be a four-letter word.

In reality, I should not have been surprised at the lack of recognition. True to form, when things go right, the bigwigs get the credit. When plans go awry, the little guys get the blame.

On my return to duty, I found a command to attend HQ Personnel the following day at 10:00 a.m.

I did so and was admitted to the presence of Chief Inspector Hooker, who, with a smile on his face, bade me sit down. He had the inevitable file on the desk in front of him.

"Well, William, or would you like me to call you Bill?"

"You can call me Allan, sir. Everyone else does."

He flicked the file open. "I see you have been a sergeant for eight years now. You seem to have picked up a lot of experience in that time."

"Thank you, sir. I have been lucky."

"Well, Bill, I think it is time you got a bit of uniform experience with a view to realising your potential and getting to inspector."

"Hah," I thought. "I know what's coming."

I said, "I'm quite happy in the commando unit, sir, and I do acting inspector when Mr. O'Connor is away."

"Ah, that's the thing. You see the attachment to the commandos is being restricted to three years. As far as I can see, you have been with the unit for more than that time." (I had been on it for three years and two weeks.) He smiled. "So you see, it's the ideal time for you to get some uniformed experience."

"Oh, yes," I thought, "but it's not the ideal time for me to have called the chief constable a rude name."

What I actually said was, "I see, sir. I hope the unit is not going to suffer too much. There's a few lads been there for over three years." In fact, all but three of the unit had been there more than three years. Nobody else was posted off it, and, in fact, DC Colin Putland, who had been on it when I joined, finished his police service some twenty years later, still in the unit.

Mr. Hooker ignored this and told me I'd be starting the following Monday on uniform patrol at Hove. The wheel had turned full circle then.

I said a sad farewell to the lads on the commandos at the end of the week, especially to John and Toby.

Before I close this chapter, I'd just like to confirm the claim made by Sussex Police that they offered help and any counselling required to all those officers involved in the Grand Hotel bombing.

I'd like to confirm it but unfortunately I can't, because it was never offered. Not to John, not to Toby, not to Tina, and not to me. I straightened out my personal nightmares by arranging for private counselling through my GP. This was unbeknownst to Sussex Police because I did not want them to know.

Record straight?

There is one more thing. Details of commendations were always published in the Force Routine Orders. Not long after the bombing, Orders carried a notice that every member of the force who had been involved on the night of the outrage was to receive a commendation. When Magee was caught and charged, a similar notice appeared to the effect that every single officer involved in the inquiry was likewise commended.

I thought, "Well, I'm damned. I wait years for a commendation, then three come along almost together!"

At my retirement "do" eight years later, my inspector had managed to smuggle my personal record out of HQ, with which to raise some laughs at my expense. I had a look at it. Only one commendation was recorded—that for the Peter Gifford porno job.

In 2004 Peter Taylor of BBC, who was running a programme to mark the twentieth anniversary of the bombing, interviewed me. He asked the questions. I gave honest answers. I was featured in about ninety seconds of the broadcast. I criticised nobody in the Sussex Police, only casting doubt on the Security Services' "low risk" assessment. I had been retired ten years by then.

In 2009 the Grand Hotel threw a bash to remember the twenty-fifth anniversary. Everyone who had any connection with the outrage was invited. I wasn't, nor were Toby, John, or Tina.

The leprosy pills hadn't worked, then.

# CHAPTER 17

## Hove Second Time Around: Back at My First Station

I duly reported at Hove on the Monday morning, having restocked myself with uniform at the HQ clothing store—my old stuff was hanging off me, as the fitness regime I had undertaken while with the commandos had shaved my measurements down considerably. Times had changed at Hove in that there was no longer an admin sergeant—Bill Crawford had long retired, his job civilianised at half the cost.

Admin directed me to the divisional commander's office, where Superintendent Frank Hooper was waiting for me along with his 2IC, Chief Inspector Daryl Fromm. I had and have respect for both these gentlemen. They were probably reluctant players in the game, doing what they had been told to do.

"Welcome back to Hove, Allan," said the super—obviously having done his homework. "I'm told you're here to get some uniform time in before going on the Inspectors' Promotion Board."

"That's what I was told too, guv'nor."

"Well, we don't think you're quite ready for it yet."

I stifled a laugh, as did both the senior officers. "We should get on okay, then, sirs, as we all seem to be on the same wavelength," I said.

"I'll be honest with you," said the super. "We've put you on a section that's having some problems that need sorting out."

"And I'm the man?" I asked. "In need of rehabilitation?"

"No, but going by your record you should command a bit of respect. The PCs are a very good bunch, but they need motivating." He went on to tell me that the section he was putting me with had three supervisors, an inspector, and two sergeants, who were coming over as "time-servers" and had lost the respect of the section.

Fine, I thought, maybe I can motivate the PCs, but the other three are surely your problem, gentlemen. I thought it but I didn't say it. I simply nodded sagely—I hoped they'd interpret it as such.

Daryl Fromm must have read those thoughts. "We were prepared to do things the hard way and get rid of two of them, but we found out we were getting you and thought we'd give this a try."

I told them I was no miracle worker and knew only one way to work—by leading from the front. What if the guys did not want to follow? I shrugged. "I'll give it a go."

The section I was allocated to was working the 2–10 shift. I met them at briefing that day and was pleased to see that I already knew three of them—Bob Hatley, Chris Wratten, and Billy Bond. Bob had had a spell on the commandos but had to go off for personal reasons. He was fearless and a great guy to have at your back. Billy was simply a great all-round bobby. Chris had been on my Brighton section and had also had some CID experience.

Due to Bob's considerable influence, I retained my nickname of "Abo."

Bob and Billy cornered me after briefing and confided that the section's problems derived from the fact that Inspector X and the other two Sergeants Y and Z never wanted to go out on the streets. "We call them 'The Olympic Flames,' because they never go out!" Billy told me. "There's no back up, no thanks when you get it right, only moans about your paperwork."

"The lads all know we'll get no help from them if we ever land in the shit," said Bob.

I went off at 5:00 p.m., saddened. I had one day, Tuesday, to get to know the section before they had two rest days before early turn.

The next day, not long after we completed the briefing, and the PCs had gone out, a "shout" came in that a burglar had been disturbed trying to get into a basement flat in Blatchington Road, a shopping street in the middle of Hove. I had been talking to one of the two "Olympic Flames" when I heard this, and I snatched the keys for the sergeants' car and more or less dragged my colleague out with me.

When we got to the scene, Bob Hatley was there. The offender had tried to kick the door in, and when disturbed had run off eastwards in the Brighton direction. Units were already searching in that area. The offender was described as around twenty years old and wearing a red anorak. Just then I spotted a number 49 bus drawing away from the traffic lights at the western end of Blatchington Road heading further west. I realised there was a bus stop at the eastern end of the street, and the offender had been running towards it. I got my colleague into the car, and we followed the bus, watching who got off at stops before overtaking it and boarding it at Portslade Station, a mile or so from the scene of the burglary.

Upstairs we found a young man aged twenty in a red anorak, obviously out of breath.

"How long have you been on this bus?" I asked him.

"I got on at the Old Steine," he replied, naming a large square by the Royal Pavilion in the centre of Brighton.

"No, you didn't," retorted an old gentleman seated behind him. "He got on at the top of George Street!" This was the bus stop at the eastern end of Blatchington Road.

With some difficulty I persuaded my colleague to arrest the youth, and eventually he did. It was later found that the offender's trainer had left a perfect matching sole print on the basement door, and he pleaded guilty at court.

Bob Hatley met us at the police station. "Well done, Sarge," he said to me.

"Not me, Bob. He's Sergeant Y's prisoner."

The effect on section morale was instant.

I found out fairly quickly that Sergeant Y liked to check all the section paperwork, Sergeant Z wanted to be station sergeant and supervise the jailer, and Inspector X had domestic problems and liked to discuss them with his sergeants in his office.

From then on, I was able to persuade both the other sergeants to come out a bit more often.

After a year or so, a new inspector, Paul Curtis, replaced Inspector X. He was as different as you could wish for. He was young and dynamic and able to make immediate contact with the PCs on the section. He never spent a minute more than was necessary in his office. Thanks to him, the performance of our section was soon rated the best in the subdivision. He soon climbed deservedly up the career ladder and at time of writing is chief superintendent.

About a year after my arrival, Sussex Police took part in a trial run of the extremely controversial Police and Criminal Evidence Act (PACE) of 1984, which was due to come into effect soon. This meant the appointment of a custody sergeant for the duration of the trial. Sergeant Z was desperate for the job. Paul Curtis told me I was going to do it on my shift. Each section had to supply a sergeant as a dedicated custody officer.

I was very reluctant to do it but agreed after being told it was only for the duration of the trial. I had to go to HQ for a brief two-day course on the Act, before the trial was implemented.

As far as I have ever been able to tell, the motivation for this act becoming law was the premise that all policemen are bent. In other words, they fabricated evidence, they beat up prisoners, and they banged people up in cells for days on end with no contact with anyone outside.

The perception of policemen is indeed somewhat different since the inception of that Act. They are never seen on the streets, they never answer emergency calls, and so on ad nauseam. An awful lot of that is directly due to the Police and Criminal Evidence Act.

This act was legislation written by lawyers for the benefit of lawyers firstly and criminals secondly. The pecking order of importance of people involved in any case was remodelled, with suspects at the top, followed by defence lawyers, prosecution lawyers, witnesses for the defence, witnesses for the prosecution, injured parties, and policemen in that order.

The Act was, with the Crown Prosecution Service, also responsible for the generation of the mountains of forms and other needless paperwork now required to push the simplest of cases through the judicial system.

Prisoners' entitlements were never-ending. They had to be dealt with within five hours of their being booked in at the police station. If they were not, the custody officer had to authorise their further detention, and as delays went on, an inspector, then a superintendent, and then a magistrate had to give permission for their incarceration to be continued before charging. All the minutiae of their detention had to be faithfully recorded on their custody records.

"Oh, yes," I hear the cynical cry. "The custody sergeant is always going to authorise their banging up!" Maybe in most cases he'd like to, but each authority had to be reasoned and the reasons recorded on the prisoner's custody record. As the record went up the line, the reasons had to be stronger. Any mistake on a custody record, and the case went out of the window.

The prisoner had to be fed and watered at regular times. Not so the arresting officer. I'd no problem with any of that in general. However, during periods of mad activity, such as the night I had experienced back in April 1978 in Brighton, when dozens of football supporters were arrested in a few hours, the whole system would have collapsed. Either that or Brighton would have been sacked by rampaging hooligans, with every copper sitting in the Nick doing paperwork.

I'll stop railing on at PACE except to relate a story, which happens to be true.

One night during the PACE trial, I came into Hove on night shift. It was a Tuesday and I remember that, because on the shift system the Tuesday—the second night of nightshift—is when you felt most knackered. Your body clock had not adjusted to sleeping during the day, and it needed another twenty-four hours to catch up. Long-haul airline passengers will know the feeling very well.

On this particular Tuesday, there was a message from Bournemouth, where they were also running a trial on P.A.C.E. They had in custody a certain Mr. Lockwood, who had been circulated by Hove as being wanted for burglary and had a previous history of escaping from custody.

In fact, it was a second message. Mr. Lockwood had been in custody for over five hours, and his detention had been further authorised only because circumstances had made it impossible for Hove to collect him. If he was not collected by 02:55 hours, he would have to be released—no ifs, no buts.

That night we were seriously short-staffed and had only the inspector, two sergeants, and seven constables to cover the town. On nights the three patrol cars needed two men each, and the inspector could not go in case there was a PACE problem. Nobody would authorise two PCs off the 2–10 shift to collect the prisoner on overtime.

One of the PCs on my shift was a lad called Fergie Spiller, who was not a police driver, so he was nominated. There were no prisoners in the custody suite, so Sergeant X and I drew straws to decide who would drive, and I got the short one.

It was a foul night, with heavy rain and a strong wind from the southwest. There was only one car available—an ancient three-door Metro. Driving off into the teeth of the wind and rain, it soon became evident that the windscreen wipers were not man enough for the job, the wind lifting them off the windscreen!

Peering into the deluge, I drove as fast as was safe, to get to Bournemouth before the deadline. We made it with around twenty minutes to spare. I was a bit hungry and had a headache coming on. At that time of night, Bournemouth Police Station did not have any facilities for food, and Fergie and I had to make do with cups of tea before placing Lockwood in the back of the Metro, handcuffed to Fergie, who was seated behind me.

Almost immediately, Lockwood started whingeing that he wanted a smoke. He had cigarettes in his pocket, but his lighter was in his property bag, which was locked in the boot. I put up with his wailing for as long as I could, but my headache was not getting any better, so in the mistaken interests of safety I relented and used the car's cigar lighter to get him going.

As any erstwhile Metro owner will confirm, put three grown men into one with the windows closed and within a very short time it will become fuggy and unbearable. I had already tried the fan-driven fresh air vents, but the fan motor was apparently on strike. The windows were misted up, and I had to use tissues to clear the inside of the windscreen.

As Lockwood smoked, the air in the car became rapidly unbreathable. I tried winding the driver's window down and immediately got soaked by wind-driven rain. I pulled over and wound the window down on the other side before proceeding. Within a few minutes, Lockwood began to complain that he was getting wet and cold. I pulled over again and wound it up until there was only a one-inch gap at the top and carried on.

By now, of course, there was so much moisture in the car that the misting got even worse. The demister was either cold or full-on hot, just like my temper was becoming.

Those who served in the Chichester area around the time will recall that, before the nice dual carriageway A27 Chichester to Portsmouth was constructed, all traffic passed via the village of Fishbourne. They will also remember that just before the eastbound A27 entered the

Chichester bypass, there was a right-hand bend, on the grass verge of which there stood a lamppost of enormous diameter.

Some way before reaching Fishbourne, I had overtaken a huge Spanish juggernaut, and just before I reached the Chichester bypass, the combination of tiredness, damp fuggy air, and cigarette smoke took effect and I nodded off.

I was awakened by Fergie's scream of "Saaaarge!" I could see the lamppost rushing towards me and steered away from it back to the road. Only I didn't because the continuous heavy rain had waterlogged the grass verge. The car's forward momentum continued until the Metro hit the lamppost with a loud crash.

The windscreen popped out in one piece followed by Lockwood, who was, of course, handcuffed to Fergie. Fergie was stopped by the driver's seat, the back of which slammed into my shoulder blades; Lockwood's progress out of the car was halted by the handcuffs. He lay on the bonnet of the car gazing at me with an astonished look on his face. I unclipped my seat belt and opened the door, immediately being doubled up by two ribs, broken by the seat belt. I called to Fergie to release the handcuffs.

"I can't, Sarge!"

"Why not?"

"The keys are in my left trouser pocket." His left hand was, of course, attached to Lockwood by the handcuffs. Despite the excruciating pain in my ribs, I got the key out of Fergie's pocket and released Lockwood, who was, miraculously unhurt. Apart from a seriously bruised left wrist, so was Fergie.

Suddenly, I remembered the Spanish lorry. There were no lights on the car, the rear end of which was protruding on to the road, nor would the four-way flashers work. I got Fergie attached to Lockwood again, using their other wrists and, hearing the Spaniard approaching I started to run in the direction from which it would appear. Suddenly I realised I was wearing my dark blue tunic, which I tore off, along with my shirt, which I started waving in the air as the lorry approached, my busted ribs screaming in protest.

It screeched to a halt. I knocked on the driver's door and could see a face, pale for a Spaniard, on a head that was shaking forcefully. Pedro clunked the truck into first gear and roared off.

I ran back to the car. The radio was not working either. I got Lockwood to sit in the wreckage while Fergie stood in the rain and, doubled up, I ran back to where I knew there was a phone box.

We were collected along with Lockwood's property and taken to Chichester Police Station, where Fergie and I made statements, mine under caution. Lockwood was fed (not us!), and he made a statement that he had been asleep at the time of the accident. I opted not to go to the local hospital. I knew the ribs were broken and I also knew there was no treatment for them. I was duly informed that I would be reported and could be prosecuted over the crash.

My shift had gone off duty by the time we got back to Hove. The early turn inspector told me to take a couple of days off.

I returned for Friday's nightshift and, at briefing, was ceremonially presented with a model of a Metro, painted in the proper colour, in collision with a lamppost. It had been made by Bob Hatley, who had even gone so far as to remove the windscreen and glue it to the base!

A week or so later, I was summoned to the austere presence of Assistant Chief Constable Dibley at HQ to be "advised" regarding the crash. I had received an official document telling me I was not to be prosecuted for "reckless, dangerous, or careless driving."

Mr. Dibley duly addressed me on the importance of maintaining a good standard of driving and concluded by asking me what steps I would be taking to reimburse the force for the loss of its vehicle.

Knowing full well that the old Metro was worth only a few quid as scrap, I replied using the same phrase as he had when my car had been wrecked in the Grand Hotel bombing. "As the vehicle was being used within the terms of its insurance, the matter of reimbursement is between the insurance company and the Sussex Police, sir."

Mr. Dibley looked stunned for a few seconds, and then threw his head back and laughed. "Good Lord, Sarge, you've got a good memory!"

\* \* \*

In December every year, in those days, Hove Subdivisional Social Club held a raffle. They don't have it any more, because there are now no police social clubs in Sussex, unless Brighton has retained the one there. Various firms or other beneficiaries in the town donated most of the prizes. I guess that would also be frowned upon these days.

Imagine my surprise when I came to book on for nights and found I had won the "star prize" in the 1986 draw. It was a package holiday at a location of my choice up to a certain value. Sandra and I decided on Portugal and were duly booked up at the resort of Cascais, downstream of Lisbon on the Tagus Estuary. My mother was roped in to "babysit," although the "babies" were now fairly well-balanced teenagers.

We took the holiday in August 1987, and it was a lovely break. The package included a hire car, which was placed for us in the hotel's basement garage.

The first time I drove it out, I had an eye-opening experience of driving in Portugal. At the top of the ramp from the basement garage was a one-way street. One hundred metres or so down this street was a set of traffic lights. I was still twenty-five metres from them when they changed to amber. I slowed down gently, and then braked, and from behind there came the sound of a car horn. The operator obviously had his hand on the button, as it went on nonstop until I eventually stopped at the long-red light.

I looked in the mirror and saw a small car containing only the driver, who was shaking his fist and making what I know now is a very insulting gesture in Portugal.

Now, like in many European countries, the lights sequence goes straight from red to green without the "red-amber" bit. The time interval between the light going green and the reapplication of the nonstop hooter from behind cannot have been more than a fifth of a second. I allowed the following car to pass, observing that the driver was still gesturing at me, and he did not resume looking at the road ahead for a frighteningly long time.

We drove along the coast road, and more than once I found myself confronted by coaches and other vehicles on the wrong side on some of the very sharp bends.

I had made the acquaintance of the hotel barman the previous evening. Sandra and I went into the bar, and with shaking hands I asked him for a very large Scotch. Sandra had something strong too!

"Carlos," I said, "I have driven in several European countries as well as all over Britain, and I have to tell you that Portuguese drivers are the worst I have ever seen!"

"Oh, no, señor," Carlos replied. "They are the best drivers. If they were not, they would all be dead!"

That part of Portugal was well worth visiting. As well as the proximity of Lisbon, there are some very beautiful old towns within easy driving distance. Moorish influence is everywhere, as in Sintra and Leiria, while there are some fine examples of mediaeval architecture in Mafra and the old walled town of Obidos.

There is a town called Batalha, which means "battle." It is the site of the most important battle in Portugal's history, just as Hastings was in England. Batalha and the town of Battle near Hastings have many identical features, including fine abbeys. We also visited Torres Vedras, near which were built the "lines" of the same name, two series of forts built by Wellington's armies during the Peninsular War against Napoleon to bar the French route to Lisbon.

* * *

After Paul Curtis had been at Hove a few months, it was time for my annual "assessment." He had given me a glowing write up, and when he asked if I had any problems, I expressed my dislike of the "custody officer" role. He asked what I thought of the trend towards "community policing." I replied that if he was referring to the practice of having constables on fixed beats acting as practically village bobbies, I was 100 percent in favour. I felt there was no better way of maintaining contact between the people on the ground and the force, provided the PCs were doing it for the right reason, and not just to skive away from supervisory eyes.

He told me the subdivision wanted to have a sergeant dedicated to running the eight PCs currently engaged in that type of police work, so that they would have one man to answer to instead of whichever sergeant happened to be on duty on any particular day. I told him I was more than keen to take the job.

For the next nine months or so, I had the very happy job of looking after these guys, dealing with some of the men most dedicated to carrying the banner of police work into their respective communities. No soft touches were these men, no pushovers, but very ready with a friendly ear and good advice, and terrific sources of up-to-date intelligence into the activities of their various "black sheep." All were very experienced bobbies, men like Billy Bond, Carl Collins, Paul Allen, Trevor Cox, Chris Candler, and Steve Pratt, men with years of experience and a mountain of common sense between them. I always met them on their "ground," patrolled with them and tried to work in their interest when calls were constantly being made on their services away from their beats, for tasks like court jailer or prisoner escorts. These detractions were always the bane of my life, good policemen being wasted by having to swan around court cells or being taken off the division completely. Chapter 19 has a reference to this. Nowadays these posts have mainly been "civilianised." That, to my mind, has been a positive step in the right direction. I wish I could be as positive about other manning decisions, not only in Sussex.

It's time for a quick true story about Steve Pratt. Steve was a first-class electrician by trade. He never, ever shirked his job as the community policeman for the Mile Oak area of Portslade, but when he went off duty, especially on rest days, he reckoned his time off was his own, and he used to do electrical work to a very high standard.

Now, police regulations specifically forbid serving police officers from any paid work (called a "business interest") outside the job. I quote Part 2 of the regulations regarding "business interests" under the subsection "Government":

### *Business interests incompatible with membership of a police force:*

*A member of a police force or, as the case may be, a relative included in his family, shall have a business interest if:*

*The member holds any office or employment for hire or gain (otherwise than as a member of a police force) or carries on any business.*

Needless to say, Steve's electrical activities came under this umbrella, and eventually it came to the notice of senior officers. Steve was summoned to HQ to give an account of himself and, no doubt, to be told in blunt terms that if he carried on fixing wires for reward he would find himself out of a job. A superintendent saw him, and Steve later told me the conversation went something like this…

Superintendent: "PC Pratt, I am informed that you have been doing paid work as an electrician. This is contrary to police regulations."

Steve: "Yes, sir, this is true. I can even tell you who I have done work for. Chief Superintendent W, Superintendent X, Chief Inspector Y, and, oh, Assistant Chief Constable Z."

Superintendent (overwhelmed): "I see. Tell me, PC Pratt. Are you doing anything next weekend?"

Apocryphal? Maybe. Steve always was a great raconteur, but anyway he blithely carried on working, including wiring up my house extension!

It was always a mystery to me why policemen, who only enforce the law, are forbidden from having a little earner on the side. Even something as innocuous as a window cleaning round counts as a "business interest." Yet MPs, who make the law, may have as many well-paid interests as they want, including directorships of companies with a lot to gain from having their own contacts in Parliament.

On the night of October 15, 1987, I was awakened at around 2:00 a.m. by a screaming noise from outside the house. I rushed to my bedroom window to be greeted by the sight of objects whirling past it. The girls had been sleeping upstairs and both jumped, scared, onto the bed.

I dived to the sliding door of my extension. Outside was pandemonium. Roof tiles were crashing onto my patio, and the sound of breaking glass came from the bottom of my garden. The screaming noise was the wind, and I realised I was in the middle of a unique meteorological phenomenon.

I tried to phone HQ, but all lines were engaged. After some time, I got through to Hove Police Station. The reply I got was that it was chaos, and, if I could, would I get in to assist. I said I would try.

Looking outside I could see that to try to get in would be suicide at that time, as the air was full of lethal bits of flying debris. I knew the roads would be blocked, so I waited for the wind to die enough to get onto my bicycle.

When I finally got in, the day became a constant cycle of helping the fire brigade to rescue people and responding to emergency calls of all kinds. "The Great Storm" of 1987 is well documented elsewhere, but what is almost never acknowledged is the amount of effort put in by policemen of all ages and ranks for long hours, just to get things moving again. But then, no copper ever looks for such recognition. It all goes with the job.

So do the occasional run-ins with the powers that be. It is often quite difficult to maintain an air of equanimity when dealing with whatever might be on one's plate any day. It's no different in the job, and obviously some unfortunate officer or civilian employee stationed somewhere had incurred the wrath of an influential telephone caller, because one day at briefing an item was read out. It had obviously emanated from the Ivory Tower with instructions that all subdivisional commanders were to ensure that anyone answering incoming telephone calls followed these instructions.

*"Telephone answering technique. On receipt of an incoming BT call, it is to be answered as follows. 'Good morning (or whenever), Sussex Police, Hove (or wherever) Police Station, this is Sergeant Neil (or whoever) speaking. How can I help you?' Any deviation from this formula will result in disciplinary action being taken against the person answering."*

Of course, the first result of this might well be that members of the great British public might have to wait a little longer for someone at the police station to answer, thereby avoiding putting himself, or herself, in peril of disciplinary proceedings.

Or the result might be like when I answered an incoming call on the very day of the instruction.

"Good morning, Sussex Police, Hove, Serg…"

"Put me through to the superintendent."

"Excuse me, sir. Good morning, Sussex Police, Hove, Sergeant N…."

"Just put me through to the superintendent, would you?"

"I'm sorry, sir. Good morning, Sussex Police, Hove, Sergeant…"

"Are you going to put me through to the bloody superintendent, or not?"

"Good morning, Sussex Police, Hove, Sergeant Neil speaking…"

"That's all I need to know." He then hung up.

Apparently he was a local solicitor and came to the front desk a short time later, where someone else saw him, before he was ushered up to the superintendent's office. I dived quickly into the briefing room and photocopied the instruction, highlighting the bit about disciplinary action. Twenty minutes later, I was summoned into the presence of the superintendent of the time.

"I just had to pacify a certain Mr. Y. He says that you refused to put him through to me on the phone."

"Not really, sir." I told him about the instruction and handed him the photocopy, which he read.

"What bloody idiot wrote this?" he demanded. Without waiting for an answer, he continued, "Just use your bloody common sense, okay?"

"Yes, sir. Can I ask you to tell HQ to use theirs?"

I was thoroughly enjoying my spell as community policing sergeant, which was interspersed with Saturday duties at the old Goldstone ground home of Brighton and Hove Albion Football Club.

Albion had risen to the giddy heights of what is now called the Premiership, then the First Division of the Football League. They had even got to the FA Cup final in 1983, when they had come within a few inches of defeating the mighty Manchester United before being whipped 4-0 in the replay. They then slid down the leagues.

In the 1987–1988 season, they had won promotion back from Division 3 to 2, having been relegated the previous season. Now teams like Leeds, Millwall, and Portsmouth brought their hordes of fans to Brighton. I normally found myself in the visiting supporters' enclosure during these games and had some lively Saturday afternoons.

The liveliest, however, had been in the north stand when the Albion had been playing some team from London—not Millwall. I'd had to go into the crowd with my squad of PCs to arrest some particularly obnoxious home supporters.

Back at Hove Police Station, I found that the back of my overcoat was covered in spittle.

One indignant father arrived at the Nick to get his little boy out and demanded to know why these nasty policemen had interfered with his son's enjoyment. I showed him my coat and pointed out the thirty or so gobs on the back, telling him that those were relics of the sort of friend his little boy was spending his Saturday afternoons with. When he left with his son, I was sure I could hear the smack of palm on ear all the way up the drive! We had twenty or so miscreants in that day, and a remarkable number seemed to be called Darren, Wayne, or Lee.

I made up this little ditty, with apologies to Gilbert and Sullivan...

"Three little yobs from Hove are we,

We're called Darren, Wayne, and Lee."

My period of relatively stress-free policing came to an end one day in March 1988, when Paul Curtis called me into his office.

He produced the new issue of Force Routine Orders, which announced the formation of a Sussex Police Air Support Unit, involving the use of a helicopter. Four sergeants were required to man the machine.

"You're ideal for the job, Allan," he said. "All your experience in the job, including surveillance, and I noticed in your CV that you've done two courses on aerial reconnaissance. I want you to apply."

"Come on, guv'nor," I replied. "Have you seen my history? To blame for the Brighton bomb, calling Mr. Birch a rude name (Mr. Birch was the chief constable), being rude to the chief inspector at Personnel? No chance, but thanks for your confidence."

"I'm being serious. If you don't ask, you don't get. I'm practically ordering you to apply. I'm putting my reputation on the line for you here."

Well, put like that, how could I refuse? I applied.

Within a week, I had a call from Superintendent Dick Terry at HQ Operational Support. He totally supported Paul Curtis's recommendation, and I was required at HQ for a medical examination and, if that turned out to be satisfactory, an interview.

The medical was a formality, and Superintendent Terry saw me in his office.

"Sir, I said, I'd love the job, but I don't think the chief will approve me."

"It's my decision, Allan, and anyway the chief is away in Hong Kong." He extended a hand. "The job's yours if you want it."

I still see Dick Terry occasionally. He is a member of Sussex County Cricket Club, where, as a match day Steward, I find myself on a regular basis these days.

I was sad, as usual, to leave my friends, but helicopter policing? Wow! What a challenge!

# CHAPTER 18

## Hotel 900: Policing from the Air

The helicopter, which had been given the call sign Hotel 900, was to be based at Shoreham Airport, rather than at Force HQ, Lewes, where an earlier trial had taken place. Residential streets surround headquarters and, of course, live-in students on courses have rooms that happen directly to overlook the helipad!

There were to be four sergeants in the team, these to be called observers, and there were also two sergeants who were on standby if required for holiday relief or any reason. They had taken part in the initial trial, but had opted not to go full-time from Shoreham, because they lived a bit too far away. The other three selected as full-timers were Ian Jeffrey, who had been the moving force behind setting up the full-time unit, Mike Rumble, whom I knew from my Brighton uniform days, and Nigel Nuttall from Horsham Traffic. Nigel lived furthest away, on the edge of Horsham, but could reach Shoreham very quickly via the A24/A27 route, especially at night, which was when any call-out would be most likely to occur.

I was living at Southwick at the time, and the road to the airport was downhill all the way, making it easy to get there by bicycle, and only four minutes or so by car at night.

On Monday, April 25, 1988, we all gathered at Shoreham Airport, which is the oldest commercially operating airport in the country. It had been a frontline fighter station during the Battle of Britain in 1940, being ideally placed a few hundred yards from the sea. The prevailing wind—from the southwest—meant that aircraft taking off from Shoreham were over the Channel in a matter of seconds.

It was also perfect for helicopter operations, as the chopper would be at a good altitude before flying over houses, and if heading north only the grand buildings of Lancing College stood in the way and overflying them could easily be avoided. The Adur River valley was a perfect route out to the north, and the aircraft could be routed to the east and west of the county just offshore until sufficient altitude had been reached to overfly inhabited areas. On most tasks, the helicopter could achieve operational height over the airfield if immediate fast transit was not needed.

On the first day, Ian had arranged an hour or so of fixed-wing flying when the four of us had a fly around in a small Cessna, to get the idea of observing from the air. I had, of course, had two weeks of this at RAF Abingdon, but I kept that fact to myself.

The rest of the day was taken up with setting up and equipping the "Portakabin" that was to be our base meanwhile. Everything needed to run the operation was brought in from headquarters, and we had electricians, electronics people, and radio engineers rushing around. Toilet and other facilities were to be found in the main terminal building, where a discount had been arranged on hot food in the restaurant. The Portakabin had a kettle and a microwave oven.

Sussex Police helicopter Hotel 900 over Malling Down, Lewes. Pilot is my hero Dave Williams, yours truly on his left.

Nigel, quickly known as "Nuts," turned out to be a real joker and wanted to put in a spoof requisition for leather flying helmets, goggles, scarves on coat hangers, deck chairs, and a tannoy system! He also suggested we all cultivate handlebar moustaches!

I found that my nickname had followed me again, owing to one of the sergeants on the initial test, Darryl Twibill, with whom I'd had contact on a commando job, passing the information on to Ian Jeffrey. I didn't mind at all. I'd become quite attached to it.

Before I joined the helicopter unit, I had arranged to go on the London to Brighton Cycle Ride in aid of the British Heart Foundation. This is an annual event, held in the second half of June. It had been started about five years earlier and had already achieved great popularity, and twenty thousand participants set off on the 1988 run. The distance is fifty-four miles, beginning on Clapham Common, just south of Central London, and terminating on Madeira Drive, on Brighton's seafront. I had organised a team from Hove, including some of my fixed beat officers and others from uniform, CID, and the Drugs Squad.

We were fifteen in all and had been given permission to have a nonparticipant take a van from Hove to convey the bicycles to Clapham Common. The event is not a race, but when one of my team pointed out in front of the others that, at nearly fifty, I was going to be struggling and have to be looked after, I determined not to make a fool of myself.

I hadn't done any long-distance cycling, but for years I'd been cycling to and from work so was a long way from being unfit. The hardest part of the route was, and still is, from the village of Ditchling up on to the top of the South Downs at a point called Ditchling Beacon.

I had pushed myself a lot, and all my teammates were a long way behind when I got to the bottom of the Beacon. To get from bottom to top is a distance of 1.6 kilometres—one mile—with a height difference of 170 metres, so the overall gradient is over 1 in 10. However, there is a succession of hairpin bends where the gradient is considerably steeper, up to 1 in 4 in places. I decided, "Sod it. I'm walking up here."

I dismounted and started to walk at a brisk pace. Astonishingly, some of the mountain bikes were so low-geared that I was actually overtaking some of them! My machine was a road racer with ten gears, five of which were quite high.

At the end of the ride, all fifteen of the Hove riders had finished the course, but the oldest of them was able to give the others a bit of stick, finishing ten minutes ahead of the lad in second place!

Back to business then. The job of supplying and piloting the helicopter went to a Devon company called Police Aviation Services, PAS, which had been set up when Devon and Cornwall Constabulary established the first British Police Aerial Support Unit outside London a couple of years earlier.

PAS was run by an ex-Army Air Corps officer called Mark Trumble, a tall, bald man with a quirky sense of humour. The pilots employed by Mark were all ex-military, mainly Army Air Corps, although one, who worked a lot in Sussex, was an ex-Marine pilot named Steve Bidmead. Three former Royal Navy pilots later joined us—David Kelly, Ian Brown, and Rory Cowan. The first two had seen active service in the Falklands War. Ian had in fact ended up having a brief swim in the South Atlantic when the ship on which he and his helicopter were being transported—the Atlantic Conveyor—was sunk by an Exocet missile of the Argentine Air Force.

Besides Sussex, other forces in England were in the process of setting up air support units. At the end of April, Nuts, Mike, and I made our way to Exeter, where PAS and Devon and Cornwall Constabulary had organised a course to familiarise us with all the aspects of helicopter policing.

Mark Trumble and Inspector Brett Harvey, the OIC of the Devon and Cornwall unit, ran the course. As well as the three of us from Sussex, there were representatives from Thames Valley, West Midlands, and

Warwickshire, all of whom were forces in the process of setting up their own helicopter units.

The course had the use of two helicopters, an Aerospatial Gazelle, as used by the Army Air Corps, and a Bolkow BO-105, very popular with the German police and made by the company that made Messerschmidts. The Sussex trial had used the Gazelle, but the full-time unit would have the Bolkow.

The course was that ideal mixture of intense concentration, serious study, and, in most evenings and at the weekend, fun and games. I learned more about navigation, radio procedures, and, something that had not been covered on the RAF courses, hazards particular to the operation of the helicopter, which invariably flew at a much lower altitude than the fixed-wing Bulldogs.

Things to keep an eye open for were bird flocks, power lines, and bridges. It is safer, when negotiating power lines at very low altitude, to fly under them close to the pylons and over them equidistant from pylons. We learned to use the equipment then fitted to the aircraft—searchlight (also known as Nitesun). The beam from this light could be adjusted, from a small cone to illuminate a small circle up to what amounted to floodlighting an area.

There was the tannoy, or ground address speaker, which had several obvious purposes. We did not have one on the course, but later, operationally, the Sussex aircraft was equipped with an infrared heat-seeking camera, known as FLIR—forward looking infrared.

Aerial photography and the use of gyroscopic binoculars were learned. These binoculars were ideal for reading vehicle number plates or getting a good look at a suspect's facial features. They killed the vibration of the aircraft so that your vision became clear, once you'd mastered the trick of keeping the picture steady, as it could rock and yaw if the operator was careless in his handling.

Unlike the Met Police helicopters, the county ones would be able to intervene directly on the ground, providing there was a safe place to put down. It was necessary, therefore, to be familiar with safety in leaping out of and boarding helicopters. The pilot had the sole decision on when it was safe to get out, and you learned to stand fully in the pilot's vision and wait for his indication that it was safe to approach. Never, ever approach a helicopter from behind. The pilot cannot see you and may be totally unaware of your presence. He might even turn the aircraft round, and that could hurt or much worse!

Fully cognisant of map reading, navigation, search techniques, road following methods, and the use of all the onboard gismos, we returned to Sussex.

My first day at work was Thursday, May 12, 1988, when the pilot was a quietly humourous ex-Army Air Corps officer called Paul Hannant. The first job was a search of the Itchenor area to try to find a missing six-year-old boy. Ian Jeffrey came along on my maiden live flight.

How on earth can I remember this? Well, as part of our course at Exeter, Mark Trumble had given us aircrew flying logbooks, and I kept mine faithfully up to date during my time on the helicopter.

That first trip was a good experience of how an aerial platform can clear a huge search area in very little time. Itchenor is a tiny hamlet near the mouth of Chichester hamlet. Open fields surround it on flat ground, plus there is quite a considerable length of waterfront to be searched. No, we did not find him, but we were quickly able to say that he was probably in a building somewhere and that is how it proved. He was fine and returned to his parents.

There was always a hard body of opposition to the chopper within the police service, based on its apparent cost of £600 per hour of flight. Our argument was that, properly used, the machine could actually save money. The cost of searching the Itchenor area with ground "troops" would have been considerable.

Most of the jobs that first week were searches, including one around Robertsbridge for a "misper"—police jargon for "missing person." Mark Trumble piloting, again we searched a large area and found a coat belonging to the "misper" at the edge of some woods a considerable distance from his home. This did not have such a happy ending, as his body was found nearby in the same woods.

May 16 brought my first visit to Beachy Head, the notorious "suicide spot" near Eastbourne. A car had been seen to go over the cliff edge. It was not known if anyone had been in it. Normally the Coastguards take care of the recovery of bodies from there, but we decided to save them some time and check if there had been anyone in the car. The pilot, another Army Air Corps veteran called John Ball, also wanted some practice of manoeuvreing the aircraft close to high cliffs, where air currents can be very unpredictable.

Sadly there was a body. He had been a young man in his twenties from East Grinstead. After a row with his wife, he had taken her car and then his own life. As we were down there, we recovered the body to the clifftop. At first the Coastguards were miffed, thinking we were going to take work from them, but they were okay in the end. H900 was another tool that they could use, as and when they needed it.

The following week showed more versatility for the aircraft. We did some aerial reconnaissance and took photographs for a Crime Squad operation near Crowborough. We called at HQ on the way back and airlifted an armed response team to an incident at Littlehampton before being overhead for containment as their raid went ahead.

Later that day, we positioned ourselves near Crawley, as the Metropolitan Police Flying Squad had a tip-off about an armed robbery to take place in the town. The helicopter has a special role to play when fugitive vehicles are being pursued. If we could get overhead quickly, there was no way an armed robber's car or a stolen vehicle was going to escape, and danger to the public can be dramatically reduced. In the event at Crawley, nobody made a getaway and our services were not required.

Also adding to the operational value of the aircraft was the fact that, returning from assignments, we still kept a constant watch on the ground. On June 3, returning to Shoreham from the Hayward's Heath area, we found a stolen caravan, which had been carefully hidden behind a tall hedge on farmland.

In the same week, coming back from a photo assignment in East Grinstead, we spotted some youths on motorcycles bombing recklessly among walkers on a footpath near the Devil's Dyke, on the South Downs north of Brighton. They were astonished when we dropped out of the sky in front of them and not very happy when we told them to push their bikes the best part of a quarter of a mile on to a road.

There they were met by Traffic Patrol, and I do believe had to leave their bikes there while they arranged transport for them, as they were not insured to be ridden on the road and none of the riders had crash helmets. Did I hear the word "trivial"? Maybe, in the context of the use of an expensive and sophisticated piece of equipment like a helicopter, but try telling that to the loved ones of any walkers mowed down by that reckless misuse of motorbikes.

Quite early on in the life of the unit, we ran a trial on carrying a paramedic. The Bolkow was ideal for carrying casualties on stretchers in the back as it had a wide door under the boom tailplane. The benefits of the aerial transportation of the badly injured are taken for granted nowadays, but it was all very new then, especially the use of a police helicopter.

The great advantage of carrying a paramedic on searches was that we had another pair of eyes. He sat behind the pilot and so searched to the starboard side. The pilot could concentrate ahead, while the police observer took care of the port side.

On the first one-day trial, we attended a serious road crash on the A23; the paramedic took care of initial treatment, and we conveyed the casualty to the nearest accident and emergency department with landing space.

Over the next few weeks, in liaison with the ambulance service, we adapted several pieces of kit to fit the aircraft and removed obstacles to running tracks in the back.

A working procedure for handling 'casivacs' soon evolved. The pilot put down as close as was safe, the paramedic jumped out and ran to the scene, while the police observer got the paramedic's kit out and ran after him with it. If the injury was serious, the paramedic got on with stabilising the casualty, while the observer rigged up drip lines. Only the paramedic was allowed to insert a cannula into the casualty, but thanks to the police observer knowing what to do, he could get to that point much sooner.

Meantime, if necessary, the pilot would try to get closer, still having 100 percent safety in mind. He stayed with the shutdown aircraft listening out to radio and keeping control up to date. If any more kit was required, such as the spine board, the observer fetched it. When the casualty was ready to be shipped out, the paramedic, the observer, and any other pairs of hands were utilised to make the "carry" as smooth as possible, and the stretcher was slid into the back of the helicopter.

In Sussex, we were never more than ten minutes' flying time from hospitals with accident and emergency departments, and mostly we could land fairly close to the ambulance entrance. A notable exception was the Royal Sussex Hospital at Brighton, which had nowhere for a helipad to be sited, so we would try to avoid it. If circumstances dictated that our casualty had to go there, we had to land in East Brighton Park—about a kilometre away—and transfer the patient to a road ambulance.

My most memorable "casivac" took place at the village of Loxwood, close to the Surrey boundary at Cranleigh on Sunday, July 17—our eighteenth wedding anniversary! This is traditionally one of the busiest Sundays of the year for traffic. After a week or so of dry roads, there was a sharp shower of rain that Sunday morning, and a collision took place in the centre of the village on a slippery stretch of road. At that point, there is only one road in and one out, and soon traffic was backed up in both directions.

As there was a report of someone trapped, the fire brigade had been called but could not get through. We learned over the radio en route that the local GP was in attendance, so Steve Bidmead put down in a field adjacent to the village centre. The paramedic and I got out and climbed fences to get to the scene, where a young woman aged thirty-two was trapped by the legs in her little Citroen Visa, which had had an argument with a Range Rover. Steve lifted off again and fetched a couple of firemen, with some of their cutting gear.

The GP, Dr. Norman Jones, and the paramedic were unanimous that as the lady appeared to have a serious neck injury; not only was road transport undesirable, but so was hoisting the stretcher over a five-foot fence. Steve called me back to the aircraft, and, on his directions, with me standing on the skids (in a harness) advising him of telephone wires and other obstacles, he shoehorned the helicopter onto the road, which the locals had cleared to make space.

Inching our way past power and telephone lines, we finally put down with about half a metre space all round for the rotor blades.

The casualty was loaded in, and we took off using the same procedure. Ten minutes later, the stretcher was off-loaded at Guildford Hospital. Happily, the lady made a full recovery over a number of weeks.

Back at base, we got a telephone call from Dr. Jones. "I was in the pub at Loxwood in the afternoon, and this guy came in," said the doctor. "He said, 'Did you see that bloody police helicopter land in the village this morning?' The landlord said he had, and the guy said, 'Yes, but did you see the bloody accident it caused!'"

The job continued into autumn with numerous searches and car chases. We also discovered that police dogs were very keen on riding in the chopper, and we frequently had one with its handler in our base at the ready to be transported. The idea, when a dog was called for, was to drop dog and handler where the fugitive had last been seen, then fly on ahead, turn and search back along any track the dog was following. We had a number of successes doing this, especially with the FLIR at night.

One late evening, we had returned to base just before midnight, when we intercepted a message about an intruder being disturbed at a girls' boarding school, a minute's flying away. We responded and were searching the grounds when the FLIR picked up a moving heat source on the school roof, then hiding behind a chimney.

We flew around the school with the searchlight probing in the grounds, but with the burglar held fast in the FLIR. Eventually he believed we had not seen him and stepped out from behind the chimney, making obscene gestures at us while we filmed him in glorious infrared!

A dog had been called, and the handler found his way onto the roof. The burglar was duly arrested and taken to the local police station at Shoreham.

Before going off duty, we got a call from the duty sergeant. "The guy we brought in says the police helicopter is a waste of time and money, and it took an old-fashioned dog to nick him."

On my way home, I dropped the video from the FLIR in at the station. The next day the DC in the case phoned us and said we should have seen the offender's face when he saw the video and when he was told the magistrates would see it too.

In 1988 the Conservative Party conference returned to Brighton. The force hired another helicopter for the duration so that there was always at least one aircraft over the Brighton Centre. Altogether that conference and the lead-up to it used up 52.25 hours of flying time. At £600 per hour, you can work out the cost for yourself!

I had become quite a proficient aerial photographer and was often called upon. One day we got a call from the Regional Crime Squad, who wanted to get a warrant out on a farm near Godalming in Surrey. They believed large numbers of stolen Range and Land Rovers were being stored there before being exported. Security at the farm was very tight, including alarms on the approach road, and they could not get close enough to get evidence. Their target was, they said, very influential in the area, and they would need more than just "say-so" to get their "brief," or warrant.

Now, the pilots and I had been working for some time on a way of using two of the navigational beacons scattered around the county to zero into any point within a ten-metre square. Rather than fly to and fro past the farm, we decided to fly in or above the low cloud prevailing on the day, get directly overhead, then, with me harnessed and on a skid, drop out of the cloud, grab some quick pictures, and then get out. Steve Bidmead was the pilot, and he was spot-on.

I got half a dozen shots, and we flew to HQ, where the photo lab was on standby. The pictures were developed and showed, quite clearly, about a dozen Land Rovers lined up in the open.

We rendezvoused with RCS at Surrey HQ and handed the evidence over. They obtained a warrant and executed it no more than two hours after I had taken the pictures. The Land Rovers had gone, and in addition, all the outbuildings were empty. However, the photos gave the Crime Squad enough ammunition to crack the job on interrogation.

I said earlier that even apparently negative flying time, such as returning to base, could be used fruitfully, simply by the crew keeping their eyes open. Returning from Crawley one day, we heard a report about a road accident on the back road between Balcombe and Handcross. A traffic car had been despatched but could find no trace of an accident.

As we were passing, we flew along that road and there it was! A car had hit the verge at speed and somersaulted clean over a hedge, where it was invisible from the road. We landed and checked but the car was empty. Five minutes later, we found the driver staggering along a nearby lane, concussed but otherwise unhurt.

Coming back from Chichester another day, we intercepted a call about a teenaged horse rider having ridden hysterically into Slindon College, screaming that she had found a dead body on the Downs. In her traumatic state, she could not remember where she had ridden from, so we volunteered to do a wide area sweep.

Within five minutes, we found the body of a man lying on a shotgun, later found to have been discharged. Nearby, leaning against a bench, was a motorcycle, through the index number of which the man was quickly identified as coming from Surrey.

A later inquest decided on accidental death, but I have never been happy with that, for various reasons. Going by bloodstains, the man had been shot beside the motorbike. The trail of blood led down from the motorcycle to where the body lay. The trail was steady, not intermittent as you might expect if the man had rolled down the slope. The victim also had a drugs connection on police file.

The decision reached was that he had driven on to the Downs intending to camp, had got off his motorbike holding the shotgun, and had somehow contrived accidentally to shoot himself.

Life on the helicopter proved to be a succession of a big variety of jobs. Just going briefly through pages of my flying log, I came across items like "Diving accident Brighton. Diver lifted from beach to Haslar Hospital with the bends." Because of the nature of the sickness, this casualty was conveyed to Haslar Hospital Gosport at just a couple of metres above sea level and just offshore. Any gain in altitude involves a drop in air pressure, and as the casualty had surfaced too quickly without proper depressurisation, it was important not to exacerbate his condition.

There are many examples of area searches, including one on Bonfire Night at Chichester, where it became obvious that people on the ground were deliberately firing rockets off in our direction!

There were photo assignments aplenty. Aerial photograph is the best way of assessing a large area prior to any operation. It can also be a wonderful tool in planning for specific events—for instance, football at Brighton and Hove Albion, racing at Goodwood, and many other police operations.

Occasionally a job would come along that would turn into a real heart-warmer, making everything totally worthwhile.

December 21, 1989 was a horrible day with fog, low cloud, and heavy rain. We received a call from the Maternity Unit at Southlands Hospital, asking if we could possibly help. They had a newly born baby with a potentially fatal condition that could not be treated there. The nearest hospital with the facilities required was at Portsmouth. The child would not survive more than an hour or so, and no road vehicle could make the trip in time in the prevailing conditions.

The duty pilot was Dave Williams, an extremely resourceful ex-Army Air Corps sergeant. The weather was quickly checked and was the same across the whole of the South of England. Dave sat deep in thought, looking at a map, and then jumped to his feet. "We can do it!" he cried. "Get HQ to ask Portsmouth Football Club if they can turn on the floodlights at Fratton Park. While they are doing that, ring that hospital extension at Southlands and get them to shine car lights across the grass area at the back. Tell them we are on our way and they need to do it right now!" He ran out to start the helicopter up.

John Tullett, the paramedic, and I made the phone calls, and then ran to the aircraft, and we took off. Southlands Hospital is less than thirty seconds' flying time once airborne. We were well aware of the highest object in our way—the hospital incinerator chimney—and its position in relation to the grass area at the rear. The chimney stood out on FLIR as it was still warm, and we stayed above it until we saw hazy lights converge on the grass.

Dave dropped the aircraft in exactly the right spot, and an ambulance raced across the grass towards us. I leapt out to make sure it didn't get too close to the blades. A nurse jumped out of the back of the ambulance carrying a large box, which transpired to be an incubator containing the tiny form of an infant. She was accompanied by a doctor.

John Tullett had to stay behind and work his way back to the airport, as it became obvious that the nurse—a midwife—had to come with us. The doctor and the incubator took up the other seat.

We took off and I contacted the ops room. They confirmed that the lights at Fratton Park were being switched on and also that there would be an ambulance waiting at the side of the pitch. The hospital was only a few minutes' drive away for the ambulance.

We followed the line of the coast at a height well above any obstruction, and we were still several miles from Fratton Park when we spotted the floodlights. We'd had a further message from Ops telling us to land as close to the waiting ambulance as possible, as the pitch was waterlogged.

Dave got us in safely, and as soon as was safe, baby, doctor, and midwife got out and made their muddy way to the ambulance. We returned via the coast and, positioning ourselves over the Shoreham Airport beacon, we landed home. John Tullett was waiting for us in the terminal.

The baby, Jason Willcox, survived and, in fact, visited us at the airport on the occasion of his first birthday, to be reunited with Dave and me. A lovely feeling and Ms. Willcox had another on the way! We asked her if she wanted to book her ticket now!

On his first birthday Jason Willcox comes to say hello to his saviour, Dave Williams (L). Yours truly on the right trying to make intelligent conversation, impressing neither Jason nor his Mum!

The warm glow generated by this incident has stayed with me. If we had stuck to the letter of the law and not flown in the conditions, Jason would not have survived. If it had gone wrong, the apparatchiks at the Civil Aviation Authority would have crucified Dave Williams from the comfort of their nine-to-five armchairs.

Dave moved on from Sussex to one of the Yorkshire forces, and I read in the papers about how he had averted a serious rail accident. He had flown at almost ground level in front of and facing a speeding train to persuade the driver to stop, thus avoiding ploughing into a derailed train ahead.

Such heartwarming events as Jason were not the norm, but we all prided ourselves on giving the best possible service to the job, and therefore to the people of Sussex.

Rory Cowan arrived as a pilot in late 1989. He had been a test pilot in the Royal Navy, and between us we wrote a navigation book for the Sussex helicopter, enabling us to land anywhere in the county using navigational beacons, within ten metres of target.

This was quite a job and unfortunately is now completely obsolete with the advent of "GPS" satellite navigation.

I mention Rory as he was of the Penicuik Cowan family that had been paper mill owners in the past and had also donated several landmarks to the town, such as the fountain in the square and the Cowan Institute, which had become the town hall. I once sent Rory a postcard from Penicuik—a photograph of the old Cowan Institute, with the caption, "Tell Daddy this place is in serious need of repairs."

I came off the Air Support Unit in May 1981 after three years, as I wanted my last two or so years in the job to be as a basic, or "real" policeman, on the streets and up front. Anyway, another sergeant was aching to come on the unit. He was better qualified than I was, with private pilot experience, so that was a good excuse.

# CHAPTER 19

## Worthing Second Time Around:
## Seeing My Time Out

It was a quiet "leaving do" in the garden of the Royal Oak at Shoreham. It was timed for when the aircraft was "off-line" for a service, obligatory after a certain number of flying hours, by laws enforced by the Civil Aviation Authority.

It had been an interesting three years, but I had become restless at the hours of sitting around waiting for things to happen, and I was actually in the air for less than an hour a day on average.

I had spent a year compiling a book listing every town, village, hamlet, and crossroads in Sussex with navigational coordinates and distances from at least one directional beacon, known as VOR—short for VHF omnidirectional radio range. These beacons are scattered throughout the country and are a good way of fast navigation without recourse to maps, although all the pilots preferred to fly with maps on their knees, as they also contained information about height limits for flying and areas under Air Traffic Control rules.

The navigation book was a good tool, but of course it very quickly became obsolete with the advent of global positioning systems—GPS.

My posting was to Worthing, where I had worked in the mid-1970s. The police station had not changed a bit, but the way of running it had. Where there had been a chief superintendent, now the officer in charge was one rank lower at superintendent. There were one or two fixed beat officers, all in the west of the town, and police officers patrolling on foot in the town centre were a total rarity, as had been the case on my return to Hove. Once more I was on "C" section!

I had to see the superintendent, of course, and was informed that the shift was suffering from a certain lack of leadership. Again, it seemed that supervisory officers were reluctant to venture out of the station.

I was to discover very quickly that the section had a nucleus of hardworking young constables, including four excellent thief-catchers. Two of these, PCs Sean Scott and Chris Carter, were nothing short of completely outstanding.

The problem was the Police and Criminal Evidence Act, as I had discovered during the trial at Hove, and the additional presence of the Crown Prosecution Service, which had spawned another police department—the Process Office. Coppers arresting offenders could say good-bye to the streets on arrival, as the most basic of offences involved completing sheaves of forms.

In addition, prisoners' rights were absolutely paramount, and all their needs had to be attended to promptly. The police canteen had virtually gone except for lunchtime, so that shift officers had to rely on bringing in sandwiches, or buying a takeaway on the way in for meal breaks.

Not so the prisoners. They had to be provided with hot, nourishing meals. These were fixed up by the canteen, except at weekends, when they would be collected from one of the hotels in the town. After a while of this, someone realised that it would be a whole lot cheaper to install a freezer and stock it up with frozen ready meals to be cooked up in a microwave oven in the custody area.

For an insight into how the balance of power had shifted into the defence camp, I give you two examples. The first did not occur in Worthing, but immediately affected it and every other police station in the country.

An offender was brought to a police station—not in Sussex. As is standard practice, he was asked at the time of his detention if he needed a solicitor to represent him. Yes, he would, and nominated his own brief, call him Mr. Smith.

Mr. Smith arranged to turn up at the police station at a given time to be present at his client's interview. They all sat down at the table, and the tape recorder was turned on. When it got to that part of the procedure where the prisoner was asked if he wanted legal representation, the prisoner was sitting at the table with Mr. Smith, his own chosen lawyer, alongside him, so the interviewing detective felt it was superfluous to ask him that question. When the case came to court, it was thrown out because the DC had not asked the question.

Another concerned a case I was in charge of. I had arrested a horrible little habitual thief called Bain for stealing something or other. He wanted a solicitor to be at the interview and did not have a preference, so he got the "duty brief."

Four of us duly sat down in the smallest interview room at the station—Bain, his solicitor, a young WPC on her learning curve, and me. As soon as the tape recorder was switched on and we'd gone through the procedure, yes, including asking him if he wanted legal representation (incidentally, he replied to that, "Who the f*** is this if he's not a lawyer?") and I was ready to start the questioning, Bain turned to his solicitor. "Give us a fag, would you?"

Now Worthing Police Station by now was a strictly "no smoking" environment, except in the cells, of course. As the solicitor went to his pocket, I said, "I'm sorry, you can't smoke in here."

The solicitor said, "And why not?"

I explained about the "no smoking" rule, and the lawyer replied, "He is entitled to have a cigarette."

I said, "If he wants a cigarette, he will have to return to his cell." I indicated the size of the room, which was no more than two metres square, without ventilation. "I for one do not wish to subject my lungs to secondhand smoke in this little room."

The solicitor then told me that if I denied his client a cigarette, this would amount to oppressive behaviour. I suspended the interview and asked the WPC to fetch the duty inspector for a decision. The inspector subsequently consulted with the superintendent, and the upshot was that I was instructed to let Bain have a cigarette.

I refused, on a point of principle, to continue the interview. The inspector had to sit in the smoke-filled room while I had an interview with the superintendent instead. Not a pleasant one, either. It culminated in my intimating my intention of referring the matter to the Police Federation and the burgeoning "Health and Safety" Department.

I was in court when Bain and his lawyer attempted to get the case thrown out on the grounds of oppressive behaviour and unreasonable delay to his interview. Happily, the senior magistrate had some choice words for Bain before telling him the case would continue. After unsuccessfully trying for an adjournment, Bain was convicted—all very minor stuff, but a pointer to how things had been going and would continue to go.

About this time, Littlehampton, just along the coast, had been suffering a series of late evening house burglaries, similar enough to have been committed by the same person or persons. Some senior officer decided to do something about it, and his solution was to form a temporary "burglary unit" based in the town. Someone remembered my surveillance experience, and I was asked to run it. I asked for, and got, two experienced detectives. I tried to get my two best thief-takers but could not have them. Instead I got a young, active PC who had gained a reputation for being inventive. We were given covert radios, similar to the Regional Crime Squad's, and set about taking a look at known house burglars resident in the town. To begin with, this meant observing them and looking for any possible pattern.

It was not long before we had a decent suspect, an old lag in his sixties. He was drawing a state pension and was not doing any other work. However, we observed that he was a daily visitor to one of Littlehampton's betting shops.

One of my DCs had a line to the manager, and we found that as well as being a regular customer, he was also a regular loser to the tune of a lot more than his pension every week. He had not been convicted for some years, but we found he had been released from prison just before the start of the burglary series. I set up surveillance on his address, and, sure enough, he emerged about 9:00 p.m. It was dark and we kept the follow loose, but he was totally unaware, taking no avoiding action.

After walking along several quiet streets, he saw a house that obviously appealed to him, being in darkness. He went over the garden wall, and we just surrounded the place and waited for him to emerge, having called a marked car to be handy. When he emerged, the uniformed crew stopped him and found him to be carrying a plastic bag full of jewellery and trinkets.

Within a week, we had solved Littlehampton's crime wave, and we returned to our normal duties. After several uneventful evenings, everyone knew we had the right man.

I had been at Worthing a few months when we had a change of superintendents. The new incumbent was Mike Bowron. He had only joined the police in 1980 and had had a dizzying rise through the ranks.

My initial reaction to the news that he was coming to Worthing was one of searing scepticism. The sergeant in charge of the Process Department, Bill Carcas, whom I'd known at Brighton, told me not to preconceive Mike Bowron, as he had been his tutor at Brighton when Mr. Bowron came back from Initial Training School.

I confess that only reinforced my preconceptions. I'd had too much of the masters of paperwork. I wanted a leader, not yet another administrator.

I was so wrong!

General impressions of Worthing were that was a sleepy coastal resort, inhabited by people who tended to be in their mellow autumnal years, and most of the time this was the reality, apart from the hard core of habitual minor criminals mentioned in my earlier chapter on the town.

In fact, on Friday and Saturday nights, it became a magnet for young people from miles around with its half-dozen or so nightclubs. It was Brighton on a smaller scale. Those were the days when pubs had to finish serving at 11:00 p.m. and be clear of customers by 11:30, unless they had an extension, which would be granted only in the event of a "special occasion."

Drinks in the pubs were generally a lot cheaper than those sold in the nightclubs, so the form for most of the punters was to get tanked up there before joining the queues at the clubs. Unsurprisingly it was not unusual for hundreds of intoxicated young men and women to be disgorged on the streets of the town in one sudden flood. Obviously, this was a catalyst for trouble, and on Friday and Saturday nights, Worthing used a similar system to that used in Brighton—six or so fit young officers in a minibus, with a sergeant in charge.

My first duty in "The Van," as it was known, was a very busy one, and soon I was left with only the driver, everyone else being in the police station with prisoners. I had to sweep up a couple of PCs who were working late on out-of-town beats to keep the unit on the road.

Four weeks later, I was back in charge of "The Van." Meantime, Mike Bowron had arrived as the new superintendent and turned up at our briefing at 10:00 p.m. He introduced himself before asking if he could come out with me in "The Van." He hastened to add that I was still in charge of the unit and he would be just one of the crew. He was just curious to see the town from our viewpoint as it happened and not from behind a Monday morning desk. He got off to a very good start in my eyes and those of the PCs.

Out on patrol we went then and had the usual "chucking-out time" calls. These were all settled by way of quiet words, and the streets quietened down again by 12:30 a.m., the usual time for the crew of "The Van" to come in for refreshments, able to go out again to oversee the emptying of the nightclubs from around 1:30 a.m. It was my experience that the doormen and stewards at the clubs were capable of handling anything up till that hour.

This night, though, we had a "shout" at about a quarter to one from one of the nightclubs, incidentally one of two that were only a couple of hundred yards from the police station. The call was that four people had been ejected from the club and were now causing problems out in the street.

We duly rolled up to be confronted by four shapely women in their twenties, all attired in almost identical black mini-dresses and high heels and not a lot else. That was problem number one—we had no female officer on duty. Problem two was that they were aggressively drunk and trying to force their way back into the nightclub, screaming foul abuse at the doormen.

I got out of the van with three or four of the crew and asked the women to be on their way peacefully. It was my turn to be subjected to the abuse. Now the last thing you need is to get involved in a wrestling match trying to subdue and arrest drunks. The problem magnifies a thousand times when the drunks are skimpily clad and, yes, quite good-looking young women.

I was trying to arrange a way of taking these women in one by one when Mike Bowron stepped from The Van. Now Mike was a slim young man and a very good-looking one at that. Dressed in his superintendent's uniform with all the braid, he looked a winner.

The four women stopped and gazed at him. The self-appointed leader said, "Here! Who's he?"

One of her companions said, "Cor, he's a bit of all right! Who are you, mate?"

Mike did not stop to draw breath, but swept his arm towards The Van. "If you'd all like to step into my vehicle, I'll tell you."

The four, whom we later christened "The Wicked Witches of the North, South, East and West" obediently got on board. Mike told them they were all under arrest for causing a breach of the peace.

They were detained until sober and then released without charge after a few words of advice were given, gratis.

Superintendent Bowron grew hugely in my estimation after that. He grew even further later. The reason will be revealed in Chapter 20.

As can be the way with rising stars in any occupation, he did not stay long at Worthing. Soon after my retirement, he moved to Kent as an assistant chief constable. He is now the commissioner of police for the City of London, approaching his own retirement now, I believe.

I had only a few months left of my service when I was asked to run the "Minor Crimes Unit." This was a small team of one DC, two PCs, and me, and the idea was to take the weight off CID by dealing with and processing lesser matters like shoplifting, thefts of and from vehicles, and the like. It all worked very well, and I remember no problems with the Process Office. All files went through me and were generally very simple matters that would be dealt with frequently by way of a caution.

The one matter that sticks in my memory is the case of the elderly German lady, living on her own in Lancing, who was a compulsive kleptomaniac. Her speciality was in stealing soft toys and the like from charity shops. She would hoard these in her little bungalow until she had enough to set up a stall at a local "car boot" sale on the Adur Recreation Ground in Shoreham. On two occasions very close together, she was arrested outside charity shops, being processed, cautioned, and released. On the third occasion, I went to her bungalow and searched it, finding a room stacked floor to ceiling with filched soft toys and models plus a number of aluminium flower holders that she had stolen from graveyards. This time she was charged, put before a court, and duly handed over to Social Services for psychiatric treatment.

About this time, I had the germ of an idea. I had over twenty-seven years of experience in "the job," nearly all of it on the front line. At fifty-five years of age, I could retire with a lump sum, known as "commutation" and a pension, or could carry on in my rank one year at a time, with annual extensions decided on by HQ. Carrying on meant I would still be paid at the same rate and would have the same deductions, including pension contributions. This meant that there were a couple of snags to carrying on. One was that I should be working effectively for half pay. I would not be receiving my pension and, to me more importantly, although I would still be paying superannuation contributions at a whacking 12 percent, my pension, when I received it, would not increase by a single penny a month. Finally, not having received my lump sum, I should not be able to pay my mortgage off, and interest on that was then around 13.5 percent and I should not have the balance to invest.

Why, though, should all my experience not be put to the use of the service, ergo, the community at large? Yes, there were plenty of opportunities to work as a civilian for the job, but these were all admin type positions, where I should not be able to use much of my frontline knowledge.

I prepared a report along these lines.

---

I would retire as normal on December 28, 1993 and would collect my commutation—my lump sum.

My police pension would commence on December 29, 1993.

On Monday, January 3, 1994, I would resume as a uniformed police constable.

I would be paid at the rate of a constable with twenty-two years' service.

I would be self-employed on an annual contract and therefore responsible for paying my own income tax and National Health contribution.

I would waive rent allowance, but take three weeks' paid leave during the course of the year's contract.

My duties would follow a twenty-eight-day cycle with eight of these days taken as rest days and one as an additional rest day.

I would undertake to spread my duties between 7:00 a.m. and 2:00 a.m., with the following as a suggestion for the first month. In the event of special occasions requiring additional policing, these duties might be varied.

Week 1

| | |
|---|---|
| Mon | 0700–1500 |
| Tue | 0900–1700 |
| Wed | 1000–1800 |
| Thu | 1000–1800 |
| Fri | 1800–0200 |
| Sat | 1800–0200 |
| Sun | 1100–1900 |

Week 2

| | |
|---|---|
| Mon | Rest day |
| Tue | Rest day |

| Wed | 1000–1800 |
|-----|-----------|
| Thu | 1000–1800 |
| Fri | 1600–0001 |
| Sat | 1800–0200 |
| Sun | 1100–1900 |

**Week 3**

| Mon | 1200–2000 |
|-----|-----------|
| Tue | 0700–1500 |
| Wed | Rest day |
| Thu | Rest day |
| Fri | 1800–0200 |
| Sat | 1800–0200 |
| Sun | 1100–1900 |

**Week 4**

| Mon | 0700–1500 |
|-----|-----------|
| Tue | 0900–1700 |
| Wed | 1400–2200 |
| Thu | 1000–1800 |
| Fri | Rest day |
| Sat | Rest day |
| Sun | Rest day |

In the four-week cycle:

| | |
|---|---|
| 0700–1500 | 3 days |
| 0900–1700 | 2 days |
| 1000–1800 | 5 days |
| 1100–1900 | 3 days |
| 1200–2000 | 1 day |
| 1400–2200 | 1 day |
| 1600–0001 | 1 day |
| 1800–0200 | 5 days |

This spread allowed opportunities for the service of process, statement taking, and other inquiries. Duty Sundays, being taken as 1100 to 1900, especially offer this facility. On Fridays and Saturdays, I would be available for the different, more direct kind of policing required.

A monthly additional rest day could be taken on the Monday of week 5 (at the beginning of the second twenty-eight-day cycle) so that in weeks 9, 13, 17, and so on Monday is an ARD. (The ARD, taken once per month, adjusts the duty cycle so that in a four-week period a total of 160 hours is worked, making a forty-hour week.)

I should work on the town centre "1 beat." As far as I can ascertain, this beat is rarely covered by a foot patrol. It contains the town's main shopping streets and a large number of licensed premises (bars), as well as some quite dense housing areas, the Pier and Lido, a few nightclubs, and a length of seafront.

It is central to this idea that I should not be taken off it to cover duties such as escorts, court jailer, or duties pertaining to persons in custody, unless I am responsible for their being there.

I should carry out all tasks expected of a uniformed beat constable, including service of process, execution of warrants, taking of statements, attendance at incidents including road traffic accidents, regular visits to licensed premises, gathering of intelligence, and so on.

I have made some inquiries at the Inland Revenue, Station Approach, and I can be given a small, secure room close to the main door, where I could write reports, have items including process, inquiries, and charged radio batteries delivered, and take my refreshment breaks. I need never come to the police station except with a prisoner or on another urgent operational matter connected with my beat. The contract would be subject to review prior to being renewed and should be renewed only with the approval of both parties to it, the Sussex Police and myself.

As this was a new concept, I first showed it to the Police Federation— the nearest there is to a trade union in the police. I half-expected it to come back with, at a minimum, a lot of hemming and hawing, but was pleasantly surprised when it was received with enthusiasm. Mike Bowron submitted it to HQ with a strong recommendation in favour of the year's trial run.

A few weeks later, when I was sitting in on the 2–10 shift briefing, I was surprised when an assistant chief constable turned up.

I sat in on shift briefings when I had information to convey. This briefing turned into an embarrassment for one of the PCs, Dick Lancashire, who had had a struggle arresting an offender the previous day. This offender had been bailed from Magistrates' Court, and I warned the shift that (1) he was violent and (2) he had tried to make a complaint against Dick that he had indecently assaulted him during the arrest. I passed it over to Dick to tell the story. Dick related the offence and the fact that the offender had resisted arrest before coming out with the timeless sentence, "He was a right handful!" Even the ACC dissolved in laughter.

The ACC asked me to stay behind after the briefing, as he wanted a word. "About your report to retire and stay on, it has been considered at the highest level, and I'm afraid we have to reject it as you have put too many conditions on it."

"What conditions were these, sir?" I asked.

"All this stuff about not being called into the police station for escorts and court jailer and all that. We have to make best use of our assets."

"That's what I was hoping to achieve, sir. Without blowing my trumpet too loudly, I would have thought that with my experience I'd be an asset best left out on the beat. That's what everyone who is anyone seems to want—uniformed bobbies seen on the beat."

"The decision has been made, Allan, and that's the end of it." Well, at least he'd called me Allan! Mind you he had been a uniformed inspector at Brighton when I arrived there in 1977.

Sadly, that was that. I heard some time later, that another force was trying the idea out, their Federation branch having heard about my idea from mine. You can imagine my disbelief and extreme sadness when I found out, shortly after my retirement, how the Sussex Force corrupted my idea and my offer.

A certain chief superintendent, under whom I had never served, so obviously cannot comment on his methods or performance, retired shortly after I did. He was given his commutation lump sum (considerably more than mine had been owing to his vastly more senior rank), and placed on pension (ditto).

He was immediately taken back on in the rank of police constable and instantly promoted back to chief superintendent on full pay. Prudence and the threat of high blood pressure precluded me from trying to contact the Sussex Police Authority to inquire just how much this little maneuvre was costing the taxpayer. I would also have liked to point out how little, in comparison, my offer would have cost and how much more local efficiency it would have achieved, not to mention how my idea could have been a winner in the hands of the Public Relations Office. In addition, this little move must have caused considerable chagrin among serving senior officers of the ranks of chief inspector to superintendent, whose promotion paths had been effectively blocked.

In these days of economists and accountants quantifying every aspect of life in financial terms, how much hard cash had Sussex Police tossed aside when you try to put a value on twenty-seven and a half years of sheer experience?

"Allan, old son, you are out of it now. Stay out of it," said my little inner voice.

Time for yet another "leaving do," then.

# CHAPTER 20

## An Annus Horribilis: When It All Went Horribly Wrong

I had a few weeks to prepare for my final "leaving do," as I had been saving up all overtime worked to be taken as "time off," and it had been adding up. It enabled me to catch up with maintenance around the house and garden and to sniff the air with regard to what I was going to do with my future.

The "do" took place in the now sadly defunct Social Club at Worthing Police Station. My last inspector, Stuart Harrison, organised and ran it and his father, my former DI, Gordon, came along. There were also gratifying numbers of people from former units that I'd worked in.

I had brought Sandra and the girls along and felt very proud that they could hear in speeches made that it looked as though I had achieved what I had set out to achieve—the respect of my peers, far more important to me than rank or financial reward.

Stuart Harrison had managed to smuggle my personal record out of HQ personnel, and everyone got a few laughs at my mug shots.

As I mentioned earlier, I sneaked a peep at the record and saw that despite what Force Orders said at the time of the Grand Hotel business, I had not had my two commendations officially recorded.

I suppose that's what you get for calling the chief constable a four-letter word, but the fact only reinforced in my mind that I had been right to do so. Someone up in the Ivory Tower had exhibited some cheap mean-mindedness, and I already indicated where the buck stopped.

For the first time, I also saw the letter written to the Sussex chief constable by the chief supt. in South Wales regarding the job in Penarth, outlined in Chapter 15.

Stuart presented Sandra, Jo, and Hannah with lovely bouquets, and I confess that when the time came to give my speech, I just filled up and was probably incomprehensible. Or maybe I was just drunk!

It was a proud finish to the year. It had not started out that way.

In December 1992, The Queen, in her Christmas speech, referred to 1992 as her "annus horribilis." 1993 was ours.

In retrospect it had all begun to go wrong in the summer of 1990. Jo joined the Royal Air Force with the intention of becoming a dog handler. While in her initial training at Swinderby in Lincolnshire, she began to suffer severe headaches and what were diagnosed as migraines, and she was released by the RAF on medical grounds.

It started to get worse in October 1992 when Sandra and I took Jo for a holiday to New England, to see the "fall colours," and to Canada to visit my aunt, her sons, and their families. It was while we were in Montreal that the monster she was to fight for the rest of her young life first showed its hand in earnest. Jo began to develop not only headaches, but also serious twitching around her face and mouth. She found frequently that she was unable to swallow food.

On our return to Southwick, she saw her GP, who referred her on to a neurologist. He, in turn, arranged for her to go into Hurstwood Park Neurological Unit at Hayward's Heath in January 1993. Jo had a brain tumour, and it was not known at that stage whether it was benign or malignant, serious or lethal.

We took Jo to Hayward's Heath at the beginning of February for x-rays and examination. A day or so later, we were contacted and asked to bring her in for emergency surgery on Wednesday, February 10.

The neurologist, Mr. Ward, took Sandra and me to one side, explained the seriousness of the operation, and, I can see in hindsight, prepared us for the possibility that Jo might not survive it. Owing to the location of the tumour, another possibility was that she might survive but be paralysed.

Sandra and I stayed at the hospital until Mr. Ward came out and advised us to go home for the night, as he would not be able to give any useful information until the morning. We arranged to return to the hospital at 11:00 a.m. next day. We would be informed by phone of any change.

I have no recollection of the drive home that day.

The next morning, I rang the hospital and was informed that there was no change, but we were more than welcome to come in.

Before we got there, Jo had emerged from deep unconsciousness, and we were able to see her. She was all wired and tubed up and could not communicate other than by touch. Her head had been partially shaved, and she had a hideous crescent-shaped wound at the side of her skull. Occasionally she would tremble and go into a fit. Each of these seizures was frightening, but the first was the worst, until the ward sister explained that these were a reaction to the probing in her brain and they would die off gradually.

Mr. Ward took Sandra and me aside, and the bombshell followed. The tumour was inoperable. He explained that it was what is known as an astrocytoma, so-called because it was roughly star-shaped and the points of the star penetrated into the depths of Jo's brain. Her only hope was in radiation and chemotherapy, neither of which was going to be much fun for her. In addition, he told us kindly, it could be all in vain. He said the best possible scenario was that Jo might live for three more years. That said, he told us, Jo was going to get their very best shot.

That evening I started a diary to write my feelings down. This is what I wrote that first day before my emotions overwhelmed me.

Lying there so pale, almost yellow, a baby again with wires and tubes leading off to the most modern of life-supporting gadgets.

Your blood pressure constantly monitored along with your pulse, respiration, fluid, food and drug intake.

Remembering how, as a baby in the hospital at Bishop's Stortford, all those yesterdays ago I could soothe your distress by stroking your tiny forearm with the tip of my finger. I tried it again when the pressure on your tortured brain took you over the edge into a fit, and it still works, my darling.

The next days were a blur. This is an excerpt from what I wrote the following evening.

I know she is terrified of what is happening to her and what is going to happen in what is left of her future and she is looking to me— Dad—to make it better.

But this time I can't make it better. Oh, Darling, I wish it were just a skinned knee, a sprained ankle, a broken leg, a fractured skull. I only wish I could change places. It would be a very good bargain indeed for me, because at nearly fifty-five years of age I have had a much better innings than lots of people half as old again.

I was due back at work after rest days, but Mike Bowron gave me open-ended compassionate leave. That was all by the by, as I was required as a witness at Magistrates' Court on the following Wednesday. I was informed I could not be excused. I still wonder just what it takes for PC or Sergeant Plod to be excused from a court attendance. Once again I swanned around in the court waiting room, and in the end the lawyers did a deal and I was not required after all. As I was expected in court again the next day, I decided it would be as well to get back to work, as we were told we should be able to take Jo home on Saturday, February 20.

That morning an official-looking letter had arrived from the "Adur District Council." It was addressed to Jo, but in the circumstances I opened it. It was a demand for an amount of money allegedly owed by Jo in respect of what is now universally remembered and detested as the "poll tax." It was in the form of a "final demand" and stated that in the event of the money not being paid within a very few days, steps would be taken physically to recover it.

Now I was aware that Jo had disputed her poll tax bill as, during the year in question, she had moved out for six months to live with a friend in Portslade, in the adjoining council area, while her friend's mother took a temporary job abroad. As far as I was aware, Jo had settled this, and had paid Hove Borough Council for the six months in question. The tax was payable to the local authority in whose area the taxable person resided.

As she was not in a position to discuss the matter, I telephoned Adur Council first thing on Monday morning. I was put through to the "recovery officer." I informed her that Jo would not be able to do anything about this demand as she had just undergone a serious operation. Could the business of her alleged outstanding tax please be put on hold until she had recovered enough to be able to deal with it?

The reply was, "That's not my problem. Either she pays the money or we enforce collection of the debt."

"How do you intend to enforce the collection?"

"We get a court order, and the bailiffs will call and collect goods to the relevant value, plus costs," she replied.

"I don't think you understand me. My daughter underwent a very serious but unsuccessful operation for the removal of a brain tumour less than two weeks ago," I informed her. "Please postpone this until she can do something about it."

"As I said, it's not my problem. Either she pays in the next few days or we take action to recover the debt."

I hung up without a word, but dashed a letter off to the finance officer of the council, whose name was Clapp. In it I reiterated that Jo had undergone serious brain surgery and that her survival was not guaranteed. I protested the inhumane attitude adopted by his employee in the recovery office and suggested that maybe she was having a bad day. Again I asked that the matter of the money allegedly owed by Jo might be left in hand until Jo could sort it out, after her hoped-for recovery. I delivered this by hand to the council office.

I got a reply from Mr. Clapp within two days, making no apology for his employee's attitude but stating that it was the council's duty as laid down by the government to collect any outstanding money, and steps would be taken to effect collection as stated.

After a sharp exchange of letters, which got me absolutely nowhere, I wrote out a cheque for the amount in question (£258.99) and a second cheque for £25. I wrote another letter stating simply that the demanded money was enclosed plus an extra £25 to cover the administrative costs the council had no doubt incurred.

I received no acknowledgement, but the full amount was taken from my bank account including the extra £25. Regrettably, in my rage, I ripped the council leader's letter up. I wish now that I had kept it as a monument to bureaucratic inhumanity. I have to add at this point that every dealing I have ever had with Adur District Council and its successor has left me feeling royally ripped off.

The day before that, I had rung a national cancer charity, having been told that they would offer help and support. The male person I spoke to told me they had enough on their plate and did not want to know. I am not making that up. Needless to say, I have never donated a penny to that charity since and always switch the TV sound off when any of their begging ads come on.

Jo's therapy got under way when her wound had healed enough, and life became a whirl of getting her to hospital for appointments. I had to return to work, and Sandra did most of the taxi work.

As part of her treatment, Jo had been put on steroids and her weight ballooned. She had rightly been proud of her lissome figure, and we had to work a bit at preventing her becoming more depressed at her physical change. Additionally, her lovely long honey-blonde hair all fell out and we bought her a wig, which she never wore as she said it made her look like a tart! She much preferred to show her baldness or cover it with a hat or a headscarf.

June brought a welcome break in the doom and gloom. During the summer of 1992, Jo and her great friend Nikki, through a brilliant piece of observation and initiative, had been instrumental in helping the Metropolitan Police to solve a serious lorry hijack and recover property stolen during it. For this, on June 23, 1993, she and Nikki received Sussex Police "Three Nines" awards from the lord lieutenant and chief constable.

By then Mr. Birch had collected his routine knighthood. I don't know if he remembered anything, but he did not come near me, so that there was no unpleasantness to mar a very proud occasion. The photograph of the presentation is on my sitting room wall by the door. It is the first and last thing I see entering and leaving the room.

At the police station one day, Mike Bowron called me into his office. His fiancée, Karen—a WPC at Worthing—was also there. Karen was quite the equestrian, as was Jo, so they had hit it off when they met at the Police Club one evening. Mike wanted an update on Jo's progress and listened carefully. He then told me he had been in touch with the Force Welfare Office and told me that they would give me up to £1,000 so that I could take the family on holiday. This was wonderful news. I went home and sifted through my finances and discovered that I could probably double that thousand. We had a family conference, and everyone was in agreement with Jo's suggestion that we go to the American Wild West. When I told Mike Bowron, he suggested I go to Panorama Travel in Hove and see what deals they would do. It had been the same company that provided the raffle prize that I had won back in 1986—the holiday in Portugal.

That August the four of us flew to St. Louis, where we caught an onward flight to Phoenix. Panorama arranged all the flights, car hire, and the first two nights at a very generous discount.

On the day of our outward trip, there were enormous electrical storms the length of US Midwest, and all east-west and west-east flights were disrupted. When we finally got away from St. Louis, there were only seven passengers on the plane—the four Neils and three girls from Chicago, air stewardesses making their way to Las Vegas "on vacation." The flight path took us around the fringe of the storm into Mexico and out again, and the view from the windows of the plane of the electrical pyrotechnics ten thousand feet below was quite unforgettable.

Panorama had booked us in for the first two nights at La Quinta Hotel on the northern side of Phoenix, and the hire car was waiting. I shall never forget the sensation of walking out of the air-conditioned Sky Harbor Airport into the car park, where, even as late as 10:30 p.m., the temperature was in the nineties Fahrenheit!

Like most cities in the United States, Phoenix is well served by first-class roads. With the hotel being just off Interstate 17, a straight follow on from Route 60, alongside which was the airport, we were at the hotel in just a few minutes, having been kindly supplied a map by the Avis girl.

The girls excitedly called out the exotic names of the intersections on the way: "Indian School," "Camelback," "Bethany Home," "Glendale," "Northern," "Dunlap," "Peoria," "Cactus," and "Thunderbird," before the intersection for the hotel, "Greenway." The night staff was ready for us, having been alerted by the girl at the Avis car hire desk.

The hotel was perfect for us. It provided a continental breakfast with, of course, unlimited coffee and juice, it had a lovely swimming pool and outdoor Jacuzzi, both of which we made good use of, as they were mostly ignored by other guests, who seemed to be mainly commercials. In its location just off the interstate freeway, it is ideal as a base for exploring the area. The next day, after a swim, we set off to explore the mountains to the south of Phoenix and the Citrus Hills. It was all so new to us—the desert heat and dryness and the unfamiliar cacti and other flora.

The next day, we explored the Apache Trail, and the girls panned for (and found) tiny grains of gold in an abandoned gold mining settlement, which was all done up as a Wild West town, complete with saloon and jailhouse!

For the rest of the holiday, we travelled all over the region. We stayed in places like Las Vegas and Mesquite in Nevada, Flagstaff, Prescott, Williams (on Route 66), and Holbrook in Arizona, and Gallup in New Mexico.

Marble Canyon, where the accommodation was 100 percent run by Navajo Native Americans, was unforgettable. Apart from Las Vegas, we stayed at motels, all at least very good standard and some quite excellent. We saw the wonderful Grand Canyon from both rims, and had many, many superb experiences.

We explored the Navajo Nation, which is a semi-autonomous land area of 26,000 square miles (67,339 square kilometres, 17 million acres), occupying all of northeastern Arizona, the southeastern portion of Utah, and northwestern New Mexico. It is the largest land area assigned primarily to a Native American jurisdiction within the United States.

Maybe I should write another book about that fortnight. There is so much I could say about it and so much we crammed into those two weeks.

I will mention one strange quirk of the American psyche. In Las Vegas, we visited one of its many huge casinos. The girls went to one of the employees whose job it was to circulate around, keeping the punters well supplied with change and gambling chips. Jo cashed ten dollars into quarters with which to play the one-armed bandits. The girl asked Hannah how old she was, and Hannah was disgusted to discover that she had to be twenty-one years old to play the machines. This disgust was not assuaged by the fact that the next day we stopped off in Mesquite, Nevada. While the other two got sorted out, Hannah and I took a stroll down the main street, which was like somewhere out of a Wild West movie, right down to the tumbleweed rolling down the road! We found a hardware store and decided to look inside for a souvenir. One entire wall of the store was covered with a comprehensive display of firearms, from little revolvers like the sort Wild West heroines kept in their garters, right up to hunting rifles and semi-automatic weapons.

Hannah stood open-mouthed, staring at the display. The storeman came over. "You interested in buying yourself somp'n, ma'am?"

"What, you mean guns?" asked Hannah. "I'm only nineteen years old."

"You got proof o' that, ma'am?"

"Well, yes. I've got my passport here."

"Take yore pick, ma'am. You's old 'nough!"

"But they wouldn't let me play the machines in the casino!" exclaimed Hannah.

"Oh, no, ma'am. You's too young for that kinda stuff, but you ain't too young to defend yusself."

We'd booked the last night back at La Quinta, and after a leisurely breakfast and swim, it was time to drive back to the airport and say a fond farewell to the Wild West and the best period by far in a trying year.

* * *

Before our holiday, Hannah had got herself a boyfriend and decided to move to Carlisle to be with him. Neither Sandra nor I wanted this to happen, but it was not the best time in the world to argue, and we let her go with our blessing, although the young man was not to our taste. After all, she was nineteen years old, an age when I had been expected to die for my country if required to, and Jo needed all our attention and assistance.

It was not to be a long-lasting arrangement, as it transpired, and in September I drove to Carlisle to collect her and bring her home. She had begun to show symptoms of petit mal epilepsy, and medication was necessary. This was an obvious factor in Hannah's decision. At Carlisle I decided to drive another one hundred miles north and visit my mother and sisters, to put them in the picture about Jo. It was while I was there I discovered that my younger sister, Janette, had been diagnosed with breast cancer.

The mood in Mum's little house was understandably bleak, and I decided to take Hannah for a long walk in the Pentland Hills, where she had last been as an eight-year-old. We actually walked all the way through the hills to the little town of Balerno, where Janette's husband, Brian, met us with my mother, his daughter Angela, and his new grandson, Jamie. I have a photograph somewhere of the four generations together, but the most beneficial thing about the day was the walk through the hills in the autumn sunshine. Apart from

Arizona, it was the first day I had felt anything like at ease for nearly a year.

The feeling was not to last. Shortly after arriving back in Southwick, Sandra went out shopping. Jo was with her friend Nikki two doors away. Hannah was reading in the dining room, and I was upstairs on my word processor. In the dining room, we had a portable gas fire on castors and Hannah had turned it on, complaining about being cold.

I heard nothing until Sandra arrived home and started to scream my name. I dived downstairs. Hannah had experienced her first grand-mal epileptic fit, and had apparently catapulted herself out of her chair into the fire.

These fires automatically switch off if they are upended, but Hannah had knocked it into the sideboard, where it adopted a 45-degree angle but did not turn off. Hannah's face and hands were in the flames. Mercifully, she was still out of it, although the violence of the fit had subsided. We applied emergency first aid by the use of towels soaked in cold water, and I called an ambulance.

Hannah was taken to the A & E at Worthing Hospital. Sandra went in the ambulance, and I followed as soon as I felt safe driving, having ensured that Jo stayed with Nikki. I could not tell anyone how long we stayed, but eventually we had to get back for Jo.

The next morning we returned to the hospital. Hannah had been put in a ward, and I did not recognise her when we visited. Her hair had burned off the front of her head, which had swelled up to nearly twice its size. Her eyes were closed, and my first dread was that she had been blinded. Her hands were bandaged.

Amazingly, she was cheerful and philosophical, and I remember thinking that among all the negatives of the year so far, Hannah's attitude gave me some hope. Within twenty-four hours, Hannah was transferred to the Queen Victoria Hospital in East Grinstead, where they have a world-class "burns unit." This had achieved universal fame during WWII, due to the work of Sir Archibald McIndoe in treating the serious burns suffered by many, especially aircrews who had been shot down in flames. For more information, put "Guinea Pig Club" into Google.

The burns unit at the hospital is named for Professor McIndoe and is a beautifully appointed, self-contained concern within what looks, from the outside, a pretty rundown, unattractive set of buildings. Hannah underwent reconstructive surgery to her face, especially her eyebrows.

Her eyelids had also been burned, but if they had been open at the time of her fit, she would undoubtedly have been blinded. Her hands needed treatment too, and she spent about two weeks there.

At the same time, Jo had to be taken for visits to the Royal Sussex Hospital in East Brighton and the neurological unit at Hayward's Heath.

My finances had, of course, taken a bit of a kicking on our once-in-a-lifetime trip to the Wild West, and during this period, petrol prices rose by 15 percent. I tried to find out if there was any relief that the government could offer to offset the cost of these visits. As usual I could not work my way through the bureaucratic quagmire.

I had walked for the last time out of the police station as a serving officer during the week of Hannah's disaster, owing to having saved up all my considerable overtime as time to be had off.

The "leaving do" mentioned at the start of this chapter was the last time I ever went in the station again, and I visited headquarters only to go through the final ceremony of saying "good-bye" to the chief constable.

There was a new incumbent, Mr. Paul Whitehouse, Sir Roger Birch having retired a couple of months earlier. I should not have gone for the "ceremony" if he had still been chief.

Very sadly, Mr. Whitehouse was made to retire in 2001, having carried the can for the erroneous shooting of an unarmed man some years earlier. While I understand that national politics were involved in the matter, and I had long gone anyway, it looked as though the buck had stopped at the end of the line.

Farewell to 'The Job'. December 1993 with Chief Constable Paul
Whitehouse, a really good guy who later took the rap for others'
stupidity. For once The Buck really did stop there.

This was in marked contrast to the events after the Grand Hotel
bombing, when I have never been able to shake off the feeling that I
am still held to be to responsible for it. I have been proved in the clear
over and over again, but time and again over the years I have been
treated as no better than a leper when the subject is raised publicly.

# CHAPTER 21

## Life Begins Again:
## Learning to Live in "Civvy Street"

It was not completely a tearful good-bye to the job. I had loved working with some of the best people in the country and had personally never lost the motivation to catch thieves and other criminals. However, the balance between the enforcement and administration of the law had, particularly since the introduction of the Police and Criminal Evidence Act, been shifting inexorably from the former to the latter.

I was very disappointed by the force's response to my offer to work on in the rank of constable. That had been exacerbated by the force's decision to apply a corruption of my suggestion with regard to a retired chief superintendent.

Instead, I went to the local job centre to register as unemployed. It was there that I encountered another little quirk in the law.

Having reached the age of fifty-five years, I discovered that I was barred from claiming unemployment benefit. It was not a big problem to me. While not in the same league as politicians' pensions, the police sergeant's pension was enough to live on, particularly with the weight of a mortgage removed.

What did give me pause, however, was when I realised this: take a twenty-two-year-old who joined the same day as I did, maybe straight from university. He served the same time as I had and retired the same day in the same rank as I held. Now he would have been treated somewhat differently.

Having reached the age of fifty, he could commence to receive the same pension as mine. He would also have the same lump sum. However, he could claim and receive unemployment benefit for the next five years. Given that such a person would have paid in to National Insurance for twenty-seven and a half years, and I had for forty years, I considered this a flagrant injustice.

It also gave me a little insight into governmental unemployment statistics. I noticed that the phrase used in the announcement of these figures had changed at some time from "the number unemployed is 2.2 million" to "the number unemployed *and claiming benefit* is 2.2 million."

The government of the day had come to power claiming "Labour isn't working." That was in 1978, with a national unemployment figure of half a million.

I found myself wondering what, had the 1993 rules applied in 1978, Labour's unemployment figures would have been. Conversely I had a shrewd idea what the 1993 figures would have been had the 1978 rules applied. What was that about lies and damned lies . . . ?

Enough of whingeing! I was fifty-five years of age, physically fit and fairly well balanced mentally. I was playing squash regularly and refereeing two rugby matches a week, sometimes more. I was capable of working on for many years, making a few extra quid to pay for life's little luxuries. I could also contribute a bit more to the national economy by way of extra income tax and additional spending power.

I would also be making life a bit better for the unproductive—and I don't just mean the unemployed!

I inquired of the staff at the job centre about available work. The clerk asked a few questions, glanced at my CV, and directed me to the executive section.

There I made the contact that led me to discover that the villains I had been dealing with in the job were all fairly obviously crooks. This was not to be so anymore.

I was given an introduction to a company involved in consultancy in crime prevention. They also provided stuff like burglar alarms, so that you went along to talk about making your home safer against burglars and ended up recommending kit on which you copped a backhander by way of commission.

I was less than comfortable with this, especially when I found that the kit I was expected to recommend was a long way inferior to some of the other products on the market. I also uncovered some shady dealings—legal of course—between my new boss and companies in the tax haven Channel Islands. I got out at a personal cost of about £3,500—giving clients their money back, which I considered as a fair fine for my unwariness.

What to do now, then, I wondered.

Prior to my retirement coming up, I had attended a week's seminar at police HQ giving pointers on how best to handle retirement from the job. One thing that stuck in my mind was a talk from a doctor specialising in dealing with recently retired professionals. It was his assertion that people who retire from high-pressure jobs and just put their feet up and relax tended not to live for very long. Apparently the stress has to be reduced very gently.

Okay, assuming that my police career had been fairly high-stress, what should I do? I considered the options that were open to me, given my experience and qualifications.

"Got it," I thought. "I'll become a driving instructor." As they are today, the papers were full of advertisements lauding the freedom and earning potential afforded by working as a driving instructor. Best of all, in my opinion, was that I could choose my own working hours to suit my family needs.

I signed up with "the Instructor College," whose setup was at the old Croydon Airport, quite handy for Southwick. Their course was very comprehensive and impressive, and I duly took it up. I paid for it myself. I could not get government help with retraining. Guess why? I was not in receipt of unemployment benefits! So, had the notional fifty-year-old who retired the same day as I and got the same lump sum and pension decided to pursue a new career, he would have qualified for government assistance with his retraining. Isn't life a bummer?

In order to become an approved driving instructor, or ADI, a candidate had to pass three examinations.

The first of these was a theory test, where the candidate had to achieve a high mark—a minimum of 85 percent on any part but an average of 90 percent—as I remember, on three tests, including disability matters.

The second was a straightforward driving test, along the same lines as the driving test for learner drivers, but marked much more strictly, and the third was a test of one's ability to teach.

I sailed through the first test and set out to do the second. I took that at Eastbourne, the examiner being one Roger Thompson. I faithfully applied all the rules of safe police driving. At the end of the test, Mr. Thompson said, "You're an ex-policeman, aren't you?"

"Yes," said I.

"I thought so. You've failed." He went on to explain that I must drive to the same standard that the driving standards agency applied to learner drivers taking their test. That did not include straightening out bends, even when the road ahead was palpably clear, nor did it include whizzing through roundabouts without signalling, even if there was nobody to signal to. Mr. Thompson had been an instructor at the Met Police Driving School at Hendon, so had recognised the police "system"!

Chastened, I reapplied for the test and passed next time out, a few quid poorer.

In the meantime, I took a job as a taxi driver in Lancing, in order to practice driving using someone else's petrol. I must have been the only cabby in the country that never double-parked, U-turned in the wrong place, or sat on double yellow lines waiting for a fare.

One amusing interlude was when my cab was pulled over in Worthing by one of my former PCs, and I ended up signing his pocket book as "Satin 4," my taxi call sign!

The test of teaching ability was not as difficult, provided one stuck to the theory of making the pupil provide the answers rather than telling him, and I duly became an approved driving instructor.

I worked for six months with the British School of Motoring, BSM, a move I can recommend to anyone, as you very quickly learn all the admin of being a self-employed instructor, including how to deal with Driving Standards Agency bureaucracy.

In the summer of 1995, I left BSM. I had eleven pupils on my books and gave each a letter with a copy to BSM, telling them that it was their decision whether to stay with BSM or come with me when I got started on my own account. Ten opted to stay with me. I ordered a brand new Peugeot 205 diesel and asked the dealer to fit dual controls and have it signwritten on delivery.

Sandra and I then flew off to Florida, taking Hannah for a late birthday treat in the same way as we had taken Jo back in 1992. As in Phoenix, we stayed at La Quinta hotels in two locations, starting off in Orlando so Hannah could take in Universal Studios and other attractions. We stayed with the same chain at Daytona Beach. As before, I was very impressed with them.

On my return, I collected my new car, very professionally signwritten in gold on dark blue, "ALLAN NEIL DRIVING TUITION" with my telephone number, and I was away.

At home, Jo seemed to be doing well in her fight with her cancer, and the Florida interlude had done wonders for Hannah, who was making great strides with her own recuperation and had met the young man who was to become the father of my wonderful grandchildren, Neil.

Was life looking up? Definitely!

# CHAPTER 22

## The Driving Instructor: "Keeping Death Off the Roads"

As well as the ten pupils who had come with me from BSM, I found that I had picked up an eleventh—the brother of a friend of Sandra's sister. Most pupils wanted one hour a week, but about a third liked to do two hours, so I was starting away with about fifteen hours' tuition per week. This was already above my break-even figure of 12.8 hours per week, covering car finance, insurance, fuel, and servicing.

One of my pupils, Clarissa by name, was a boarding pupil at Roedean, the famous girls' school on the eastern edge of Brighton, and I had not seen her since the school broke up for the summer. She had been able to have some practice on her parents' cars, and I felt that she would be ready to take her driving test after perhaps six more lessons.

It is not always easy to judge when a pupil is test-ready, particularly as you have to book five or six weeks ahead. Pupils could go off the boil in that time, and I found that if you present a candidate for a test and he or she fails badly, the examiner makes a note of it. If you make a habit of it, it soon gets back to the chief examiner, in my case, the same Roger Thompson who had failed me on the driving part of my qualifying exams. When that happens, an instructor could find himself with Mr. Thompson in the backseat during a lesson, checking on the quality of his teaching, and dispensing some pointed advice afterwards, even, in the worst case possible, taking his instructor's ticket away.

Thankfully, that never happened to me, although I had the pleasure of Mr. Thompson in the back twice, as part of a scheduled programme of check testing.

I did have one unfortunate test blip. I had been teaching an Indian girl from East Brighton. The first time I put her up for a test, she failed very narrowly, for treating a "stop" line as a "give way." But for that, she would have passed easily.

I put her in for another test, and she got a different examiner, one who was "guesting" from another test centre. When they got back, the examiner called me over and berated me for putting the girl up for a test before she was ready; he was duty-bound to report the fact.

I protested that she had failed on only one fault a few weeks ago, but he would have none of it. Speaking to the girl, it seemed this examiner had made no attempt to put her at ease and had actually made her extremely nervous. Her test sheet was a mess of faults. She was in tears, saying she never wanted to take another test. In the end, I gave her free lessons pending the next test, as I felt somehow responsible.

I also wrote to the DSA, quoting the date of her previous test, the examiner's name, and the result and the fact that the girl had somehow had a personality clash with the second examiner. I got no reply or feedback, and, happily, the girl got on okay with the third examiner and passed easily.

If, on the other hand, you did not recognise the pupil's readiness for a test and carried on instructing him or her, you could be open to accusations of making more profit out of the pupil than you needed to. It could be a fine line to tread.

Back to Clarissa, then. She was very competent, and I had no problem booking her in for a test as soon as one was available. As it happened, the girls in her form at the school were on a bad losing streak on driving tests, and something like eight girls in a row had failed, some quite badly.

Clarissa passed with ease. It's a strict rule that after the test, pass or fail, the instructor drives the candidate home, as his or her mind would be only partially on the road, the rest of it planning how to tell friends, parents, etc.

I drove her back up to the school and parked outside Lawrence House, the sixth form building. Clarissa told me her friends would be coming out for lunch in a few minutes. I parked up, got out of the car, and got Clarissa to sit in the driver's seat before whipping the magnetic "L" for "learner" plates off the car and replacing them with green "P" for "passed" ones. I got back in. After a short time, girls began to come out of the house, and in no time we were surrounded by whooping, laughing young ladies.

Several begged me to take them on, but those already with an instructor I told to stay with him meantime. Two practices that can make an instructor very unpopular very quickly are undercutting charges and poaching pupils. I did pick up three or four new starts, though.

When it came to setting my lesson fees, I was determined not to fall into the trap of charging too little. I set my fees at exactly the same rate as the RAC Driving School, then the second-largest national school. The only thing I did for free was a half-hour assessment before taking a new pupil on, so that I could give an honest estimate of approximately how many hours of lessons would be needed to reach test standard. This was a worthwhile giveaway, as it generated so much goodwill in the long run.

Having pupils at Roedean was not entirely a blessing, as it is quite some way from Southwick, where I was living, so I tried to ensure that the girls there had consecutive lessons. It helped that one of my ex-BSM pupils was a resident of the Whitehawk Estate, only a mile or so from Roedean School, and I soon found myself with several others from the same area.

At one time, I had eleven Roedean girls on my books simultaneously. Before starting with any female pupil, I always went through the same mantra, which went something like this. I cleared it with Mr. Thompson, of course.

*The Driving Standards Agency has issued clear instructions that there must not be any physical contact between male instructors and female pupils. The reason is obvious. "Me old man, you pretty young girl, result—fraught with danger." However, there may be four instances when I might have to make contact, but only with your permission, as follows.*

*Firstly, in early lessons you may find you need help finding the correct gear, so I may ask if I can guide your hand on the gear lever. Is this acceptable?*

*Secondly, this car is dual-controlled so I can brake if necessary. However, if you are steering into trouble I may need to grab the wheel in a hurry and not have time to avoid your hand. Is that acceptable?*

*Thirdly, when we start on reversing lessons, it can be stressful for you, and you could be confused with lefts and rights, because you will be looking in the opposite direction to usual. If you are, and I want you to look over your left or right shoulder, I may want to tap you lightly on the correct shoulder. Is that acceptable?*

*Finally, I think it's no bad thing to interact with pupils. If you do something really well, I may ask for a "high five." Is that acceptable?*

In not a single case did a female pupil object to this.

During the time I was instructing, I failed to get only two pupils eventually through their tests. One was a girl from Roedean, who failed quite inexplicably four times, and we simply ran out of time before she left the school.

The second was a lady of about forty. She was from Mauritius and was a charming and delightful personality, but it was obvious very early on that we would have difficulties. Despite trying every trick in the book (and some that aren't), it took me about twelve one-hour lessons to get her driving in a straight line. Every aspect of driving was the same. After about thirty hours, I concluded I was taking money from her from nothing and asked her to consider if she wanted to carry on. Yes, she did.

Eventually I came to the conclusion that nothing I said or asked was registering. In desperation I took a tape recorder on to the car. Here is a transcript. By the way, the lady's name was not actually Amara!

Me: Amara, how far out from the kerb should you be driving?

Amara: Six inches?

Me: No, Amara. Try again.

Amara: Three inches.

Me: No, Amara. Try three feet.

Amara: Oh, three feet. Okay.

Five minutes later . . .

Me: Amara, how far out from the kerb should you be driving?

Amara: Six inches?

Me: No, Amara. Try again.

Amara: Three inches.

Me: No, Amara. Try three feet.

Amara: Oh, three feet. Okay.

I kept reminding "Amara" that we did not seem to be getting anywhere, but she was determined to carry on. After something like one hundred hours of trying, she demanded to do a "mock driving test." This was always a feature of my training programme as a pupil's driving test approached. She would not be dissuaded, and I approached David, one of BSM's most senior instructors, who conducted "mock tests" for the company, and he agreed to carry out the test.

We met in Goldstone Crescent, by Hove Park. David got into my car with Amara, and I waited in David's as they drove off. Ten minutes later, they were back with David driving.

He got out and came over. "I've terminated the test. She's dangerous. You should have told me." He was obviously ruffled.

I apologized. "I didn't want to precondition you. I didn't want her to do the test, but she insisted."

Amara's lessons went on and on. At one point, I spoke to her husband and pointed out how much money this was costing them. He was equally adamant that she carry on.

Months later, Amara began actually to show some signs of getting to grip with the theory of driving a car. Again she asked for a mock test. This time I decided to conduct it for her. I chose to do it on a Sunday morning so that we could start and finish at the Brighton test centre in the Brighton marina.

Off we went from the marina to Rottingdean, where we carried out two reversing manoeuvres and an emergency stop. Amara made several mistakes, which would have meant failure, but I was very pleased with her performance as we set off back along the A259 coast road towards the finishing point in the marina.

Now, after climbing out of Rottingdean, the A259 runs downhill past the famous St. Dunstans Home for blind ex-servicemen and women. There is a large roundabout there where a road goes off to the north and Ovingdean.

Adhering to the system used by DSA examiners, I said to Amara, in good time, "At the roundabout, take the first exit, straight ahead." I checked my mirror. I could see a bright red BMW coming fast up behind us. I made a note that Amara had not checked her mirror, but, correctly for the chosen route, she stayed in the left lane and did not signal on the approach to the roundabout.

As we entered it, Amara suddenly began to turn the steering wheel to the right. The BMW was just about to fly past us. I grabbed the wheel and Amara fought me, still trying to turn right. I managed to keep it straight, when suddenly she let go of it. I overbalanced slightly and the car mounted the verge, heading towards a flimsy-looking fence, beyond which was a hundred-foot drop to the Undercliff Walk.

The car was still some way short of the cliff when I stopped it, and the BMW was by then a diminishing dot in the distance.

There was silence in the car for some time, before I said to Amara. "If this was a proper driving test, the examiner would now get out and walk back, and you would be left here until I could walk out to you. The test is terminated, and I will drive us back to the marina, where we'll have a coffee and a chat about the future."

"Oh, please let me drive back. Please!"

Stupidly I agreed, making sure there was not a moving vehicle westbound on the road before starting back.

The road into the marina from the east passes through a short tunnel, at the end of which is a set of traffic lights. These were showing green to us. As we approached them, Amara suddenly stood on the brake and we screeched to a halt. In the mirror, I could see a car following us. There was an expression of horror on the face of the driver, an Asian lady, as she also braked hard. She managed to stop, but can only have been a matter of millimetres from my back bumper.

"Why did you brake?" I croaked.

Amara pointed at a light that controlled traffic crossing us at 90 degrees. You could just make out that it was red. "There's a red light!"

"Drive on!" I said.

The Chinese lady followed us into the supermarket car park. I got out and apologized. She was very gracious, but I could tell she was still shaken.

Over coffee in the supermarket café, I told Amara that I would not teach her any longer. Obviously, I told her, the fault was mine and she might be a lot better off finding another instructor. "Better still," I said, "take a couple of months off to consider whether you really want to drive."

I took her home and explained the situation to her husband. He smiled, "I will try to convince her, but I think she will want to keep trying."

A few months later, I was waiting at traffic lights at crossroads in Hove. Apart from the roads, there is also a pedestrian entrance to a recreation ground in one of the angles of the crossroad. I saw a BSM car waiting at the lights in the opposite direction. The driver was indicating to turn left.

As the lights changed to green, the car entered the crossroads but did not turn left. I could see a look of alarm on the instructor's face, and then realised that the driver was none other than Amara, who promptly steered the car through the gate and into the recreation ground, on what was, in fact, a footpath!

Soon after that, I got a telephone call from a young girl who wanted to take lessons. She gave her name, and I realised the surname was the same as Amara's—an uncommon one at that.

She was, in fact, Amara's older daughter, who was nineteen years of age. I told her I had failed utterly to teach her mother. Was she sure she wanted to go with me? She replied that she did.

I took her for the half-hour assessment, and could see she had some of her mother's early inability to steer. However, nothing else promised to be a huge problem and I took her on. She needed about ten hours more than the average learner, but passed her test the first time.

Not long afterwards, I found myself teaching Amara's younger daughter, who flew through the course, also passing the first time.

By the time I'd been teaching for a year, I found I was working full-time. I realised that when I got someone through the test, that person's friends nearly always came to me when they became seventeen years old.

In addition, I had picked up pupils from two other fee-paying schools, Brighton and Lancing Colleges. One of the Brighton College boys was a youth member at Hove Rugby Club, and I found myself with several other Rugby Club members on my book.

One of the Lancing College boys, Gregor Smith, was involved in an accident during his driving test, which resulted in my having to replace my car. Gregor had just set off on his test, from the Hove test centre. In the front seat was Don Strange, the chief examiner at Hove. I was waiting at the test centre when another instructor turned up and informed me that my car had been involved in a crash at the Hangleton traffic lights, a few hundred yards from the test centre.

He ran me down there. My little Peugeot was L-shaped, having been involved with a large BMW. Nobody was hurt, but poor Gregor was shaking. I got the details from Don Strange.

Gregor had stopped at a red light and had done everything correctly— hand brake, neutral gear, and so on. The lights in the other direction changed to red. Gregor prepared to move off, but, correctly, did not proceed until he had a green light. As he pulled forward, the BMW had shot the red light, passing two cars that had already stopped.

The BMW hit the Peugeot at an estimated 40 miles per hour, connecting with the front wheel, and spinning the car round.

The two drivers who had been waiting at the red light came forward with their names. One was an off-duty policeman, the other the security manager of a large local company. I collected all the details needed and arranged for my car to be towed away.

My insurance included a replacement car, but it was going to take more than twenty-four hours to deliver it, so I had to cancel all my lessons for the rest of that day and following day and a half.

A couple of days later, I received a letter from Direct Line Insurance, which company had insured the BMW driver. This letter stated that their information was that the accident had been caused by the learner driver of the Peugeot, and how did I intend to settle the matter? Of course I did not reply, but forwarded to my own insurers. They phoned me back and reassured me that with the status of my witnesses I need not worry. Sure enough, Direct Line settled with the price of a replacement car and two days' loss of earnings. My dual-controls had not suffered in the crash.

I collected my replacement car, another Peugeot 205 diesel, and carried on. Around then I began to offer the "Pass Plus" course. This was for new pupils who had recently passed their driving tests. It involved supervised practice in driving on motorways and other difficult roads, such as little winding country lanes, and driving at night. Wherever possible I included bad weather driving, which often meant arranging lessons at short notice.

I'll just mention one other amusing incident from those days. I had been teaching Michelle, a Chinese lady from Hong Kong who spoke no English—her husband always came out with her as interpreter on lessons. On the day of her test, she drove off from the Hove test centre, again with her husband in the back.

When she returned, she had passed, but when the examiner, Steve Parker, got out of the car he was laughing. He put an arm round me. "Corinne sends her love." It transpired Steve had stopped in Rigden Road, Hove, and was about to get Michelle to do a "turn in the road," better known as a "three-point turn." As he instructed her, this tall lady had rushed from a house and banged on the car roof. "I've had enough of you driving instructors using this road for practice."

Steve had wound the window down. "I'm not an instructor, madam. This lady is on her driving test."

Corinne then apparently saw my name signwritten on the car and asked, "Is this Allan Neil a Scottish guy?" Steve had affirmed that, and she had given him the message to "give me her love!" I told him I hadn't seen Corinne for years, and he told me I'd find her at the Rigden Road address. Corinne, of course, was the girl who, at fifteen years of age in 1966, had been babysitter for my sons shortly after I had joined the police.

A second incident occurred on a driving test in Worthing, conducted by a very suave examiner whose name escapes me at time of writing. The learner was driving along a straight bit of urban road when a police car with blue light overtook it and the driver was pulled over. A tall, young PC got out and walked nonchalantly back to the passenger side. The examiner wound the window down. The PC looked in at the examiner, and then the driver. "Ah," he stammered, "a case of mistaken identity!" He walked quickly back to the patrol car, pretending to talk into his radio.

Again the candidate passed, and I was greeted by a laughing examiner, who told me of the incident. "By the way, his number is." I know the PC, and he is a great guy, so I won't embarrass him anymore, should he read this.

Towards the end of 1998, with the new car reaching a high mileage, owing in part to greater distances involved in the "Pass Plus" lessons, I was presented with the problem of whether to buy a replacement, thereby committing myself to another three or four years of instruction.

There were things I had wanted to do on my retirement from the police, but, of course, with the situation with Jo and to a lesser extent with Hannah, I had had to put "on the back burner."

I decided to retire at Christmas and go off to Australia in January, to see if I could be reunited with my two boys. I bought tickets to leave in the third week of January and stopped taking new pupils on.

Even that plan went awry. A week before my due departure, when I was busily telling my remaining pupils that they'd have to change instructors, Hannah went to visit her uncle, Sandra's brother Lionel, in Southwick. She did not get a reply, but as the door was unlocked she went in and discovered Lionel's body in the hallway.

I rescheduled my trip and, interspersed with Lionel's funeral arrangement, I continued with my dwindling band of pupils.

A week before my rearranged departure, my final two learners had tests arranged. The first, Karen, was my last Roedean girl and she sailed through. The final one, named Barry, did not. I arranged another test for him four weeks ahead, but I was going to be in Australia by then. I made arrangements for his father to be on my car insurance so that he could use the car to supervise Barry on practice up to his test and drive him home afterwards.

That was it, then. Allan Neil, Driving Tuition, was no more.

# CHAPTER 23

## Good-bye Jo: The Very Worst Time of My Life

During the period of time between my retirement from the police and my starting off as a driving instructor, Jo had been continuing her therapy and we all began to be more hopeful. She had regained her normal figure and her hair had grown back, albeit curly brown rather than the original honey blonde.

She had found a job with a Hove pharmaceutical firm. It was a bit of a dead-end job in the packing department, but it was something to occupy her. Her workmates seemed to be very friendly, and she had found a boyfriend, Lee. He was a fishmonger by trade, but had gone to work at the pharmaceutical company, as things were slack on his home front. He and Jo seemed to hit it off, and we were happy for both of them.

Everything was going well for Jo, as far as we could tell. She had inherited my taste for world travel and had enjoyed holidays in the US and Mexico with her old friend Rachel, the Canary Islands with another great friend, Lisa, and a couple of weeks in the Gambia and another in Cornwall with Lee.

When it hit, the downside caught all of us totally off guard.

In December 1996, I got a phone call from my sister Catherine, telling me that our younger sister Janette's breast cancer had spread to her brain.

Just before Christmas, Jo was coming downstairs when she seemed to lose her balance, and fortunately I was in a position to catch her before she did herself any damage. Sandra was at work.

Jo's speech was slurred, and she could not stand without support. I called the GP and a doctor came out. I explained everything to him. He shook his head. This was classic, he told me. Gently, he explained that Jo did not have long to live. "Weeks," he said, "rather than months."

She had an appointment due some six months ahead at the Royal Sussex Hospital. I phoned and tried to get this brought forward urgently. There was no chance. I phoned Sandra to get her home. She came straightaway.

In the next few days, I tried everything I knew to get Jo seen urgently. The result was the same everywhere—a shaking of heads that I could not see but could easily envisage. "I'm sorry," "I'm, sorry," "I'm sorry." When our normal GP, Dr. Christine Habgood, returned to duty, she came round straightaway, and from then until the end she was just marvellous, often calling with her children in the car on her way to or from the shops.

On Boxing Day came the bombshell from Penicuik. Janette had lapsed into a coma, and I should be prepared for the bad news. On New Year's Day, I got the news. Janette had died. She was only fifty years old.

We did not tell Jo, but I think she picked it up somehow. Her condition deteriorated so that she became bedridden.

In early January, I travelled to Penicuik for my little sister's funeral. I had to explain why I had come alone. Everyone was sympathetic except my mother. She was distraught. Jo was her first granddaughter.

By the end of February, Jo was fighting hard for her life. Sandra's sister Janet, a hospital sister, came over from Fareham to stay with us. This meant we could take care of Jo at home, rather than consign her to a hospice. I tried to stay with the driving instruction as a means of trying to keep my mind off what had become the inevitable.

Around March 8, 1997, Jo went into a coma for most of each day, with diminishing periods of lucidity. I dropped all my lessons except those where a driving test had been arranged. I found myself walking the streets of Southwick and Portslade at three in the morning, trying to exhaust myself so that I could sleep.

On March 14, I had to take a pupil to a driving test. It was all I had on that day. She failed quite badly, and the examiner started to rabbit on at me. I think I was quite rude to him, saying I had more important things on my mind than whether a silly seventeen-year-old girl could drive a car.

He must have got the message, for the next time I saw him he was very friendly to me. Maybe he heard on the instructor grapevine, as I had placed some of my pupils with other instructors.

The next day, the fifteenth—the Ides of March of 1997—Jo did not emerge from her coma at all. Janet was wonderful, as was Dr. Habgood, who called several times.

At 7:25 p.m., with Sandra, Janet, Lee, and myself telling Jo how much we loved her, she slipped peacefully away, and life was never going to be the same again.

I phoned my sister Catherine and asked her to break the news to our mother at a suitable moment. I could not face telling her myself, being unable to comfort her from more than four hundred miles away.

The funeral was at Worthing Crematorium. I had the address made by a nonreligious speaker, as Jo had made it perfectly clear in a lucid moment that she did not want a preacher or any religion at her funeral.

My mum was beside herself with grief. In a few short months, she had lost her younger daughter and her first granddaughter. Poor Mum never had it easy, from first to last.

This was what I wrote for Jo.

## Too Brief a Life

Jo was born on December 22, 1971, at Bishop's Stortford in Hertfordshire. The Maternity Hospital in Stortford is situated about four hundred metres from the border with Essex, and Joanne was always jokey about missing out on being an "Essex Girl."

She was a beautiful, laughing baby, firstborn of Sandra and Allan, the first granddaughter for Sandra's parents, Sid and Eva, and the paternal grandparents, Jessie and Willie, and a shining light in what was a dark, dark winter—even the three-day week of the Edward Heath government could not dim her parents' joy at such a perfect gift.

When Jo was a few months old, the family moved from their flat in Bishop's Stortford into a small, cosy dwelling called Boundary Cottage, it being on the parish borders of the Essex villages of Quendon and Ugley, so that from being nearly an Essex girl, she just avoided, by a few inches, becoming an Ugley girl.

Boundary Cottage was a perfect little house with a large garden for a toddler to explore, but it had one snag. It was directly on the A11 trunk road, which, prior to the construction of the M11, was the main link between London, Norwich, Felixstowe, and the Norfolk Broads.

Traffic was heavy and constant and included many huge juggernaut lorries, cars, and caravans. One day Jo managed to evade detection and got to the edge of the A11, where her horrified parents found her sitting on the verge with thirty-ton trucks whizzing by a couple of feet away.

Soon Dad's job took him to Sussex, and the family moved to Fishersgate in Southwick when Jo was two years of age. She was given the upstairs back room and was nightly tucked up to sleep, at first in her cot, later in her bed. Meanwhile, little sister Hannah had arrived, and one morning Mum got up early, looked in on Jo, and found (more horror) that Jo had worked out how to open her bedroom window and was happily perched on the window sill, feet dangling over the concrete backyard, watching the dawn goings on in the garden.

The family moved twice again in a short time until they settled as a happy foursome at their present address in Southwick in December 1978. The photograph album is full of pictures of Jo with her sister and parents, laughing and having fun.

Jo made friends easily, especially when she went to "The Big Girls' School"—Portslade Community College. Friends that she made there have been with her since, even though some have moved away from the area—Rachel to America, Heidi to London.

She also maintained friendship with all her cousins, especially Karen, who is working in Cuba and, sadly, cannot be here.

All through her life, Jo had an affinity with any creature having four legs and fur or two legs and feathers, but in her teens she became madly keen on horses. She had many albums of photographs that she took of horses, all named with summaries of their characters. Jo's idea of a perfect holiday was getting cold and wet and cultivating saddle sores.

In 1988 Jo collected her GCSE results, but the idea of higher education did not appeal to her. She found the chance to indulge her passion for four-legged friends by working with the dogs at Corals Greyhound Stadium in Hove. She had a particular favourite there who must have had the worst form record of any canine in the country, and one night, when Mum and Dad turned up to watch the racing, she urged them to put a bet on him as nobody else ever did. A quick look at the form book convinced the parents to put their couple of quid elsewhere, and guess what? Jo must have tied a rocket to his tail, because her dog romped home in first place at about a hundred to one!

In May 1990, Jo went into the RAF, but with one thing and another, including headaches, maybe a precursor of things to come, she stayed only briefly.

She worked at the Grand Hotel in Brighton for a couple of years, gathering more friends on the way, before starting at Custom Pharmaceuticals in Hove, where she stayed right up to the day when she found she could work no more.

Jo loved to drive and, having passed her test, missed no opportunity to get out on the road. Through her love of horses, she had a good friend, Avril, who, with her husband, runs a horsey farm in Aberdeenshire.

Jo borrowed Dad's Sierra, her own Metro being too small, and set off, having assured her father that she would stop off to see another friend, Olly, two hundred miles up the road, then stop at her gran's two hundred miles further on, before going on the final two hundred–mile leg to Avril's. Dad later found out she had driven the full six hundred miles in one go, stopping only for fuel, such was her eagerness to collect more saddle sores.

Even then she had not had her fill of driving, as she returned to Sussex the longest way round that she could find—via Ben Nevis!

For her twenty-first birthday present, Jo went with Mum and Dad to New England and Canada in the autumn of 1992, her first holiday abroad since a lovely week in Denmark ten years earlier and a few short trips to France and Holland. It was on this trip that the first serious symptoms showed of the monster that she was to fight for the rest of her young life.

During the latter part of 1992, she and her great friend Nikki, through a brilliant piece of observation and initiative, were instrumental in helping police to solve a serious lorry hijack and recover property stolen during it. For this, she and Nikki received Sussex Police "Three Nines" awards from the lord lieutenant and chief constable.

In February 1993, at the age of twenty-one, Jo underwent a painful and desperately serious operation to try to remove a tumour from her brain. As it turned out, the surgeons were unable to remove it owing to its location among the controls for several vital organs. Jo spent a week that felt like eternity on life support, before going to a recovery ward and then home.

She was put on a course of steroids, which ballooned her from her normal trim 7.5 stones to over 10 stones, followed by radiation, during which all her hair, her pride and joy, fell out.

In August 1993, the family, including sister Hannah, went on an unforgettable holiday to the Wild West—Arizona, Utah, Nevada, and New Mexico, believing the end for Jo might be nigh, but, typically, she fought back and the tumour went into recession.

Jo then went about enjoying life to the full and more holidays followed—Connecticut and Mexico with her great friend Rachel, who works in America and, sadly, cannot be here, the Canary Islands with another lovely friend, Lisa, and then several trips with the man in her life, Lee, to Africa and various trips to Cornwall.

Jo was never one for the boys. All her friends were girls, and she was a great mate to them. However, at Custom Pharmaceutical she met Lee, who got the Jo cold shoulder at first. However, he persisted, and Jo finally agreed to go out with him. It went on from there, and it soon became obvious that here was a special partnership, the two of them becoming inseparable.

Late in 1996, the monster began to reassert itself, and Jo began to show hideously familiar symptoms. Her GP advised her to stay off work in December, but she insisted on going back. Sadly, it was not long before her friends, and she had many at Custom Pharmaceuticals, brought her home.

She fought a phenomenal retreating battle against her implacable foe, but it had all the weaponry, and on February 28 Jo collapsed and became bedridden. Still she fought and fought, but on March 8 she lapsed into almost constant sleep, entering her final coma at 3:30 a.m. on her final day on earth. Even then she did not give up, and it was not for another sixteen hours that she finally floated away into eternity, leaving this world a poorer, sadder place, seeming to return it to the darkness that existed just before her birth those brief twenty-five years ago.

Jo's friends have all stayed faithful to her because, above all, she was straight and honest with them and would have killed to defend them.

Her father found this poem among her belongings. It sums her up to perfection. I think it is called "Carpe Diem"—"Seize the Day." Lee had written it down for her.

*We walked a path of graceful rivers,*

*So sublime a setting,*

*Swans swimming in this river long,*

*Dancing reeds in shallows caress,*

*Words should be put to song,*

*And spoken to a love.*

*Oh, but when I saw the sun did stroke your hair so fair*

*And eyes did match the sky.*

*Alas, but I saw a heart of thine, so blind,*

*I wish I'd said,*

*Though always true,*

*I wish I'd said,*

*I love you*

*Thou art as graceful and missed as this day*

*Carpe diem.*

Now we all think it, darling Jo. We didn't say it often enough. How much we love you.
Farewell, my love. Our love.
Farewell.
That was it, then. Life went on with a huge hole in it.
Good-bye Jo.

# CHAPTER 24

## Mission Australia: Finding My Long-Lost Sons

Sheila had migrated to Australia with her new husband, John Golding, in early 1974, taking Stephen and Gregor and their half-sister, Julie, along. Within a few months, I heard from Marion Blundell that Sheila and John had split up.

I explained in an earlier chapter that Sheila had politely but pointedly declined any help from me. I had written but got no reply. I learned from Marion Blundell that Sheila and the children had moved and that she was under strict instructions from Sheila that she was not to let me have the new address, even though, at the time, there was no prospect of my going out to Australia. We had a new baby to consider, and Gatwick had just been taken over by Sussex Police. My wages had fallen through the floor, so that was that for the time being.

Life after that seemed to consist of one crisis after another, and it was not until early 1999 that I was in a position to go.

I hadn't fancied the idea of travelling from London to Sydney in one jump. As far as I could see, all the "direct" flights involved very short stopovers of no more than a couple of hours in Hong Kong, Bangkok, Singapore, or similar. In my view, these stops only lengthened the duration of the flight and, anyway, who wants to spend a minute longer than necessary in an airport? Getting paid for doing that was bad enough. Anyway, for many years, I had hankered after the experience of circumnavigating the globe. I made the decision to do just that.

I decided to give myself three weeks to find my sons, with the other three weeks divided between Hong Kong, Melbourne, Fiji, Hawaii, Los Angeles, and New Orleans.

The London-Hong Kong opening leg was going to mean twelve hours of continuous flying, so I thought it might be a good idea to reserve an aisle seat. The aircraft was to be a Boeing 747, with two aisles in economy class, meaning four aisle seats in each row. I rang British Airways to reserve such a seat but was informed that I could not do so until I checked in at the airport.

Accordingly, I ensured I was at Heathrow Airport in good time, and was number one in the check-in queue for the flight. I asked the check-in operator for an aisle seat and was astonished to find that they had all been allocated already. Apparently the flight started off from Frankfurt, and passengers joining there had first choice on seat reservations.

On boarding I found myself between the two biggest Chinamen in the world, each well over twenty stones in my estimation. I caught the flight attendant's attention and asked if I could be moved. She informed me that the flight was completely full, so off we went, a third of my lateral seating space being taken up each side by these two oriental monsters.

Immediately upon takeoff, the guy in the aisle seat immediately lapsed into a state of total unconsciousness. I'd had a pint of something nice in the departure lounge, and after about three hours in flight I began to feel the need. The ogre in the aisle seat was totally impervious to my nudges, and I began to cross my legs tighter and tighter.

About eight hours into the flight, the giant groaned and wriggled, and then heaved himself out of his seat. He went towards the toilets, and I tried to overtake him by running up the other aisle, only to be thwarted by someone getting out of his seat in front of me.

I ended up with one other passenger between him and me in the toilet queue, which began slowly to diminish. Eventually the huge Chinaman let himself into the toilet just as the captain came on the public address to announce that we were flying into turbulence and everyone must return to his seat.

At that point, the friendly giant emerged and the girl in front of me went into the toilet.

A stewardess tapped me on the shoulder and insisted that I return to my seat. I tried to tell her that this was an emergency, but she insisted I return.

The huge Chinaman looked at me balefully as I asked him to let me pass to my seat.

I was seriously considering the plastic bag in which the in-flight magazine had been provided when, mercifully, I fell asleep.

I awoke in time to rush to the toilet before we went on final approach to Hong Kong. I would not have believed my bladder could hold so much, when I finally managed to void it.

I had not booked any accommodation in Hong Kong, mainly because the *Lonely Planet* book on the city told me there was so much in Nathan Road, Tsim Sha Tsui, that I would find it easily at a much better price.

A fellow traveller in the Heathrow departure lounge had also tipped me off that the best way to get to Nathan Road was to board one of the hotel courtesy coaches at the airport, as nobody ever checked. He had given me a list of the hotels concerned, and I quickly found a courtesy coach displaying the sign, "Sheraton Hotel." The driver took no notice as I climbed aboard, and as it stopped outside the hotel I picked my backpack up nonchalantly and got off.

I found Nathan Road easily and was immediately accosted by a crowd of hotel touts. I was planning to be in the city for only three nights and accepted one for 100 Hong Kong dollars a night.

It was on the fifteenth floor of a building called Chungking Mansions and was nothing more or less than a firetrap. The "room" was about six feet by four feet with a combined toilet/shower big enough to accommodate a midget. I spent no more time in the room than necessary for sleeping! Even that was not easy one night when a couple moved into the next room. Their emotional activities were only too audible through paper-thin walls!

My last driving test success had been a girl from Roedean School called Karen Tong. She had given me her telephone number and instructions to ring her, as she was going to be home on Easter Holiday. Her parents would show me around Hong Kong.

I rang her in the morning. They were not available that day but would meet me on the next. Meanwhile I explored the city, including the commercial district, known as Central. It was all very new and exciting to me.

The following day, Karen and her parents met me. First of all, they treated me to my second experience of dim sum. The first had been in Brighton when I had succeeded in getting another Chinese lady through her test. However, the Hong Kong experience was the ultimate dim sum. The restaurant was on the sixth floor of a huge commercial building known as the Ocean Terminal and must have had around 150 tables. Even so, we had to wait for a table to become free.

Afterwards, Karen's father went off on business, and she and her mother showed me around many of the sights of old Hong Kong. It was a wonderful day and a great start to my world tour.

I expressed my intention of visiting Macau on my final day. Karen's mother was aghast. "There is shooting and violence there."

I was determined, though. Macau is an old Portuguese colony a forty-minute ride away by hydrofoil.

I loved it. It looked as though someone had taken Lisbon and dropped it in China, removed all the Portuguese, and replaced them with Chinamen. The food was delicious—a combination of Portuguese and many different kinds of Chinese cuisine.

The economy was based on gambling and prostitution. I thought I had experience of how prostitutes worked from my time on the Vice Squad, but these girls were nothing like their Brighton equivalents. Instead of accosting you from shop doorways, these girls came straight out and physically grabbed you!

There had been turf wars, involving gun battles, when the Portuguese had pulled out a couple of years earlier, but one of the warring "tongs" had prevailed. I was near the incredible "floating casino" when a large limousine pulled up outside. Three very large Chinamen with suspiciously bulging jackets got out and took positions, looking up and down the road. A comically small man followed them. He was dressed very sharply, including patent leather shoes and white spats, a total caricature from some Hollywood movie about "the Mob." The three goons then hustled him into the casino, and the limousine went off with a swish of tyres.

That was Macau, then. I made a promise to return for a longer visit, which I did in 2002.

The flight from Hong Kong to Sydney was by Qantas and was much more comfortable, only memorable for an unexpected bit of turbulence just as my spoon was poised to deliver tomato soup into my waiting mouth and my buff-coloured jumper acquired a large orange stain!

Several times during the flight, announcements were made reminding passengers that no foodstuffs, agricultural products, or seeds were permitted to enter the country without licence. In the arrivals terminal, huge notices were displayed to the same effect, each being placed adjacent to "honesty bins" where contraband could be dumped, no questions asked.

As I reached the customs area, an unfortunate Indian lady had had her gifts of herbs and spices discovered, and they were all being entered on an official-looking form by a grim-faced customs man.

Another, with the same facial expression, indicated that I should place my backpack on his table.

"Are you bringing any food into the country?" he asked.

"No," I replied, "unless you count the Qantas soup on my jumper." I indicated the stain.

"Oh, very funny!" He scowled blackly and I thanked heaven that he was not armed!

"Open your pack!" I did, and he tipped all the contents onto his table.

Now, while in Hong Kong I had not had time to wash any clothes, and it had been a bit humid during my stay there. All my smelly underclothes, shirts, and socks were in a black bin liner.

"What's in the bag?" enquired my new friend.

"Dirty clothing," I replied.

"Oh, yeah?" He opened the bin liner and dumped the contents on the table, taking an involuntary step backwards. The glare he gave me should really have fried my brains, but I was too busy trying not to laugh out loud!

"Put it all back and go through." He ground out through clenched teeth.

I took my time folding all the clean stuff and replacing it before stuffing the laundry back in the bin liner. At the adjacent table, the official was still making an inventory of herbs and spices.

I hoisted the pack on my back. "Have a nice day." I smiled, but the officer was already on his way to the washroom!

I later discovered that, in the opinion of one Aussie, part of the entrance exam for customs includes being shown a selection of extremely funny jokes and cartoons. Even the hint of a smile from the examinee results in an automatic failure!

Okay, I was here. Let the search begin.

I had felt it might be a bit unfair to make a huge drain on family finances, so in order to keep accommodation expenses to a minimum, I had booked in at a backpackers' hostel called "Billabong Gardens" in the Newtown area of Sydney near the university. This was just off King Street, renowned all round the world for the variety of restaurants to be found there. One of its great claims to fame was that it had been the location of the first McDonald's ever to go belly-up!

One of the quirks about Billabong was that most of the rooms contained three sets of bunk beds. The system was that when a bed was vacated it went to the next person to check in, whether male or female. For the first night, I was a sixty-year-old man in a room with five teenage girls! You will have no difficulty imagining who was the most embarrassed.

Shortly before my departure from the UK, Marion Blundell had passed away. Corinne had searched the house and found three possible addresses for me. All were in suburbs of Sydney: Beverly Hills, Revesby, and Bankstown.

I tried Beverly Hills first but found that the address did not exist anymore, as it was under a new motorway junction. I did not actually have an address in Revesby, but thought I might try estate agencies and schools. Everyone was friendly and sympathetic but I got nowhere.

It then occurred to me that, according to Corinne, Sheila had married again, and I didn't have the name of the new man, other than his first name was Brian. I knew, again through Corinne, that the boys had taken the surname Golding but reckoned they'd have been too old to be readopted by Brian. However, it was something to consider when looking at names.

By around 5:00 p.m. on that day, pooped after the flight and the walking, I decided to relax, making my way to Circular Quay, between the Harbour Bridge and the Opera House. A ferry was about to leave for Manly and promised a daylight view of the harbour on the way there, and a night view coming back. On the way, I formulated plans for forthcoming days.

The next day, I hopped on a train to Bankstown, emerging from the station into what looked like downtown Ho Chi Minh City! There were Vietnamese restaurants and shops and a busy Vietnamese market.

I checked the address I had, but the occupants had been there only a month or so, and the previous occupants did not fit the description.

I visited a few addresses of people called Golding, gleaned from telephone books, and, having trudged miles in temperatures hovering around the 30-degree mark, my feet were giving me reminders of my age, and I was getting nowhere.

I switched to electoral rolls, normally to be viewed in libraries or civic centres, checking against the names Golding and Neil and looking for addresses where the voters were Sheila and Brian. After hours of this, my eyes came out in sympathy with my feet.

I was on the point of giving up for the day when I got a hit on a Sheila Ann Golding at 9/5 Mercury Street Narwee. I found it on the map and got there by train.

I was having difficulty working out the numbering system and ended up knocking on number 4. The occupant was an old Dutch gentleman, who had known her well, but she had moved away some four years previously. He remembered Gregor and Julie, but not Stephen. He had no forwarding address but directed me to number 3, saying the woman in there had been friendly with Sheila.

She denied all knowledge, but had a son of around Julie's age who thought she had moved to a house in Shorter Street, Beverly Hills. He had lost the address and didn't have a phone number. He recalled that it had been a low number, possibly 25 or thereabouts, but definitely with two digits.

There was no Shorter Street, but there was Shorter Avenue, and it was not far from Narwee. I prayed it had been a low number because on the map it belied its name and was a very long road. The low numbers were not far from the motorway junction under which lay the previous address. I checked every other house on both sides of the road between numbers 10 and 35. It took a long time, but there was no luck and everybody knew the identity of his or her neighbours.

I was getting quite downhearted by now. On returning to Billabong Gardens, I discovered I had a new roommate, another Allan. He was in his thirties and that made a change from the teenage girls. He asked if I fancied a coffee, and we went to a coffee bar in King Street.

I found out that he was a resident of another borough in Greater Sydney. I asked why he was staying in a hostel, and at first he was very cagey.

However, after a "loosener" or two, it came out that he was "on the run." Not from the police, I should add, but from the government, or agents working on the government's behalf. They were trying to locate him to serve a writ on him to prevent him talking to the press. In order to avoid them, he was changing his whereabouts every week.

His tale was that he was a civil servant working in the Department of Aboriginal Affairs. He had become aware of serious malpractices in the department and its field agencies and had become a "whistleblower." There had been an article published in a national newspaper and ABC, the Australian Broadcasting Corporation, was working on an exposé. The government—I believe that of New South Wales—was desperately trying to find and silence him.

I told him about my search and that I had some inquiries to carry out in the morning. He told me that he would give the matter a little thought. If he had been able to go in to a government office, he could probably have been able to find them, but that was obviously out of the question.

The next day, I travelled out to Strathfield. There was a two-mile walk to the library on what was already a very warm, humid day. My spirits rose when I found a John Golding living with a Greg Golding at an address in Greenacres. That transpired to be another eight-kilometre-round hike, as there was no station nearby and no buses went that way.

The John Golding transpired to be an old pensioner living in his son's house, so it was another three hours wasted.

Another idea that Allan had given me was to try the Housing Department at Campsie, which he believed covered Mercury Street, Narwee. I went to the council offices, where they kindly let me use their phone, as the housing offices were several miles away. I got a good lead there, though, as they were able to tell me that Sheila had moved to an address covered by the Bankstown office. The kind gentleman at Campsie wrote the address of Bankstown Housing Department down for me, and I made my way there.

At Bankstown my quest came to a sudden halt on the buffers of bureaucratic protocol. I spoke to a woman there who refused point-blank to give me any assistance. After some persistence, she allowed me to speak to her supervisor, who would say no more than that it was policy not to divulge confidential information to unauthorised people like me. No amount of pleading would move him.

It was back to footslogging, then. I had another John Golding to check out, this time in Ashfield, another train ride and a mile or so to walk. I rang the number in the phone book, but there was no reply. I guessed he would be at work and decided to try later. I had a huge Greek fruit salad and yogurt for lunch.

I found the Ashfield address after walking nearly two miles in the wrong direction. It was a block of flats with worldwide cooking smells emanating from everywhere. There was no reply at the address, but the Turkish neighbour informed me that the occupant was Chinese or Vietnamese and had been there for only about three months. He had not known Mr. Golding. I'd lost even more time going down another dead end.

Back at the hostel, Allan was out and I had yet another teenage female as a roommate. This was a girl called Sophie, who came from Loxwood in West Sussex. Naturally we got to talking, and I found that the people in the village still talked about the police helicopter landing outside the pub. She had been eight years old at the time. Her boyfriend was due to join her at the hostel, and when she told me his name and his old school, The Weald at Billingshurst, I realised that I knew him from refereeing him playing at scrum half for the school's Rugby XV.

When Allan got in, he told me it had occurred to him, and he had checked the fact, that Sydney Central Library holds up-to-date microfiches of electoral rolls for the whole of Australia and I could have saved myself a lot of shoe leather and sweat.

I decided that information called for a celebration so we went off to a local pub—the Marlborough Hotel. They had a pub quiz on, which I entered with some confidence, only to find that all the questions were Australia-themed, and Allan and I came rock bottom!

I was outside the library when it opened the next morning. The amount of information was mind-stretching. I did not find any trace of a Stephen William Golding or Neil, nor did I find Gregor Allan Golding or Neil. Sheila's sister Norma was also living somewhere in Sydney, and I found a couple of Norma Blacks not far from Central

Sydney. I made a note to check these. I did not know if Norma was married. I found two Julie Goldings. One was Julie Anne, which I knew to be Sheila's daughter's full name. She lived some way out towards the Blue Mountains. The other was simply Julie Golding. She lived in Knight Street, no more than ten minutes from the hostel. By the time I left the library, my eyes were streaming from concentration on blocks of small print.

Allan had made another suggestion. I had told him that Sheila had gone to university and had graduated in social studies. I had learned that from Corinne, as I had learned so much else that she had found out only after her mother's death. Allan thought I might be able to locate her by visiting the office of the Australian Association of Social Workers in the middle of Sydney.

There I met a very helpful receptionist, who went through the information on disk. They did not have a Sheila Golding, although they did have three Sheilas on their books in the greater Sydney area. Bearing in mind that Sheila had married again, there was good chance she could be one of them. She promised to get her senior's permission to disclose their addresses and telephone numbers, but as she was out for the rest of the day, could I ring in the morning?

By now I was pretty much flaked out, physically and emotionally. I decided to take a break by visiting Bondi Beach. By the time I got there, it was raining heavily and there was not a single surfer or beach bum in sight. I got a bus and train back to Newtown, and at about four o'clock, after a shower and a change of clothing, I set off out to check the Julie Golding who lived in Knight Street. I found the street and rang the bell on a house displaying the number "2." A tall, blonde girl came to the door.

I told her, "I'm looking for Julie Golding."

The girl shook her head. "Never heard of her."

I said, "Sorry to bother you. This is 2 Knight Street, isn't it?"

"No. This is Rochford Street. Knight Street is over there." She indicated across at an angle of 45 degrees. I thanked her and made my way to the street indicated.

As soon as the door of number 2 opened, I recognised her, though I had not seen her since she had been five years old.

"Hello, Julie," I said.

"Should I know you?" she asked, squinting at me.

"I'm Allan. Your mum's ex-husband."

"Oh, bloody hell!"

"Can we talk for ten minutes?"

"As long as I can have a fag! Come in."

I told her of my quest. She told me both the boys had moved quite recently, and she did not have their addresses or phone numbers.

"Can you ring your mum and get them off her?"

"She'll do her nut if I tell her you're here."

A word of explanation is needed. Among the many things I found out from Corinne after Marion's demise had been the fact that, although Sheila had married again, her husband thought that John Golding had been her only previous husband and that I did not exist. She and Brian had visited Marion, and she had sworn her to secrecy. Marion had told Corinne and made her promise she would not tell me. Corinne had not seen me for years, so she thought nothing of it.

I assured Julie that my purpose in coming to Sydney had been only to find her brothers. There was no need for her to know I was there. "Tell her you want to invite them round for a barbie!"

She picked up the phone and went to another room. Ten minutes later she was back, and I could tell she had told Sheila everything.

"Mum says I've to ring Steve, and if he doesn't want to talk to you, that's that. Gregor isn't on the phone. Okay?"

I had no choice. She punched in a number and left the room again. Two minutes more passed, and then she came back, holding the phone out to me. "Here you are. It's Steve."

My stomach churned. I half-expected him to tell me to bugger off home. I said, "Steve?"

A deep, rich voice said, "When can you get here?"

I said, spirits leaping high, "If I knew where 'here' was I'd tell you."

"Cronulla!"

"Where's that?"

"You're at Julie's. Go to Erskineville station, just round the corner, and get a train to Sydenham. Change onto the southbound Bondi line. Cronulla's the last station on the line. When you get there, ring me on the number Julie has. I'll be with you in a couple of minutes."

I decided not to go back to the hostel for anything. Everything I had of any value was in my pockets.

There are twenty-one stations between Sydenham and Cronulla, and the train seemed to take forever. Eventually I got there and rang Stephen. Less than five minutes later, a tiny Japanese car bowled into the station forecourt, and a huge young man unrolled from it.

Stephen was a bit bigger than he had been when I had last seen him twenty-five years previously. He was now well over six feet tall and somewhere around the sixteen-stone mark. He enveloped me in a smothering bear hug. "Jeez, I thought you'd never get here!"

He drove back to a tidy block of flats in Kurnell Road, and I met the incomparable Vicki, then his girlfriend and now his wife. In contrast to Steve, she was tiny—not much over five feet tall and no more than seven and a half stones!

We spent hours going over everything that had happened in the previous twenty-five years. Well, some of it anyway, as we realised there was so much to tell. First of all, I had to realise that I was speaking to a fully grown, apparently well-adjusted man and not the ten-year-old boy he had been when I had last seen him. One mystery was cleared up. Neither he nor Gregor were on the electoral roll because neither had taken Australian citizenship. Steve said, "We have both got to go in to work in the morning, but you'll be okay here on your own."

I decided, however, to go back to Newtown and get my things together, before checking out of the hostel in the morning. I would then go to Gregor's address, which Steve had given me, and bring him back to Cronulla. According to Steve, he would not be working, Friday being the start of Easter weekend, so that should not be a difficulty.

Steve and Vicki meantime would arrange some time off for the following week. All sore feet forgotten, I caught a train back to Newtown, my mind whirling so that the twenty-one-station journey seemed to take an instant.

Allan was in the room and was delighted with the result. It was after 9:00 p.m., but I dragged him out of the hostel to an Andean restaurant that he had told me about and treated him to a cracking meal of roast alpaca washed down with a bottle of beautiful red Chilean wine.

In the morning, I remembered to ring the helpful lady at the Association of Social Workers office and said good-bye to Allan, who had neither address nor telephone to stay in touch.

Gregor's address was in the little town of Morrisset, some ninety kilometres, or fifty-six miles north of Sydney. It had a railway station on the Sydney to Newcastle main line with hourly trains. The return fare? $A13! At that time, it was equivalent to about £5.

On arrival it looked almost like my idea of an outback town with the railway station on one side of the main street and some shops and a pub on the other. The overcast sky and threat of rain did not fit with the picture, however. One of the shops was an estate agent. I went over and asked for directions. The girl gave me a map. "It's a fair way—about four or five kilometres."

I asked about taxis. She looked over to the station. "He'll probably come back for the next train."

There were no buses going in that direction. I decided to walk. I'd gone about a kilometre when it began to rain, and soon it was coming down quite hard. I reflected that it had rained at one time or another every day so far in Australia! This was a bit contrary to my preconceived idea of clear blue skies and surfing sun.

I was wet through, but in high spirits, if a tad apprehensive as I got to the address, which was a very attractive-looking single storey wooden house at the end of a long front lawn. Steve had already told me Gregor was house sitting pending planning permission for demolition and the erection of a new house on the site.

The front door was tucked in behind the garage. I knocked and waited, again unsure of the reception I would get.

The girl who answered the door was tall and slim and was wearing glasses. I asked if I could speak to Gregor. She didn't ask who I was but walked back into the house. Gregor then came to the door. Unlike Steve, he was around my height and build and had blue eyes just like my mum's.

I said, "Hello, Gregor. I'm your dad."

He took half a step back and then hurled himself at me, hugging me madly. That made two out of two unexpectedly and undeservedly marvellous receptions—much better than I expected or felt I deserved. He practically dragged me indoors and introduced me to the girl, Kaye.

He sat me down and fetched a couple of cans of beer, and we started to talk. The dammed up years were just swept away, and I learned about the life he had had in Australia. It had not been easy for him. An earlier girlfriend had committed suicide after he called the relationship off. He was plunged into unbelievable guilt, which resulted in a mental breakdown and time in a psychiatric hospital.

He was not working, but he and Kaye were existing on a very small state pension—what we would call disability allowance. The cupboard was nearly bare, and the two cans of beer had been the last in the house.

My quest had ended sooner than I had budgeted for, and I had a good supply of spare credit on the card. Gregor had an ancient Holden car—the equivalent of our Vauxhall brand. A huge LPG tank took up the back of the car.

We drove into Morrisset, where I bought some steak, vegetables, a supply of beer for us, some wine for Kaye, plus some breakfast things. I also phoned Sandra from a kiosk and put Gregor on for a chat. He loved that.

The evening feast was wonderful, and I learned that both the boys had learned to cook under the instructions of their Uncle Lawrence, who had been killed in a rail accident a few years earlier. Lawrence had been a notable chef in some of Sydney's best restaurants.

Later that night, I learned of one of the reasons for the house being up for demolition. It had cracks everywhere at floor level, and these were infested with cockroaches. The bathroom was particularly bad. The bath panel could not be removed and despite obvious efforts to plug up dozens of holes and cracks, climatic conditions were just perfect for these creatures, which came out in their hordes at night.

Before turning in for the night, we made plans for me to return to Cronulla in the morning. It was Good Friday. Gregor couldn't come with me as his cousin, Norma's son Tristan, was coming up to visit him and he had no way of contacting him to put him off.

In the morning, Gregor and I walked in the woods along the bank of the lake and began to get to know each other, almost, it seemed, from scratch.

At lunchtime Gregor drove Kaye and me into Morrisset, where we shared a huge bag of chips. It was still raining when the train from Sydney arrived and Tristan disembarked. There was just time for us to be introduced when my train pulled in.

Reunion '99, Botany Bay, Australia. Stephen, the author, Gregor.
Yours truly flying the flag for Scotland with rugby shirt. Compare
these two big lads with those in Chapter 9!

The rest of my stay was split between the boys after a get-together in
Cronulla, where we walked the beaches and had a beer or two. It was
a process of getting to know each other after the gap of a quarter
century, and it could so easily have gone wrong. That it did not shows
the strength of the affinity between us, although we are three totally
different characters. The boys obviously took time to take their long-
lost father to their hearts again and for me to shed the guilt that had

been building up since that day on the dockside at Southampton in 1974.

The visit could probably have been longer, but I think we all needed a little time to adjust to the new aspect in our lives.

I had a few more days at Morrisset, including a drive to the Hunter Valley vineyards, and I finished off back at Cronulla, where Steve, Vicki, and I went to watch a Rugby League match between the Cronulla Sharks and Canterbury Bulldogs. This was a bit of a local derby, played in front of a full house. Standing out in the open, we were exposed to a rainstorm of tropical ferocity!

We also had a visit to Taronga Zoo and the Steve and Vicki tour of Sydney before I had to say good-bye. Steve and Vicki promised to come over to Lancing next year, and as Hannah and Neil had just announced their marriage plans, we all decided that was an ideal time for their visit.

That's it for this book. Life has gone on and could well be the subject of a follow-up to this offering.

Since Sydney I have travelled considerably and also held a variety of jobs, as well as meeting many very interesting people. Life has never quite been static. It's "The Long Downhill"—a fair choice for the title, perhaps.